Preparing Physicians to Lead in the 21st Century

Valerie Anne Storey
University of Central Florida, USA

Thomas Edward Beeman
University of Pennsylvania Health System, USA

A volume in the Advances in Medical Education, Research, and Ethics (AMERE) Book Series

IGI Global
DISSEMINATOR OF KNOWLEDGE

Published in the United States of America by
IGI Global
Medical Information Science Reference (an imprint of IGI Global)
701 E. Chocolate Avenue
Hershey PA, USA 17033
Tel: 717-533-8845
Fax: 717-533-8661
E-mail: cust@igi-global.com
Web site: http://www.igi-global.com

Library of Congress Cataloging-in-Publication Data

Names: Storey, Valerie Anne, editor. | Beeman, Thomas E., editor.
Title: Preparing physicians to lead in the 21st century / Valerie Anne Storey and Thomas Edward Beeman, editors.
Description: Hershey, PA : Medical Information Science Reference, [2019] | Includes bibliographical references and index.
Identifiers: LCCN 2018030563| ISBN 9781522575764 (hbk.) | ISBN 9781522575771 (ebook)
Subjects: | MESH: Physicians | Leadership | Patient Care Team
Classification: LCC R690 | NLM W 21 | DDC 610.69/5--dc23 LC record available at https://lccn.loc.gov/2018030563

This book is published in the IGI Global book series Advances in Medical Education, Research, and Ethics (AMERE) (ISSN: 2475-6601; eISSN: 2475-661X)

British Cataloguing in Publication Data
A Cataloguing in Publication record for this book is available from the British Library.

Advances in Medical Education, Research, and Ethics (AMERE) Book Series

ISSN:2475-6601
EISSN:2475-661X

MISSION

Humans are living longer now than ever as a result of advances in the medical field. Having the tools available to train knowledgeable and ethical future generations of doctors and medical researchers is essential to continuing to advance our understanding of the human body and develop new ways of treating and curing sickness and disease.

The **Advances in Medical Education, Research, and Ethics (AMERE)** book series highlights publications pertaining to advancements in pedagogical practice for developing future healthcare professionals, research methods, and advancements in the medical field, as well as moral behavior and practice of healthcare professionals, students, and researchers. Featuring research-based book publications that are highly relevant to the healthcare community, this series is ideally designed for library inclusion at medical universities and research institutions as well as personal use by medical professionals, researchers, and upper-level students entering the field.

COVERAGE

- Clinical Research
- Conflicts of Interest
- Ethics in Medicine
- Healthcare Pedagogy
- Medical Curricula
- Medical Simulation
- Patient Data
- Professional Development
- Research Methods
- Scientific Misconduct

IGI Global is currently accepting manuscripts for publication within this series. To submit a proposal for a volume in this series, please contact our Acquisition Editors at Acquisitions@igi-global.com or visit: http://www.igi-global.com/publish/.

The Advances in Medical Education, Research, and Ethics (AMERE) Book Series (ISSN 2475-6601) is published by IGI Global, 701 E. Chocolate Avenue, Hershey, PA 17033-1240, USA, www.igi-global.com. This series is composed of titles available for purchase individually; each title is edited to be contextually exclusive from any other title within the series. For pricing and ordering information please visit http://www.igi-global.com/book-series/advances-medical-education-research-ethics/132365. Postmaster: Send all address changes to above address.

Titles in this Series

For a list of additional titles in this series, please visit:
https://www.igi-global.com/book-series/advances-medical-education-research-ethics/132365

Exploring the Pressures of Medical Education From a Mental Health and Wellness Perspective
Christina Ramirez Smith (University of the Bahamas, Bahamas)
Medical Information Science Reference • ©2018 • 349pp • H/C (ISBN: 9781522528111) • US $225.00

Impact of Medical Errors and Malpractice on Health Economics, Quality, and Patient Safety
Marina Riga (Health Economist-Researcher, Greece)
Medical Information Science Reference • ©2017 • 334pp • H/C (ISBN: 9781522523376) • US $200.00

Advancing Medical Education Through Strategic Instructional Design
Jill Stefaniak (Old Dominion University, USA)
Medical Information Science Reference • ©2017 • 349pp • H/C (ISBN: 9781522520986) • US $205.00

Organizational Culture and Ethics in Modern Medicine
Anna Rosiek (Nicolaus Copernicus University in Toruń, Collegium Medicum in Bydgoszcz, Poland) and Krzysztof Leksowski (Nicolaus Copernicus University in Toruń, Collegium Medicum in Bydgoszcz, Poland)
Medical Information Science Reference • ©2016 • 448pp • H/C (ISBN: 9781466696587) • US $225.00

Handbook of Research on Advancing Health Education through Technology
Victor X. Wang (Florida Atlantic University, USA)
Medical Information Science Reference • ©2016 • 588pp • H/C (ISBN: 9781466694941) • US $335.00

Optimizing Medicine Residency Training Programs
Jayita Poduval (Pondicherry Institute of Medical Sciences, India)
Medical Information Science Reference • ©2016 • 300pp • H/C (ISBN: 9781466695276) • US $220.00

For an entire list of titles in this series, please visit:
https://www.igi-global.com/book-series/advances-medical-education-research-ethics/132365

IGI Global
DISSEMINATOR OF KNOWLEDGE

701 East Chocolate Avenue, Hershey, PA 17033, USA
Tel: 717-533-8845 x100 • Fax: 717-533-8661
E-Mail: cust@igi-global.com • www.igi-global.com

Editorial Advisory Board

Table of Contents

Detailed Table of Contents

This chapter considers the growing awareness on both sides of the Atlantic of the importance of leadership in complex healthcare systems, and of the need for formal leadership training for both physicians and administrators. As healthcare systems evolve and physicians face more administrative and regulatory burdens, it is imperative for them to build leadership competencies. In fact, there is a need for a pipeline to be created of emerging physician leaders who have already mastered competencies and skills required of successful leaders. This strategic action is necessary, as experience has shown that the skills, competencies, and traits of successful physicians do not necessarily correlate with skills, competencies and traits required of physician leaders in our current healthcare system. Further, the heroic style of paternalistic leadership is less successful in an era of system complexity, quality control, and personnel diversity. A more preferable leadership style is that of shared leadership where a vision is created towards which team members are intrinsically driven to achieve. These factors have cumulatively contributed to the increasing cognizance that more training programs are needed to make comprehensive leadership development widely accessible to a greater number of potential physician leaders.

This chapter is grounded on the premise that healthcare in the United States is on the precipice of massive change. In anticipation of the impending effects of economic and political challenges, both locally and nationally, Lancaster General Health (LG Health) embarked on a unique, decade long physician leadership development journey that culminated in the graduation of 21 physicians and administrators, who collectively constitute a priceless network of physician and administrative professionals who are helping to lead healthcare change in their community. Value, as seen from these multi-dimensional leaders, delivers on a promise for a healthier future in the Lancaster community, one in which all care providers champion the needs of their constituents to achieve their desired healthcare goals.

This chapter is written through the reflective, and analytic lens of a Business School Dean with thirty-five years in higher education, and focuses on the trends and future of the healthcare industry. Specifically, the chapter examines the planning, implementation and identified outcomes of a cohort designed Executive MBA program. The issues highlighted in the first half of the chapter relate to 1) investing in individuals and the organizations they serve; 2) enhancing organizational capacity; and 3) implementation of pragmatic strategies to ensure an organizational leadership pipeline. The second half of the chapter suggests strategies as to how Chief Executive Officers, healthcare organizations, and partnering higher education institutions can develop both individualized master program's and professional training to ensure the development and retention of an energized healthcare leadership pipeline consisting of individual team leaders and change agents

This chapter describes evidence-based strategies found to most effectively maximize the Return On Investment (ROI) of physicians' formal leadership training programs.

Recognizing that no two prospective physician leaders are exactly the same, formal leadership training programs cannot be most effective if these do not allow for organizational and situational differences as well as critical differences among physicians' demonstrated personalities and leadership styles. When selecting prospective physician leaders, the authors advocate for an individualized process which requires "Diagnosis Before Treatment," "Three Dimensional Screening," and the application of "More Effective Alternative Strategies" in order to avoid committing the "12 Deadly Sins."

Chapter 5 contends that complex 21st century healthcare systems require leaders capable of making strategic decisions grounded on sound medical and healthcare knowledge and practices. Traditionally these two domains have been viewed through a binary lens but the author argues that in the 21st century, these domains are best viewed through a unitary lens. The chapter focuses on the organizational and individual benefits to aspiring physician leaders who complete both a medical degree (MD) and a master of business administration (MBA) degree by examining the impact of an MBA on clinical leaders and the organization they serve.

Healthcare delivery in the United States is an ever-evolving field that is changing across multiple economic and cultural levels. Healthcare delivery systems are being affected not just by emerging technological capabilities but by ongoing changes in the structure and role of health systems themselves, as well as in the diversity of the communities they service. The older model of physician-provider is likewise evolving, and today's clinician requires the skill set necessary to navigate this new healthcare delivery environment. This chapter describes the development and implementation of a clinical leadership MBA curriculum designed to provide physician leaders with a strategic perspective on healthcare decision making that encompasses a broad range of structural, technological, financial, cultural, and ethical considerations.

This chapter provides an insight into the value of tacit knowledge and how this contributes directly to the concept of human factors in the context of multi-disciplinary teamwork. In considering the notion of implicit or intuitive knowledge and how this can be taught in practice, the authors draw on the field of creative praxis as a means of harnessing knowledge from other (often under-acknowledged) signature pedagogies of direct relevance to medical practice. The authors focus on the significance of situational awareness and context of medical and healthcare provision as a means of driving debate around the value of affective domain learning and its role in 21st Century physician practice. These are bracketed under the category of non-technical skill acquisition, which is linked heavily, in the published literature to date, with holistically positive patient outcomes.

This chapter fills an important gap in the literature on healthcare systems leadership by presenting (1) a rationale and approach from the perspective of a healthcare systems chief executive officer for understanding the strategic planning, resources and expenditures associated with efforts to prepare, hire, evaluate, develop, and support clinical leaders; (2) a theoretical foundation and framework for a systems approach to an organizational healthcare leadership pipeline; and (3) a sample case study examining the outcomes of a strategically developed leadership pipeline. Further, the authors identify the resources required to put in place and operate clinical leadership pipelines—pipelines for preparing, hiring, supporting, and managing clinical leaders—based on one large healthcare system.

Foreword

The delivery of health care is rapidly undergoing change to redesign existing systems of care, payment, and collaboration to achieve better health outcomes for all Americans. This is occurring within the context of a nationally recognized goal—The Triple Aim—to increase care quality and the patient experience, reduce per capita health care expenditures, and improve the health of populations. Key to effecting success in these activities are physician leaders.

Preparing Physicians to Lead in the 21st Century—a text for both practitioners and academia—is a compendium of initiatives aimed at assisting physicians and others towards collaborative thinking and leadership through additional education such as MBA programs. Collaboration is key to advancing any organization's march towards its vision, values, and mission, and particularly in healthcare. As described in Chapter 5, an essential element to this is developing physicians to "advance their critical clinical insight into management decision-making."

The book's 10 chapter titles explicitly describe how advancing physician leadership skills prepares the right physicians to be exceptional leaders in the 21st century (Chapter 4). Thus, clinical leadership programs need to be designed to provide physician leaders with a strategic perspective on health care decision making that encompasses a broad range of structural, technological, financial, cultural, and ethical considerations (Chapter 6).

During my nearly 50 years in health care, I have experienced many twists and turns in the evolution of the current health care delivery system. The two elements that have always been the key underpinnings for excellence are the quality of the care delivered and the leadership competence and capability to affect this. Today, key discussions and action around population health, engagement of patients, families and clinicians improving care processes and health outcomes, within and outside the health system, demand excellence in these two important parameters. And essential to this is the development of health care leaders and multidisciplinary teamwork. As described in Chapter

9, "Situational awareness and higher order critical thinking skills" leads to organizational and clinical excellence. As more physicians gain insight and engage in collaborative and leadership thinking, the advancement of the goals of The Triple Aim will be accelerated. Executive and clinical leadership under the leadership and guidance of governing boards can take important steps to improve inpatient and outpatient care and reduce costs with initiatives to address population health and community needs. This book describes and recommends the educational actions that enhance this physician capability. Value based health care needs value-based decision making.

Physician leaders are an essential element.

Carolyn F. Scanlan
Hospital and Healthsystem Association of Pennsylvania, USA

Preface

Good medical leadership is becoming increasingly vital to the provision of high-quality healthcare. Leadership development should be an essential component of the education of all medical staff. Physicians must not only be strong academically and clinically but must begin early in their careers to develop a set of knowledge, skills and behaviors that will enable them to engage and lead in highly complex, rapidly changing environments. This will not occur by accident, but must be the responsibility of every individual physician, the organization they work in, and the system as a whole. Different leadership methodologies are available to do this, and each individual will find some more pertinent to them than others. Whilst mentoring relationships, and strong professional networks are all excellent ways for future medical leaders to start developing the requisite skills and experience there is a need for a more systematic approach.

Such a systematic approach to physician leadership (as opposed to a current 'piecemeal' approach) requires an organization to work in partnership with a higher education institution to develop a program with dual purposes i.e. to increase the quality of leadership on both an individual and organizational level. Authors in this book while acknowledging the benefits of coaching, mentoring, and networking argue that by developing an organizational cohort of high potential future medical leaders through a targeted program from a provider with a highly regarded reputation, the quality of systemic leadership will be improved. Contributing authors argue that the development of a healthcare leadership pipeline will further enhance both individual and organization professional capacity and enhance the quality of organizational decision-making.

Whilst the premise of authors in this book is that the development of physician leadership enhances organizational leadership others look towards physician leadership programs as a strategy for developing a cadre of physicians who will take up management positions and influence policy decisions ensuring that they are scientifically justified rather than politically prudent.

As an increasing number of physicians graduate from leadership programs so there will be a need for current healthcare organizational leaders to take a closer look at physicians' career development. Traditionally career progression this has been based on technical and academic ability at the expense of the so-called 'softer' attributes that contribute to good leadership, such as strong emotional intelligence.

This book is current and reflective of the complex healthcare landscape. There is an increasing recognition that leadership competencies need to be developed by all physicians in order to improve the quality of the service within a specialty, practice or unit or to provide a firm foundation for physicians aspiring to significant positional leadership roles, particularly that of chief executive.

ORGANIZATION OF THE BOOK

The book is organized into 10 chapters. A brief description of each of the chapters follows:

Chapter 1 draws the readers' attention to the increasing administrative and regulatory burdens physicians face and highlights the need for them to develop leadership competencies. The chapter sets the scene for discussions presented by various authors as to how leadership competencies and skills should be developed and practiced. It also identifies the importance of establishing comprehensive leadership development programs that are accessible to a greater number of potential physician leaders.

Chapter 2 outlines an effective strategy that healthcare organizations can take to ensure that leadership is well grounded to meet the current challenges of healthcare network systems. Realigning leadership goals to meet network system collective goals rather than individual organizational goals can be challenging. The chapter authors explain how Lancaster General Health embarked on a unique, decade long physician leadership development journey that culminated in the graduation of 21 physicians and administrators, who collectively constitute a priceless network of physician and administrative professionals who are helping to lead healthcare change in their community.

Chapter 3 is written through the reflective, and analytic lens of a Business School Dean with thirty-five years in higher education and focuses on the trends and future of the healthcare industry. Specifically, the chapter examines the planning, implementation and identified outcomes of a cohort designed Executive MBA program. The issues highlighted in the first half of the chapter relate to 1) investing in individuals and the organizations they serve; 2) enhancing organizational capacity; and 3) implementation of pragmatic strategies to ensure an organizational leadership pipeline. The second half of the chapter suggests strategies as to how chief Executive officers, healthcare organizations, and partnering higher education institution's can develop both individualized master program's and professional training to ensure the development and retention of an energized healthcare leadership pipeline consisting of individual team leaders and change agents.

Chapter 4 describes evidence-based strategies found to most effectively maximize the Return On Investment (ROI) of physicians' formal leadership training programs. The author's argue that as no two prospective physician leaders are exactly the same, formal leadership training programs cannot be most effective if they do not allow for individual, organizational and situational differences. When selecting prospective physician leaders the authors advocate for an individualized process which requires "Diagnosis Before Treatment," Three Dimensional Screening," and the application of "More Effective Alternative Strategies" in order to avoid committing the "12 Deadly Sins.

Chapter 5 contends that complex 21st century healthcare systems require leaders capable of making strategic decisions grounded on sound medical and healthcare knowledge and practices. Traditionally these two domains have been viewed through a binary lens but the author argues that in the 21st century, these domains are best viewed through a unitary lens. The chapter focuses on the organizational and individual benefits to aspiring physician leaders who complete both a medical degree (MD) and a master of business administration (MBA) degree by examining the impact of an MBA on clinical leaders and the organization they serve.

Chapter 6 describes from a macro level the development and implementation of a clinical leadership MBA curriculum designed to provide physician-leaders with a strategic perspective on healthcare decision-making that encompasses a broad range of structural, technological, financial, cultural, and ethical considerations. The authors argue that healthcare delivery in the United States is an ever-evolving field that is changing across multiple economic and cultural levels requiring today's clinician to further extend their skill set in order to navigate this new healthcare delivery environment.

Chapter 7 describes from a micro level a capstone course of a clinical leadership MBA curriculum. Students act as internal consultants and apply the knowledge they acquired from previous courses in the MBA curriculum (e.g., strategic thinking, competitive analysis, statistics, forecasting, financial analysis) to generating the capstone product. Students form teams of complementary backgrounds and expertise (e.g., president physician services, director of nursing, community medicine physician, rheumatologist) to develop and write a strategic plan, demonstrating a comprehensive understanding of business knowledge and the competitive healthcare environment.

Chapter 8 identifies teamwork and collaboration as the critical skills needed to be developed in a physician leadership program. To promote this approach in a physician leadership program, the authors use team structure as an essential component of classroom structure to encourage completion of real-world projects and assignments relevant outside of the classroom environment. The authors demonstrate how teams were formed and evaluated in courses involving the marketing of healthcare systems services and healthcare system mergers and acquisitions.

This chapter also describes components in the development and implementation of a clinical leadership MBA curriculum designed to provide physician leaders with a strategic perspective on healthcare decision making that encompasses a broad range of structural, technological, financial, cultural, and ethical considerations.

Chapter 9 provides an insight into the value of tacit knowledge and how this contributes directly to the concept of human factors in the context of multi-disciplinary teamwork. In considering the notion of implicit or intuitive knowledge and how this can be taught in practice, the authors draw on the field of creative praxis as a means of harnessing knowledge from other (often under-acknowledged) signature pedagogies of direct relevance to medical practice. The authors focus on the significance of situational awareness and context of medical and healthcare provision as a means of driving debate around the value of affective domain learning and its role in 21st century physician practice. These are bracketed under the category of non-technical skill acquisition, which is linked heavily, in the published literature to date, with holistically positive patient outcomes.

Chapter 10 fills an important gap in the literature on healthcare systems leadership by presenting: (1) a rationale and approach from the perspective of a healthcare systems chief executive officer for understanding the strategic planning, resources and expenditures associated with efforts to prepare, hire, evaluate, develop, and support clinical leaders; (2) a theoretical foundation and framework for a systems approach to an organizational healthcare leadership pipeline; and (3) a sample case study of how a strategically developed leadership pipeline is implemented and observed outcomes. The sample case study describes the resources required to put in place and operate clinical leadership pipelines—pipelines for preparing, hiring, supporting, and managing clinical leaders—based on one large healthcare system.

Valerie A. Storey
University of Central Florida, USA

Thomas E. Beeman
University of Pennsylvania Health System, USA

Acknowledgment

The editors would like to acknowledge the help of all the people involved in this project and, more specifically, to the authors and reviewers that took part in the review process. Without their support, this book would not have become a reality.

First, we would like to thank each one of the authors for their contributions. Our sincere gratitude goes to the chapter's authors who contributed their time and expertise to this book.

Second, the editors wish to acknowledge the valuable contributions of the reviewers regarding the improvement of quality, coherence, and content presentation of chapters. Most of the authors also served as referees; we highly appreciate their double task.

Valerie A. Storey
University of Central Florida, USA

Thomas E. Beeman
University of Pennsylvania Health System, USA

Introduction

Since physicians are the major drivers of care, it is becoming increasingly imperative that a cadre of top-level physicians is cognizant of effective business practice. These physicians have to understand how care is provided, how to risk stratify a patient population, lead diverse multispecialty groups, understand the great complexity that is a healthcare system, and unify rather than divide the practitioner teams. With physician burnout being well documented, it seems that empowering physicians to prepare for and take on major leadership roles is an imperative. The major complaint of many physicians is the disconnect between organizational leadership and the clinicians on the front lines. It is a difference of perspectives and how both groups approach the issue. For organizational leaders, it is a matter of looking at patients in the aggregate, for physicians it is about one patient at a time. How does a physician then step back and look holistically at his/her patient as part of a system of care and of finite resources and perhaps equally how does the organizational executive leadership team comprehend what it is to care for a very sick needy patient who is right before one's eyes? One could argue that it is the MD/MBA that can best bridge that gap.

Peter Drucker (1985) tells us that hospitals are the most complex form of human organization we have ever attempted to manage. Compounding this complexity is the fact that most of the hospital's professionals, not merely physicians, but nurses, social workers, pharmacists, accountants, engineers and therapists, have not been taught how to work within a cooperative framework. Rather they have a clear sense of place identifying with specific professional roles. Perceived expansion of this professional role to embrace leadership, teamwork and collegiality frequently meets with resistance, which slows the implementation of any new innovative approach. Implementation therefor becomes inconsistent. Gaining insight from front line physicians on their specific reasons for resistance provides opportunities for meaningful conversations and deeper engagement in the organization with the ultimate aim of transitioning influential physicians in their professional field into organizational change agents.

Contemporary business theorists acknowledge that the traditional approach to resistance presents several concerns. Resistance is typically defined as a willful opposition, which must be overcome (Ford & Ford, 2009, 2010). The reasons, thinking and emotions that accompany resistance are complex. Behaviors leaders perceive to be resistance may not, in fact, be resistance (Ford & Ford, 2009). Rather they may be a legitimate response to what are perceived as the goals of the organization from a narrow, limited, individual perspective.

The completion of a personalized crafted graduate credential from an academic institution designed to address the needs of healthcare systems may help to ensure that physician leaders view the organization holistically enabling issues and ultimately decisions to be made in an organizational rather than an individual context.

Effective leadership is critical for optimizing cost, access, and quality in healthcare and can be recognized as "problem-led" leadership (Ancona & Gregersen, 2018). In a large organization or complex healthcare system physician leadership can be an intermittent activity as physicians with enthusiasm and expertise step up as needed, and readily step aside when, based on the needs of the project, another team member's strengths are more central. In this way organizational personnel have the opportunity to pursue their own deep expertise, while gaining enough familiarity with other organizational knowledge realms to make the necessary connections. Strategic decision-making teams can then be fluid but in such an environment the key leadership talent is to know how to put together a team. Creating a pipeline of effective health care leaders requires developing leadership competencies that differ from the usual criteria of clinical and scientific excellence by which physicians have traditionally been promoted to leadership positions. Specific competencies that differentiate effective problem-led leaders from average leaders, especially emotional intelligence and its component abilities, are essential for effective leadership. Contributing authors in *Preparing Physicians to Lead in the 21st Century* recommend that leadership training should be broadly available to nurses, administrators, and physicians.

BACKGROUND

Many of the authors contributing to *Preparing Physicians to Lead in the 21st Century* focus on the development, design, implementation, and impact of a specific program developed in partnership by Saint Joseph's University Haub Business School and the Lancaster General Healthcare system (LG Health). The program was specifically designed to meet both organizational and individual needs of a positively identified cohort as this model is well suited to mature adults who have a wide range of experience, are strongly motivated, and recognize that learning can be colleague as well as instructor driven (Barnett & Muse, 1993).

The particulars and themes running throughout the book pivot on the link between the quality of leadership, management and team working to clinical outcomes, and how this linkage can be developed and improved. Some recurring points are the need for partnerships between healthcare systems and program providers, and the need for organizational leadership support. The transdisciplinary nature of work and practice situations is a theme evidenced in program capstones and the growing understanding of the increasing need for physician leadership and voice in organization strategic decision making.

STRUCTURE OF THE BOOK

The book is in 2 sections. Section 1 considers why we need to change, and Section 2 deals with how to create the change. The intent is to explore useful ways of framing approaches to the preparation and development of future healthcare leaders to ensure that they are well prepared to meet future healthcare organizational challenges.

Section 1 gives the context (i.e., what is happening in healthcare and the issues calling for reform). It is also a clarion call to educate physicians who have sometimes stood on the sidelines and called foul but did not get engaged in helping reform the system themselves. The book argues for physicians to take the lead in the change they want to see. The delivery of healthcare still remains a physician driven dynamic with a great number of the decisions on resources being made by physicians at the side of the patient. It calls for physicians to take a leadership role in the transformation of healthcare and in order to do so, have the business acumen to lead the change.

Section 2 largely deals with the types of things physicians should learn to be able to be the chief executive officer (CEO) or chief operating officer (COO) of a healthcare organization and partner with others to take control of a system run amok with regulation, costs and uncoordinated care. By preparing physicians to lead the authors hope that not only will healthcare improve and costs go down, but also that care providers will once again experience the joy of their healing profession.

Contributing authors throughout the book emphasize that in order to meet the challenges of an increasingly complex landscape, physician leadership development should be an organizational priority. Organizational investment in physician leadership training and the creation of an organizational leadership pipeline enhances the organization's capacity to match emerging leaders with increasing roles of responsibility. Such leaders are able to apply a holistic, strategic decision making lens to achieve organizational efficiency, effectiveness, increased patient and physician satisfaction, and improved clinical outcomes.

REFERENCES

Ancona, D., & Gregersen, H. (2018). *The power of leaders who focus on solving problems.* Retrieved from https://hbr.org/2018/04/the-power-of-leaders-who-focus-on-solving-problems

Barnett, B. G., Basom, M. R., Yerkes, D. M., & Norris, C. J. (2000). Cohorts in educational leadership programs: Benefits, difficulties, and the potential for developing school leaders. *Educational Administration Quarterly*, *36*(2), 255–282. doi:10.1177/0013161X00362005

Barnett, B. G., & Muse, I. D. (1993). Cohort groups in education: Promises and challenges. *Journal of School Leadership*, *3*, 400–415.

Browne-Ferrigno, T., & Muth, R. (2003). Effects of cohorts on learners. *Journal of School Leadership*, *13*, 621–643.

Drucker, P. (1985, May/June). Visions of empire: Some problems with the corporate model of hospitals. *Hospital Forum*, 50–52. Retrieved from www.healthfutures.net/text/w-visemp.doc PMID:10272322

Ford, J. D., & Ford, L. W. (2009). Resistance to change: A reexamination and extension. *Research in Organizational Change and Development*, *17*, 211–239. doi:10.1108/S0897-3016(2009)0000017008

Ford, J. D., & Ford, L. W. (2010). Stop blaming resistance to change and start using it. *Organizational Dynamics*, *39*(1), 24–36. doi:10.1016/j.orgdyn.2009.10.002

Siefert, K., & Mandzuk, D. (2006). Student cohorts in teacher education: Support groups or intellectual communities? *Teachers College Record*, *108*(7), 1296–1320. doi:10.1111/j.1467-9620.2006.00694.x

Warren, O. J., & Carnall, R. (2011). Medical leadership: Why it's important, what is required, and how we develop it. *Postgraduate Medical Journal*, *87*(1023), 27–32. doi:10.1136/pgmj.2009.093807 PMID:20935344

Section 1
Physician Leadership

Chapter 1
Advancing Healthcare Leadership:
Physicians as Agents of Change

Valerie A. Storey
University of Central Florida, USA

ABSTRACT

As healthcare systems evolve and physicians face more administrative and regulatory burdens, it is imperative for them to build leadership competencies. In fact, there is a need for a pipeline to be created of emerging clinical leaders who have already mastered competencies and skills required of successful leaders. The heroic style of paternalistic leadership is less successful in an era of system complexity, quality control, and personnel diversity. A more preferable leadership style is that of shared leadership where a vision is created towards which team members are intrinsically driven to achieve. These factors have cumulatively contributed to the increasing cognizance that more training programs are needed to make comprehensive leadership development widely accessible to a greater number of potential clinical leaders. This chapter explores physicians and agents of change.

DOI: 10.4018/978-1-5225-7576-4.ch001

INTRODUCTION

Physicians have an intrinsic leadership role within healthcare services and have a responsibility to contribute to the effective running of the organization in which they work and to its future direction. Today, approximately 5 percent of hospital leaders are physicians, and that number is expected to increase rapidly as the health system moves toward value-based care (American Hospital Association, 2014). In fact, Arroliga, Huber, Myers, Dieckert, and Wesson (2014) argue that failure to train physicians, as healthcare leaders will have a long-term negative impact on society. The physician's frequent role, as head of the healthcare team and commander of considerable clinical resources require that greater attention is paid to management and leadership skills regardless of specialism. Role acknowledgement and aspiration to enhanced roles whether in subspecialty practice, management and leadership, education or research is likely to facilitate greater clinical engagement.

The traditional healthcare promotion model based on favoritism and cronyism (Dye, 2016) seniority, productivity, and academic credentials (Sonnino, 2016) is becoming increasingly obsolete not least because it promulgates and replicates the now rejected "great man theory" of leadership, and overlooks systems leadership due to naiveté and lack of understanding. On a more positive note, since the late 1980s there has been an increasingly positive trend of hospital chief executives officers (CEOs) taking a more equitable approach to in-house leadership and management by providing leadership training for medical staff leaders or heads of departments (AHA, 1991).

Whilst this trend is encouraging, to date no uniform approach has emerged for the development of physician leadership and management skills resulting in an erratic rather than systematic approach to healthcare organizational leadership. This has led to quick fix, discrete leadership programs being developed rather than sustainable programs to improve physicians' leadership capacity. Consequently, standards and demonstrable leadership competencies vary between programs. It is therefor essential that program variability be addressed both at the micro (program) and macro (professional organization) level as evidence grows linking physician leadership to performance of units. As a result, a growing number of practitioners, administrators, and academics are advocating for formal leadership training to be embedded in the education, and professional development programs of physicians throughout their career.

There is also a drive to see physicians take on more significant leadership roles throughout the healthcare system. The achievement of these aims will require physicians to develop strong personal and professional values, a range of non-technical skills that allow them to lead across professional boundaries, and an understanding of the increasingly complex environment in which 21st century healthcare is delivered (Warren & Carnall, 2017).

CONCEPTUALIZING LEADERSHIP

For more than a century, scholars working to define the dimensions of leadership have been concerned with (amongst other topics) how leaders motivate and inspire, facilitate and elicit high performance, build quality relationships, manage individuals and teams, and assign rewards. In fact, over 65 classification systems have been developed (Northouse, 2016). Generally, these classifications can be placed into six different classification systems. First, leadership can be viewed as the focus of group processes. Suggesting that the leader is at the center of group change and activity (Bass, 1990). Second, leadership can be conceptualized from a personality perspective i.e. a mix of personal traits and characteristics, suggesting that these traits encourage others to accomplish tasks. Third, leadership can be defined as an act or behavior referring to what the leader actually does to bring about change. Fourth, some define leadership in terms of the power relationships, which exist between leaders and followers, and that change occurs due to compliance. Fifth, leadership can be viewed as a transformational process that moves followers to achieve more than is usually expected of them. Finally, leadership can be viewed through a capabilities lens i.e. knowledge and skills that makes effective leadership possible.

If the general population was asked, "What do you understand by the word leadership?" It is likely that the majority would respond with a practical example or with the statement, "I know it when I see it." One commonly accepted definition is that proposed by Northouse (2016) who conceptualizes leadership as a process in which the individual influences individuals to achieve a common goal. In this definition leadership is an interactive exchange between the leader and the followers. Generally, the interaction is successful due to the influence of the leader, and the effect on followers. The leader is also influential in developing the goals for the group (followers) resulting in a collective purpose. Evolving definitions in the 21st century emphasize the leadership shift from controlling and maintaining followers into building relationships and empowering followers to participate in decision-making (Cunningham & Cordeiro, 2003).

SECURING ORGANIZATIONAL SUCCESS

Physicians in the 21st century need the knowledge and skills to be successfully accomplished at both leadership and management. A successful leader requires an understanding of the leadership process whereby they can influence a group of individuals to achieve a common goal but they also require managerial, operational knowledge to ensure that the challenges are preempted and addressed before they become a prohibitive preventive issue to the envisaged change.

Kotter (1990) argued that management's function is to create order and control in organizations whereas leadership provides support, to produce change and movement. Further, management's goals are stability and order contrasting with leadership, which has the goal of adaptive and constructive change. Kotter states that both management and leadership are necessary in an organization. Not having one or the other can be problematic.

CONTEMPORARY APPROACH TO LEADERSHIP AND MANAGEMENT

Leadership and management theorists are currently advocating for distributed and shared models, in line with the preferred cultures and structures of organizations, leaning towards empowered teams, and distributed responsibility. A key distinction between this contemporary mode and traditional models of leadership is that the influence process involves more than just the downward influence of subordinates by a positional leader. Leadership is distributed and shared amongst a set of individuals instead of being centralized in the hands of a single individual that acts in the role of leader (Pearce & Conger, 2002). Each team member's individual experience, knowledge and capacity is valued and is used by the team to distribute and share the job of leadership through the team in response to each context and challenge being faced. Evidence shows that distributed and shared leadership can increase risk-taking; innovation and commitment, which should result in improved care for the patient and an organization that is responsive, flexible and successful (Smith, n.d.).

Successful distributed and shared leadership however is dependent on successful self-leadership. Leaders need to understand themselves and their impact on others, through self-regulation, self-management and self-control. To be self-aware is to ask: "What impact am I having?" Who is better at this than me? "This is not working, what do I need to change"? Self-leaders need to learn to lead themselves before they can lead others in the team or organization (Houghton, Neck, & Manz, 2002).

PARADIGM SHIFT: RE-PROFESSIONALIZING PHYSICIANS

The paradigm shift from a senior level management approach to a distributed and shared leadership approach impacts both the organizational culture and the individual as it raises questions about the relationship between leaders and followers. In the traditional model, the knowledge – power relationship lies in the hands of senior level management i.e. the people who hold positions of dominance. These leaders have controlled the agendas and the truths. The proposed new leadership paradigm will challenge this norm and it could be argued "re-professionalize" physicians.

The knowledge base for what makes for success under conditions of complexity, such as a healthcare system, is becoming more insightful. We know that successful organizations must become learning organizations. We also know that to cultivate and sustain learning in any organization there is a need to be able to engage all voices to not only tackle known tough problems but also to help confront problems, which have not yet been addressed, whether at a micro or macro level (Fullan, 2001).

In order for physicians' to be primed for this new leadership paradigm they need to be prepared at all stages in their career to not only participate in decision-making but to lead the decision-making process, particularly when issues of patient safety and quality, managing costs, reducing readmissions, managing the continuum of care and adopting quality-based compensation are the focus (Dye, 2016). Leadership priming requires that physicians be steeped in four core capacities: 1) knowledge, skills and collegiality; 2) leadership competencies; 3) emotional intelligence; and 4) change agency (see Figure 1). This will increase their effectiveness and ensure they have the skills to mobilize team members to become more willing to solve problems.

It is essential that the four core leadership capacities with demonstrable, and measurable skill outcomes (see Table 1) be continually developed throughout a physician's careers.

Figure 1. Re-professionalizing physicians: contemporary healthcare leadership paradigm

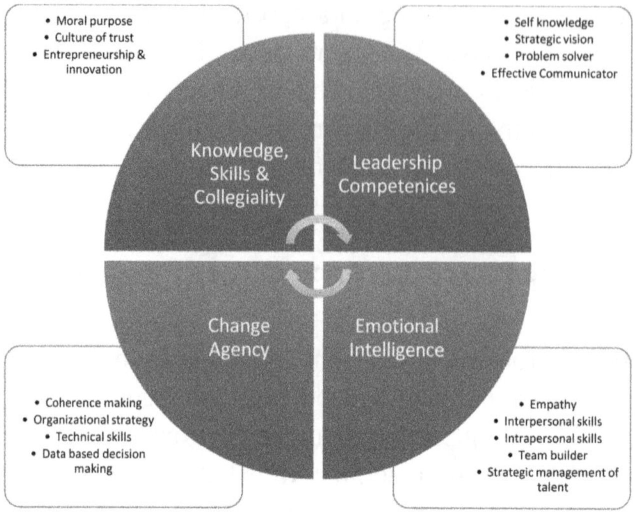

Table 1. Four core leadership capacities with demonstrable skill outcomes

Four Core Leadership Capacities	Demonstrable Skills Outcome
1. Leadership competencies	Self knowledge
	Strategic vision
	Problem solver
	Effective communicator
2. Emotional Intelligence	Empathy
	Interpersonal skills
	Intrapersonal skills
	Team builder
	Strategic management of talent
3. Change Agency	Coherence making
	Organizational strategy
	Technical skills
	Data based decision making
4. Knowledge, Skills and Collegiality	Moral purpose
	Culture of trust
	Entrepreneurship & innovation

USING THE RIGHT DRIVERS FOR SYSTEM SUCCESS

The world of healthcare has become multifaceted as the model of individual hospitals serving all patients' needs is no longer viable. Now, the healthcare world focuses on healthcare systems and networks of care (Kirtman & Fullan, 2016). This is a complicated shift that requires clear organization direction, and viable improvement. The United States of America (USA), United Kingdom (UK), and a growing number of countries are trying to drive reform with better standards, assessments, education and professional development.

Policy makers who are in a hurry to change the healthcare system, and think they can legislate to success are using the wrong drivers. To change the system, leaders must adopt a change culture, which nurtures organizational learning by embracing distributed and shared leadership from all levels and units within the organization. Increased autonomy, enhanced accountability and empowering personnel are necessary but not sufficient in the pursuit of high quality care. Making change actually happen takes dynamic leadership. Physicians must act as partners to their colleagues, and work with others to change systems when it is necessary for the benefit of patients.

Organizational culture is powerful when created by the organization as opposed to one leader. Culture (in contrast to leadership) will always trump any initiative and determine whether a new program or strategy will work or not (Kirtman & Fullan, 2016). Healthcare systems that focus on the right drivers for cultural change and identify and support collaborative leaders within all levels of the system will more likely implement sustainable improvements. According to Lencioni (2012), the right drivers for organizational success and excellence are:

1. Minimal politics
2. Minimal confusion
3. High morale
4. High productivity
5. Low turnover of talented leaders

LEADERSHIP AND PHYSICIANS

In the 21st century, organizations are progressively focused on the process of leadership rather than on individual leadership. Historically, the conceptualization of leadership theory was formulated through a male lens and subsequently applied to males and females (Shakeshaft & Nowell, 1984). Theory development was limited to males as corporate leadership positions were exclusive to males. Consequently, leadership styles evidenced in historically male professions perpetuate even as professions become gender equitable. The problem with this paradigm is that the male dominated leadership style does not reflect current leadership practices or organizational paradigms. In the late 19th and early 20th century the dominant leadership style in a complex organization would be transactional i.e. a strong leader who maintains the status quo, and focuses on efficiency, control, stability, and predictability. In the mid-20th century, organizations began to look for a transformational leader i.e. a leader who raises employees to higher levels of motivation, and promotes a vision which followers are keen to buy into (Savage, Duncan, Knowles, Nelson, Rogers & Kennedy, 2014). Towards the end of the 20th century the concept of servant leadership gained momentum, such leaders focus on the service aspect of their role and lead with humility rather than pride (Greenleaf, 1977). Today, there is an increasing emphasis on leadership traits and soft skills, (as opposed to hard skills which are the hard skills and technical knowledge needed for a job), sometimes referred to as feminine aligned practices. In a study with executive business leaders Robles (2012) identified the most important 10 soft skills as perceived by organizational leaders: integrity, communication, courtesy, responsibility, social skills, positive attitude, professionalism, flexibility, teamwork, and work ethic.

As professions become increasingly gender equitable so the individual leadership model of top-down, heroic/paternalism has transitioned to viewing leadership as a process requiring a more collaborative approach, where the leader helps the team develop a vision and empowers team members to accomplish the stated goals. This 21st century systems approach is especially appropriate for healthcare systems where tasks are complex and highly interdependent as it enables all personnel to have the opportunity to contribute to the leadership task where and when their expertise and qualities are relevant and appropriate to the challenge being addressed (Serio & Epperley, 2006).

HEALTHCARE LEADERSHIP DEVELOPMENT

National organizations such as The American Association for Physician Leadership (AAPL) have recognized for some time that early career physicians are becoming increasingly interested in developing leadership skills in order to positively affect their working environment. In 1975, AAPL began developing education and mentoring programs to facilitate physicians' leadership skills through both generic and bespoke face-to-face and distance learning programs in order to facilitate the ability of physicians to respond to the rapid changes in healthcare irrespective of their career stage (see Table 2).

The association believes that physicians best understand the intricacies of healthcare, and equipped with the appropriate leadership skills, are perfectly suited to becoming the change agents within their healthcare delivery system (AAPL, 2017). These programs however are voluntary and come at a financial and personal cost. For some, the cost will fall on the shoulders of the commissioning healthcare system, and whilst this removes the burden of a personal financial cost it does not alleviate the personal time cost on what is already a stressful, and consuming professional schedule.

Developing leadership skills is also a priority of the Physicians Foundation, as it recognizes the need for physicians to thrive in today's healthcare environment, influence the future of the profession and deliver high-quality, cost-efficient care. Rather than providing leadership programs for physicians, the Physicians Foundation has provided grants to fund universities and organizations to develop physician leadership programs that help physicians build leadership skills that drive toward healthcare excellence. The Physicians

Table 2. Physician leadership programs

Graduate #	Physician Leadership Programs
100K	*100 Leadership courses*
	Certificate Courses
1,200	*4 Master degree programs*
	Ph.D. in development
2,200	*Board Certification (Certified Physician Executive)*
	200 in house leadership courses, annually
	3,200 online courses sold, annually
21,000	*Graduated from Physician in Management series*

Source: American Association for Physician Leadership

Foundation has funded nearly 40 leadership programs over the past few years concentrating on new approaches and models that support physicians desiring to become leaders in the profession e.g. University of Massachusetts Medical School, North Carolina Medical Society Foundation, Connecticut State Medical Society Physicians' Health and Education Fund, Hawaii Medical Foundation, and the Physicians' Institute. These programs focus on topics critical to the development of core physician leader curricula, such as:

- *Leadership*
- *Healthcare Finance*
- *Organizational Behavior*
- *Conflict Resolution and Negotiation*
- *Coaching and Mentoring*
- *Building High Performing Teams*
- *Quality & Performance Measurement*
- *Operations Management*
- *Strategic Management*
- *State & National Health Policy (The Physicians Foundation, 2018)*

In addition to professional associations, healthcare systems and organizations have also identified the gap that exists in healthcare leadership development for physicians. For example in 2006, the Cleveland Clinic founded the Cleveland Clinic Academy, which developed leadership courses for physicians in both standalone formats as well as experiential learning format. The academy has trained over 6,000 physicians worldwide (Hess, 2013). Programs emphasize the need for teaching components of emotional intelligence and teamwork training during medical school and residency.

The American Academy of Pediatrics developed the Young Physicians' Leadership Alliance (YPLA), a 3-year training program designed to develop leaders and build a leadership community amongst early career pediatricians and pediatric subspecialists. The program includes the sharing of leadership principles, behaviors, and tools that can benefit early career physicians in achieving their personal and professional objectives (American Academy of Pediatrics, n.d.).

The American College of Surgeons runs a short but intense 3-day leadership course, which aims to provide surgeons with an understanding of leadership at all levels of an organization and provides them with the skills that are essential to effective leadership. Difficult leadership issues such as navigating the operational and human aspects of change, cultivating commitment to a shared vision and goals, building teams, and developing strategies for leading up, down, and across the institutional environment are all addressed in the curricula (The American College of Surgeons, 2017).

An example of a leadership program developed to meet a group need is the Executive Leadership in Academic Medicine (ELAM) program designed to support the advancement, and continuing success of women leaders in schools of medicine, dentistry, and, most recently, public health (Richman & Magrane, 2011). ELAM teaches that leadership can be exercised by anyone at any level and that every ELAM graduate can demonstrate her leadership skills and make a positive contribution to her institution regardless of the position held (Richman & Magrane, 2011). This innovative national program is organized around three curricular threads: 1) organizational perspectives and knowledge (a mini-executive MBA); 2) emerging issues in leadership and academic health administration; and 3) personal and professional development. Learning communities, and mentoring facilitate an ethos of ongoing collaboration, personal and professional support for alumnae (Morahan, Gleason, Richman, Dannels, & McDade, 2010).

PROFESSIONAL PIPELINE FOR PHYSICIAN LEADERS

The development of a Professional Pipeline for Physicians Leaders (PPPL) by healthcare systems, professional organizations, and partner higher education institutions reflects the belief that healthcare systems can do much to develop and support physicians as effective leaders if they reshape traditional, often haphazard professional development for aspiring physician leaders. The intent of the pipeline is to improve physician leadership by means of an intentionally crafted system of clearly stated expectations, selection gateways, and opportunities for professional growth for physician leaders, implemented at scale. Course selection is guided by stated expectations or competency matrices, which map required leadership competencies to specific courses.

The PPPL represents a developmental perspective for fostering leadership capacity in physicians, from nurturing potential talent during education programs to ensuring career-long learning through professional development. An intentional and mindful approach to supporting the development of physician leaders throughout their professional careers is critical to healthcare systems. How the profession enacts phases of the pipeline and the quality of these experiences serve as a message to physicians and clinical colleagues alike. Developing aligned competency curricula for aspiring physician leaders requires the strategic and intentional coordination of efforts by multiple stakeholders: healthcare systems, higher education, professional organizations, and state departments. Each entity possesses a stake in developing highly qualified physician leaders. Attention given to relationships among program features including leadership practices, allows the profession to better delineate effective and ineffective strategies to enhance the leadership pipeline.

Processes need to be in place to test the power of the pipeline to affect clinical performance and quality of patient care.

LEADERSHIP STANDARDS AND COMPETENCIES

In both the USA and the UK there is now an acknowledgement that formal training in the multifaceted components of leadership is highly desirable for healthcare leaders. Leadership is a competency-based behavior that has to come from everyone involved in healthcare. Physicians work in multidisciplinary teams focused on the needs and safety of the patient where leadership becomes the responsibility of the team.

In order to ensure that providers and programs deliver rigorous, authentic and applicable curricula there has been a move by associations and regulators to develop accepted leadership standards and competencies to ensure a consistent approach to leadership development. Academic programs are taking steps to ensure that their competency models are tied with the realities and needs of physician leadership practice.

Figure 2. Professional pipeline for physician leadership (PPPL)

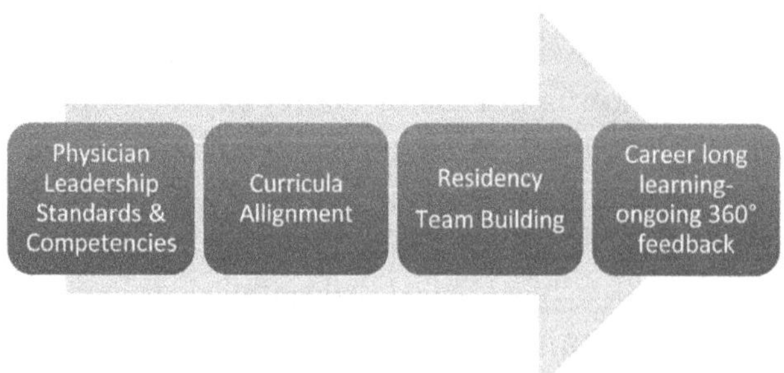

In 1999, the Accreditation Council on Graduate Medical Education (ACGME) a private, non-profit council that evaluates and accredits more than 9,000 residency programs across 135 specialties and subspecialties in the USA endorsed six general competencies to integrate in curricula (ACGME, n.d., Rider & Keefer, 2006).

1. Patient care
2. Medical knowledge
3. Practice-based learning and improvement
4. Interpersonal and communication skills
5. Professionalism
6. Systems-based practice.

For the first time there is reference to a leadership approach embedded in the sixth core competency "systems-based practice." Program graduates must be able to demonstrate an awareness of and responsiveness to the larger context and system of healthcare and the ability to effectively call on system resources to provide care that is of optimal value. Mastery of these competencies facilitates in physicians the ability to become collaborative leaders, with a vision for the entire realm of healthcare.

The Association of American Medical Colleges (AAMC) also identified core competencies for their leadership programs. Unlike previous examples the AAMC targets institutional graduate medical education (GME) leaders who oversee GME quality, accreditation, administration, and financing in their AAMC member medical schools and teaching hospitals rather than active physicians. Nevertheless, the recently introduced Leadership Development Certificate Program is of interest as the curriculum is grounded on the new GME leadership framework, which outlines four domains of leadership competencies:

1. **Foundational Attributes:** Personal attributes and capabilities essential for high-performing GME leaders. They are the individual foundational characteristics that facilitate success in the GME leader role and exemplify an effective role model and teacher to aspiring leaders.
2. **Leadership Capabilities:** Leadership performance capabilities that GME leaders must effectively demonstrate or manage to achieve success in the role. They are the underlying leadership roles and capabilities necessary to fulfill the mission of the institutional GME leader.

3. **Knowledge and Skills:** Fundamental skills and knowledge essential to performing key functional and environmental aspects of the GME leader role.
4. **Entrustable Professional Activities:** The activities and responsibilities that GME leaders must successfully execute to achieve professional proficiency. They specifically define the profession, outcomes expected by stakeholders, and are achieved through the integration of the other three domains. They are measured in terms of both process and performance outcomes. Institutional GME leaders achieve EPAs through their position of authority and through the work of teams (*Association of American Medical Colleges AAMC, 2017; Institutional GME leadership competencies).*

INTERNATIONAL PERSPECTIVE

Since the 1990s, there has been a strong push for improved physician leadership and increased medical involvement in the delivery of healthcare in the UK (Chantler, 1999). In 2005, the Royal College of Physicians stated that the complementary skills of leadership and followership should be integral to physicians' training to support professionalism. Reviews on the future of healthcare within the United Kingdom (Darzi, 2007; 2008) also highlight physician leadership as an essential component of quality care.

In 2009, the Academy of Medical Royal Colleges and the National Health Service (NHS) Institute for Innovation and Improvement in conjunction with a wide range of stakeholders published the *Medical Leadership Competency Framework* (MLCF). This document defines the skills and competencies needed by physicians to engage effectively in the planning, provision and improvement of health care services. The framework built on the concept of shared leadership where leadership is not restricted to people who hold designated leadership roles, and where there is a shared sense of responsibility for the success of the organization and its services. The General Medical Council state,

Being a good doctor means more than simply being a good clinician. Every day, doctors provide leadership to their colleagues, and vision for the organizations in which they work and to the profession as a whole. The definition of leadership has undergone an evolution in recent years. We recognize that some doctors are formal leaders who are accountable for the performance of their team, department or organization. But we think that the responsibility for identifying problems, solving, and implementing the appropriate action is shared by the team as a whole. This is what we mean by shared leadership. (Ethical Guidance Management for Doctors, n.d.)

Notably, leadership had already been identified as an essential requirement of all physicians as laid out in the General Medical Council's (GMC) publications *Good Medical Practice, Tomorrow's Doctors* and also *Management for Doctors* (2006) which set out the wider management and leadership responsibilities of physicians:

1. Managing employment issues
2. Teaching and training
3. Planning, using and managing resources
4. Raising and acting on concerns
5. Participating in service improvement and development

The aim being to ensure that the development of leadership competence becomes an integral part of a physician's training and learning. To this end *Guidance for Undergraduate Medical Education: Integrating the Medical Leadership Competency Framework* and the *Medical Leadership Curriculum* (2010) has been incorporated into the 58 specialty curricula of the Medical Royal Colleges and Faculties. There are five domains, and within each domain there are four elements, and each of these elements is further divided into four competency outcomes (see Table 3).

Table 3. Medical Leadership Competency Framework (MLCF, 2010). NHS Institute for Innovation & Improvement, and Academy of Medical Royal Colleges (p.11).

1. Demonstrating Personal Qualities	**2. Working with Others**	**3. Managing Services**	**4. Improving Services**	**5. Setting Direction**
1.1 Developing self-awareness	2.1 Developing networks	3.1 Planning	4.1 Ensuring patient safety	5.1 Identifying the contexts for change
1.2 Managing yourself	2.2 Building & maintaining relationships	3.2 Managing resources	4.2 Critically evaluating	5.2 Applying knowledge & evidence
1.3 Continuing personal development	2.3 Encouraging contribution	3.3 Managing people	4.3 Encouraging improvement & innovation	5.3 Making decisions
1.4 Acting with integrity	2.4 Working within teams	3.4 Managing performance	4.4 Facilitating transformation	5.4 Evaluating impact

The MLCF applies to all physicians and is intended to be acquired across their medical career at each appropriate level (undergraduate, postgraduate and continuing practice). The framework is currently being used in NHS organizations to inform the design and development of programs. Additionally, it is being used to assist individual physicians with personal development planning and career progression.

In 2011, the Academy of Medical Royal Colleges formally endorsed the establishment of a Faculty of Medical Leadership and Management (FMLM) to promote excellence in physician leadership in public health, primary and secondary care and at all stages of the medical career from medical student to medical director. In 2015, FMLM published the second edition of *The Leadership and Management Standards for Medical Professionals (see* Table 4*)* to provide clarity regarding the expectations of physicians in leadership and management roles. The intention is for the standards and competencies to be aspirational and stimulate improvement and consistency in medical leadership.

The 4 standards and 48 behaviors (competencies) are designed to work across all levels and are grounded in the General Medical Council's guidance, *Leadership and Management for all Doctors* (2012) (which replaced *Management for Doctors, 2006*). The foundation for the crafted standards and domains are leadership frameworks, models, and research on medical leadership, management and engagement.

FMLM also launched a 360° feedback tool (2016) for individuals at team, operational and strategic levels.

DESIGNING A LEADERSHIP PROGRAM FOR PHYSICIANS

Pearl and Fogle (2017) writing in the Massachusetts Medical Society, New England Journal of Medicine (NEJM), argue that graduating students from medical schools in the U.S. lack the fundamental business and leadership

Table 4. The Leadership and Management Standards for Medical Professionals

1. Self	2. Team Player/Team Leader	3. Corporate Responsibility	4. System Leadership
1a. Self-awareness development	2a. Effective teamwork	3a. Corporate team player	4a. System leadership
1b. Personal resilience, drive and energy	2b. Cross team collaborations	3b. Corporate culture, improvement and innovation	

training needed to effect healthcare changes, and simultaneously maximize quality and reduce cost in clinical practice. They highlight the need to take an interdisciplinary approach to physician's training in order to extend their knowledge and skills in three key business disciplines: leadership, teamwork, and data analytics. All of which are courses offered in business schools as part of their core curricula.

However, physicians participating in NEJM's, Catalyst Insights Council's Leadership survey (2017), identified interpersonal skills as the top attribute needed to successfully lead other physicians (90%), outpacing clinical skills (69%), negotiation skills (59%), administrative skills (31%), knowledge of healthcare legislation (22%) and financial acumen (14%). This suggests that what is important to physician leadership development from both the practitioner and academia perspective is method of delivery as well as content. The need to demonstrate interpersonal skills through simulations and role-plays, which enable skills to be practiced and new knowledge to be applied should always be a primary course/program aim.

Physician Leadership Program Models

Predominantly there are two models for developing physician's leadership skills. The distinct leadership program and then embedded leadership program.

The distinct leadership program approach (model 1) is the most common based on a "grow your own" approach in which the healthcare system nominates candidates and becomes a working partner with a university to address organizational needs. This is usually through an interdisciplinary MBA composed of courses that integrate business and leadership competencies within the context of healthcare.

The embedded leadership program approach (model 2) is still in the stage of incubation but requires leadership competencies and skills to be built into education and training programs throughout a physician's career allowing learning to be interspersed with periods of reflection, work experience, career progression and further challenges (Warren & Carnall, 2011). This model is by far the most intrusive, most costly, and most challenging to implement due to the number of stakeholders that need to be committed and involved.

Only through on-going research and evaluation will we know the longitudinal impact on physicians of the two different models.

Program Rationale

In developing a leadership program for physicians, irrespective of the model of preference it is important to clarify the aims of the program. Program designers should answer the following questions, as this will influence the program design, methodology, length, and cost. Is the leadership program for self-applicants, or a competitive program for targeted high potential future medical leaders, or a cohort of physicians across a healthcare system or state? Are program graduates expected to be agents of change at a system or organizational level? Traditionally the few leadership programs that exist have been for targeted high potential future medical leaders or for those applicants who have the resources to fund a leadership development program. The envisaged contemporary approach (model 2) is to embed leadership development modules early in a physician's career so that they develop a set of knowledge, skills and behaviors that will enable them to engage and lead in a highly complex healthcare system (Stoller, 2014). An appropriate program rationale would be to develop a program that fosters in physicians the ability to take a macroscopic view on healthcare provision and resource allocation to enable program graduates to become change agents in the healthcare system.

Curriculum

In both models, an interdisciplinary approach should be taken to course and module design to ensure that aspiring physician leaders understand all the aspects of the organization whether or not they are personally engaged in all of them.

Courses should include:

- Leadership-styles and process, emotional intelligence, interpersonal skills, communication skills, team building, change management
- Organizational culture-collegial leadership, teamwork, conflict resolution, negotiation
- Performance management, time management, mentorship
- Strategic data driven decision making-systems perspective, micro and macro level, financial knowledge-budgeting
- Finance-management and allocation of resources

Completing a self-assessment and 360° feedback tool (receiving confidential feedback from line managers, peers and direct reports) at regular intervals throughout a physician's career will give an individual an insight into other people's perceptions of their leadership abilities and behavior (NHS Leadership Academy, 2011; Sonnino, 2016). This self-knowledge can then be aligned to Sonnino's Leadership Framework (Table 5), which identifies the optimal elements and competencies of healthcare leadership development.

Course participants need to have a strong sense of self-awareness of their values and beliefs- and should be expected to demonstrate skills such as creating and communicating their vision, setting clear direction, service redesign and healthcare improvement, effective negotiation, collaboratively working and networking (Warren & Carnall, 2017).

Table 5. Leadership Framework (2016): Sonnino's optimal elements and competencies of healthcare leadership development

1. Differentiating Competencies	2. Personal Competencies	3. Task-Oriented Knowledge (may differ for physicians in different areas of health care)
Finance & Economics Team Building Communication Skills Emotional Intelligence Conflict Management Negotiation	Personal & Professional Development Introspection-Getting to Know Oneself Listening Empathy Awareness Persuasion Integrity Authenticity Equity Justice Work Ethic Role Modeling Innovation: Develop, Inspire, Challenge the Status Quo, & Focus on a Long-Term Vision Foresight Stewardship Commitment to Continuous Improvement & Lifelong Learning Balancing Work & Personal Life	Business & Administrative Acumen & Skills Technical Knowledge of Insurance & Reimbursement Issues Quality Patient Care/Healthcare Regulations Legal Issues in Healthcare & Public Policy Problem Solving Skills Being a Change Agent Emerging Issues & Strategic Planning Organization & Prioritization Time Management

CONCLUSION

Whilst the formal leader's role within a healthcare system is to create the climate in which the team can flourish through team building, resolving conflicts and being clear about the vision, physicians have a vital intrinsic leadership role. They are the organizational cultural drivers, and have a responsibility to contribute to the effective running of the organization in which they work and to its future direction. Expanded availability of comprehensive leadership development opportunities, would result not only in better prepared senior health care leaders but also in improved interactions between hospital administrators, practicing professionals, and academicians, with a culture of true collaborative or shared leadership. Only by taking a strategic and systematic approach can a pipeline of future physician leaders (and change agents) be developed grounded on leadership standards and competencies which will enable them to engage and lead strategic and transformational change in highly complex, and turbulent healthcare systems.

REFERENCES

Accreditation Council for Graduate Medical Education (ACGME). (2001). *General competencies: ACGME outcome project*. Retrieved from http://www.acgme.org/What-We-Do/Accreditation/Common-Program-Requirements

American Academy of Pediatrics. (2017). Retrieved from https://www.aap.org/en-us/about-the-aap/Committees-Councils-Sections/Neonatal-Perinatal-Medicine/TECAN/Pages/Leadership.aspx

American College of Surgeons. (2017). Retrieved from https://www.facs.org/education/division-of-education/courses/surgeons-as-leaders

American Hospital Association. (2014). *Physician Leadership Education*. Chicago: Physician Leadership Forum.

American Hospital Association Division of Medical Affairs (AHA). (1992). *Medical Staff Report*. Chicago: The Association.

Arroliga, A. C., Huber, C., Myers, J. D., Dieckert, J. P., & Wesson, D. (2014). Leadership in health care for the 21st century: Challenges and opportunities. *The American Journal of Medicine, 127*(3), 246–249. doi:10.1016/j.amjmed.2013.11.004 PMID:24280177

Association of American Medical Colleges (AAMC). (2017). *Institutional GME leadership competencies*. GRA Core Competency Task Force of the Group on Resident Affairs (GRA). Retrieved from https://www.aamc.org/members/leadership/470170/gmeleadershipdevelopmentcertificateprogram.html

Chantler C. (1999). The role and education of doctors in the delivery of health care. *Lancet, 353*, 1178-81.

Cunningham, W. G., & Cordeiro, P. A. (2003). *Educational leadership: A problem-based approach*. Boston, MA: Pearson Education.

Darzi, A. (2007). *Healthcare for London: A framework for action*. London: NHS London.

Darzi, A. (2008). *High quality care for all: The NHS next stage review final report*. London: Department of Health.

Doctors in Society. (2005). *Medical professionalism in a changing world*. London: Royal College of Physicians.

Dye, C. F. (2016, September/October). Selecting physician leaders. *Healthcare Executive*, 72–75. PMID:29693929

Ethical Guidance Management for Doctors. (n.d.). Retrieved March 12, 2018, from http://www.gmcuk.org/guidance/ethical_guidance/management_for_doctors.asp

Faculty of Medical Leadership and Management. (2016). *Leadership and management standards for medical professionals* (2nd ed.). London: Faculty of Medical Leadership & Management.

Fullan, M. (2001). *Leading in a culture of change*. San Francisco, CA: Jossey-Bass.

General Medical Council. (2012). *Leadership and management for all doctors*. London: GMC. Retrieved from: http:// www.gmc-uk.org/guidance

Greenleaf, R. K. (1977). *Servant leadership – A journey into the nature of legitimate power and greatness*. Paulist Press Mahwah.

Ham, C., Clark, J., & Spurgeon, P. (2010). *Medical chief executives in the NHS: Facilitators and barriers to their career progress*. Coventry, UK: NHS Institute for Innovation & Improvement.

Hess, C. (2013). Health care educators: New directions in leadership development. *The Journal of Leadership Studies*, *6*(4), 72–76. doi:10.1002/jls.21269

Houghton, J. D., Neck, C. P., & Manz, C. C. (2002). Self-leadership and superleadership: The heart and art of creating shared leadership. In C. L. Pearce & J. A. Conger (Eds.), *Shared leadership: Reframing the hows and whys of leadership* (pp. 126–132). Thousand Oaks, CA: SAGE Publications.

Kirtman, L., & Fullan, M. (2016). *Leadership: Key competencies for whole-system change*. Bloomington, IN: Solution Tree Press.

Kotter, J. P. (1990). *A force for change: How leadership differs from management*. New York: Free Press.

Lencioni, P. (2012). *The advantage*. San Francisco, CA: Jossey-Bass.

Massachusetts Medical Society. (2017). *Leadership survey: Ability to lead does not come from a degree*. Waltham, MA: NEJM Catalyst Insight Council.

Morahan, P. S., Gleason, K. A., Richman, R. C., Dannels, S., & McDade, S. A. (2010). Advancing women faculty to senior leadership in U.S. academic health centers: Fifteen years of history in the making. *Journal About Women in Higher Education, 3*(1), 137–161. doi:10.2202/1940-7890.1042

National Health Service (NHS) Institute for Innovation and Improvement & Academy of Medical Royal Colleges. (2010). *The medical leadership competency framework* (3rd ed.). The National Institute for Innovation and Improvement. Retrieved from http://www.institute.nhs.uk/assessment_tool/general/medical_leadership_competency_framework_-_homepage.html

National Health Service (NHS) Institute for Innovation and Improvement and Academy of Medical Royal Colleges. (2009). *The medical leadership competency framework* (2nd ed.). Coventry, UK: NHS Institute for Innovation & Improvement.

National Health Service (NHS) Leadership Academy. (2011). *Leadership framework: A summary.* Coventry, UK: NHS Institute for Innovation & Improvement.

Northouse, P. G. (2016). *Leadership: Theory and practice* (7th ed.). Thousand Oaks, CA: SAGE Publications.

Pearce, C. L., & Conger, J. A. (2002). All those years ago: The historical underpinnings of shared leadership. In C. L. Pearce & J. A. Conger (Eds.), *Shared leadership: Reframing the hows and whys of leadership* (pp. 1–18). Thousand Oaks, CA: SAGE.

Pearl, R., & Fogle, A. L. (2016). New physicians will need business school skills. *New England Journal of Medicine Catalyst.* Retrieved from http://catalyst.nejm.org/new-physicians-need-business-school-skills/

Richman, R. C., & Magrane, D. (2011). *The Executive Leadership in Academic Medicine (ELAM) program for women - Fourteen years of academic women leaders in medicine, dentistry, and public health.* Retrieved from https://www.aamc.org/members/gfa/faculty_vitae/148588/elam.html

Rider, E. A., & Keefer, C. H. (2006). Communication skills competencies: Definitions and a teaching toolbox. *Medical Education, 40*(7), 624–629. doi:10.1111/j.1365-2929.2006.02500.x PMID:16836534

Robles, M. M. (2012). Executive perceptions of the top 10 soft skills needed in today's workplace. *Business Communication Quarterly*, *75*(4), 453–465. doi:10.1177/1080569912460400

Savage, G. T., Duncan, W. J., Knowles, K. L., Nelson, K., Rogers, D. A., & Kennedy, K. N. (2014). Interprofessional academic health center leadership development: The case of the University of Alabama at Birmingham's Healthcare Leadership Academy. *Applied Nursing Research*, *27*(2), 104–108. doi:10.1016/j.apnr.2013.07.001 PMID:23993745

Serio, C. D., & Epperley, T. (2006). *Physician leadership: A new model for a new generation.* Retrieved from www.aafp.org/fpm

Shakeshaft, C., & Nowell, I. (1984). Research on theories, concepts, and models of organizational behavior: The influence of gender. *Issues in Education*, *2*(6), 186–200.

Smith, P. (n.d.). *Shared leadership: New ways of leading*. Retrieved from http://www.opi-inc.com/shared_leadership.htm

Sonnino, R. E. (2013). Professional development and leadership training opportunities for healthcare professionals. *American Journal of Surgery*, *206*(5), 727–731. doi:10.1016/j.amjsurg.2013.07.004 PMID:24011565

Sonnino, R. E. (2016). Health care leadership development and training: Progress and pitfalls. *Journal of Healthcare Leadership*, *8*, 19–29. doi:10.2147/JHL.S68068 PMID:29355187

Stoller, J. K. (2014). Help wanted: Developing clinician leaders. *Perspectives on Medical Education*, *3*(3), 233–237. doi:10.100740037-014-0119-y PMID:24865886

The Physicians Foundation. (n.d.). Retrieved from http://www.physiciansfundation.org/healthcare-grants/portfolio/physician-leadership-grants

Warren, O. J., & Carnall, R. (2017). Medical leadership: Why it's important, what is required, and how we develop it. *Postgraduate Medical Journal*, *87*(1023), 27–32. doi:10.1136/pgmj.2009.093807 PMID:20935344

KEY TERMS AND DEFINITIONS

Clinical Leadership: Individual skills, knowledge, and competencies required to effectively balance the needs of patients and team members within resource constraints and management.

Heroic Leadership: A version of "Great Man" theories, which emphasize characteristics such as charisma, energy, dominance, and intelligence.

Leadership Competencies: Demonstrable skills and qualities most strongly associated with advanced levels of leadership and desired outcomes in an organization.

Leadership Pipeline: A systematic, visible system of identifying employees for succession, combined with the processes for their development.

Leadership Style: Manner and approach of providing direction, implementing plans, and motivating people.

Management: Organization and coordination of business activities in order to achieve defined strategic objectives.

Physician Education: Varying routes to clinical leadership including MD/MBA and MBA programs to meet the needs of complex healthcare systems who require the dual skill sets of business-savvy and medical training from candidates seeking leadership positions in administration, policy, and industry positions.

Shared Leadership: Empowers organizational employees to take leadership positions in their areas of expertise.

System Complexity: Consist of numerous interacting and interwoven elements, parts, or agents defined by the structure of the system, the types of interactions between system elements, and the dynamics and patterns of the system that emerge from these interactions.

Team Leadership: Practices and values exhibited by leaders, governing a specific group of individuals who are working towards achieving a particular goal or objective.

Chapter 2
Developing Healthcare Leaders for the Future:
A Team Approach

Thomas E. Beeman
University of Pennsylvania Health System, USA

Genevieve Mak Dean
University of Pennsylvania Health System, USA

ABSTRACT

Irrespective of the healthcare delivery mechanisms that have endured to this day, consumers expect value in their healthcare, which implies high quality, reasonable cost, and an excellent patient experience. Physicians will need to not only participate in effecting this change, but also lead it, or risk losing credibility as a patient's most critical healthcare advocate. In anticipation of these needs, Lancaster General Health (LG Health) embarked on a unique, decade-long physician leadership development journey that culminated in the graduation of 21 physicians and administrators from St. Joseph's Haub School of Business Executive MBA program. Collectively, the group constitutes a priceless network of professionals who are helping to lead healthcare change in their community.

DOI: 10.4018/978-1-5225-7576-4.ch002

INTRODUCTION

Whether healthcare has a black swan looming, or some lesser disrupter on the horizon, one thing is certain: spending on healthcare has reached epic proportions (Taleb, 2010). Three trillion dollars, or 20% of the nation's gross domestic product (GDP), is placing a severe drag on the United States (U.S.) economy. What is uncertain is how long this level of spending can be sustained.

Consumers, who convert to patients for their brief office visits or hospital stays, pay an average of $18,764 for an employee-sponsored family plan (Kaiser Family Foundation, 2017). Considering that in 2016, the median household income for an American family was $59,039, it is no wonder that consumers feel that healthcare is priced outside of a reasonable range - like the US economy, over 30% of most families' income is simply too much. Similarly, businesses cannot afford to keep up with the rapid rise in healthcare pricing and disrupters, such as the collaboration between Berkshire Hathaway, Amazon and J. P. Morgan Chase is a good example of a major healthcare stakeholder deciding that the growth trajectory in healthcare spending must stop (Wingfield, Thomas, & Abelson, 2018).

Exacerbating the frustration with the costs of this system is the fact that outcomes of these expenses are not particularly impressive. According to the Peter G. Peterson Foundation, 30% of US healthcare spending goes to wasteful, ineffective, or useless services. In a study conducted by the Organisation for Economic Co-operation and Development (OECD), cited by The Commonwealth Fund in *U.S Healthcare from a Global Perspective*, the United States' per capita spending was highest, while life expectancy was the lowest amongst 13 OECD countries including Australia, Canada, Denmark, France, Germany, United Kingdom, and Japan.

Considering this, it is no wonder that "value" has become the buzzword in healthcare that is, according to Griffith (1998), "price and quality delivered to the customer". This means that "it consists of good outcomes, easy access and acceptable service" (Griffith, 1998, p. 3) and, one could add, at an affordable price. The Institute for Healthcare Improvement explains the need to move in this direction through the "Triple Aim" which focuses on:

- Improving the patient experience of care (including quality and satisfaction);
- Improving the health of populations; and

- Reducing the per capita cost of health care.

So, why are we at this juncture? The symptoms we are seeing, of high costs, with less than desirable outcomes, are the results of a system that was not designed to keep people well. Rather, healthcare in the US has focused on caring for people when they are sick. While not an intrinsically "bad" way to look at resolving a problem, a system that is only focused on problem resolution is incomplete. A more complete approach would be to consider problem mitigation, and resolution assessment and improvement, pieces that are often forgotten or ignored.

In healthcare, focusing on caring for patients when they are ill has resulted in a one-dimensional system. Incentives, systems and programs have all aligned to focus on getting sick patients "well", rather than keeping "well" patients from getting sick. Likewise, there is no feedback mechanism to assess whether the processes and steps we are taking to get people "well" are working. Put simply, the system has focused on interventional rather than preventative care. This is reflected in the payment mechanisms of current healthcare, with little or no recognition for the time of physicians and their staff to proactively reach out to patients for annual health checks, cancer screenings, etc., to prevent their needing future intensive care. No compensation is offered for building relationships that might actually mitigate interventional healthcare needs. Consequently, these perverse incentives have resulted in expensive inpatient services and interventions.

Unfortunately, the inefficiencies of the healthcare system have been largely obscured due to the fact that the majority of healthcare expenses are borne by government or private businesses. Per the Commonwealth Fund in *U.S Healthcare from a Global Perspective*, in the U.S., of the $8,713 per capita spent on healthcare expenses, only 12%, or $1,074 was "Out of Pocket" spending.

Due to this lack of line of sight, and a culture oriented to demand the very best money can buy, it is no wonder that healthcare costs have risen exponentially in the past half century. As businesses increasingly share the cost burden with their employees, the consumer's' voice is starting to be heard. As the cost line of sight comes into view, consumers are now aware that for the same issue, they may be charged two very different prices for the same test, such as in the case of Mr. Charlap, whose echocardiograms billed out at both $5,435 and $1,714. Though Mr. Charlap paid only $419 and $474, respectively, for those two bills, as cost becomes clearer to the patient, they are increasingly questioning how and where their healthcare dollars are being spent (Rosenthal, 2014).

So, what can we expect? We can be assured of a clash that will signal the end of an economic era for insurers, pharmaceutical companies, physicians and hospitals, when the business model finally collapses in response to the rising call for reform. Fortunately though, this clash can be either a reverberating death knell, or the resounding calm after the banging of a gong.

The way we choose to end this era is up to us; those who understand healthcare's complications and complexities, and know how it can be better delivered. If we can lean into the change, to help shape our future by understanding the mistakes of our past and paving the way for innovation and balance, we are more likely to move into this new era calmly but with excitement about the future, rather than remorse and grief over the loss of the past.

It is evident that in order to affect this type of change, the principal prescriber of care must be a catalyst in the transformation (Cochran, Kaplan & Nesse, 2014). Which leads us to the ultimate question that will shape healthcare reform: how do you create physician leaders who are willing to step outside of a known model, into one that is both unknown and untested?

BUILDING THE FOUNDATION

In 2008, Lancaster General Health (LG Health) sought out ways to answer this question – how do you create transformative physician leaders? A multi-pronged approach to this question ensued, one that took place over the course of a decade, but continues to pay priceless dividends back to the Lancaster community.

Being an independent community health system at the time, LG Health recognized that healthcare change in their community required the leadership of the physicians first -without their leadership, change would be impossible to influence. With the leadership of the Chief Physician Executive and the President of the Medical Group, the leadership team at LG Health started developing a leadership track for physicians. In 2008, the health system launched a new approach to physician leadership opportunities. Any physician, who wanted to lead, be a Chair or a Chief, or participate on a hospital Board or Committee, was required to attend the "Physician Leadership Academy" ("Academy").

The "Academy" met 12 times a year, once a month, for three hours, and consisted of dinner and a lecture. The 12 lectures were conducted by both internal and external experts, and covered topics around leadership, finance, and project management, with a capstone given by the worldwide executive for Guest Satisfaction from the Ritz-Carlton Hotel chain.

Over an eight-year period, at least 170 physicians attended this class. Building off the success of the program, and the momentum of engagement that was beginning to build, a subset of 20 key physician leaders were then sent to the Levinson Institute at Harvard, for an intense week-long physician leadership program.

These two programs created the critical mass for the leadership team at LG Health to consider next steps. Knowing that healthcare was in the midst of a major period of change, where physician engagement and managing risk and costs would become the new norm, the need to develop physician leaders to promote, even to serve in the role of CEO, was a guiding principle. With this in mind, LG Health contacted the University of Pennsylvania's Wharton School of Business, and identified coaches for 45 leaders, principally physicians and nurses. The program was conducted over the course of a semester, and took up most of a morning several times a month. To say that this was a "hit" would be an understatement.

SOLIDIFYING THE NETWORK

The program galvanized clinical leaders throughout the organization to work together towards shared goals. The effect was not only outstanding financial performance (7+% operating margin), but also the development of a culture where people worked together collaboratively to solve short and long-term problems. It was at this point that LG Health was able to begin to build its population health competency and transition to a system focused on value - where high quality and low cost were the new guideposts for care delivery.

The compounding effect of these programs was that the physicians were looking for more. After consultation with the Board of Trustees, the Chief Human Resources Officer and Medical Staff leadership, the Chief Executive

Officer (CEO) invited 21 physicians to participate in an Executive MBA Program as a cohort. The physicians interviewed three Philadelphia-based business schools, and ultimately, the Haub School of Business at Saint Joseph's University was selected. The physicians felt that the Dean and faculty were actively engaged in supporting them as learners, and were willing to tailor a program to meet their needs.

It was agreed that the faculty would have access to, and be able to teach from, real life issues including from inside LG Health. While 21 physicians were invited to participate, only 16 could make the full commitment, which left the door open for five non-physician leaders to participate.

The 22-month curriculum included one course per month, in which students met either online or in-person at predesignated times. At the end of the course, a capstone that took the class to Argentina and Brazil gave the students a chance to bond and learn together about different types of healthcare delivery systems. All 21 students completed their MBA, with over a third graduating with honors and, as with the other investments in leadership development, the dividends of the program were impressive.

According to Ibarra (2016), networks keep individuals informed, innovative, and in a perpetual state of learning. A network provides a "sounding board" for ideas and can help expedite processes. Well-established networks magnify the power of a single individual by leveraging the collaborative connections generated through a diverse group.

Considering the power of networking for a single individual, and then multiplying that power across the 21 individuals who constituted the LG Health MBA network, the health system was not only poised to have a deep pool of leaders from which to build succession plans but also a pool from which, and through which, dramatic change could be catalyzed.

Proof of this return on investment can be seen in the roles just a few of the cohort members assumed after graduation. Three physicians moved into system leadership roles taking on responsibility for areas that were new to the system or required reinvigoration (population health, quality, medical education). Three of the administrative leaders participating in the program took on similarly new roles in systems integration, regional operations and new patient tower project planning. In each of these examples, the individuals who took on these roles had to consider how to develop a new business, process, or approach for the health system from little to no previous infrastructure. In each case all of these leaders touched base with the MBA network multiple times, leveraging relationships established over the 22-month period as well as lessons learned from time within the program.

A web search focused on the greatest benefits of an MBA consistently identifies the importance of a network. For an individual, this often means a network that can help them to navigate advancement, whether in the form of employment or thought development. Extrapolating this benefit to an institution, particularly one whose industry is in a state of flux, one can easily assume that the monetary investment to educate these leaders is far outstripped by the priceless ability of these individuals to lead the institution through change.

For LG Health, these leaders are not only leaning into the change that the healthcare industry is undergoing – they are leading it. Numerous examples of these leadership examples abound, such as the creation of Care Connections, a super-utilizer program that focuses health system and community resources on patients with complex, chronic physical and behavioral health problems. Patients who have been a part of Care Connections have decreased their visits to the emergency department by over 40% and their hospitalization utilization by more than 50%. While objectively impressive, the true value of this work is that patients and their family members get much more of their time and life back and physician and administrative champions, working together, were at the heart of this transformation.

Since embarking on the LG Health physician leadership journey over a decade ago, LG Health has undergone some significant changes. In 2015, LG Health was integrated into Penn Medicine, a world-renowned academic medical center that is on the cutting edge of changing care delivery. Externally, changes in governmental policy with respect to healthcare laws and regulations changed dramatically between 2008 and 2018 and competitors in the Lancaster County market made shifts in response to the dynamic environment.

Change in the healthcare industry is inevitable and the clash we expected is upon us. LG Health, with its robust network of physician leaders and administrative champions is ready to take on these challenges and lead through the transformation to ultimately achieve what healthcare has always intended: improve the health and well-being of patients and their community.

REFLECTING ON THE JOURNEY

While LG Health's particular experience in developing their network of leaders was specific to their needs, it is applicable to any number of settings. The single most critical element of the successful journey is attributed to the visionary leadership of the LG Health team.

From a resource perspective, the developmental programs that LG Health invested in did require financial investments that the organization was both willing and able to support. As an example, the Executive MBA program that the 21 leaders participated in cost the health system approximately $1 million, not including any time that the team spent away from revenue generating activities to participate in required programs. Objectively, the return on this level of investment is difficult to reconcile. In 2012, the average hospital only made $12.9 million in profits – a $1 million investment in a non-revenue producing leadership development program would equate to almost 10% of the average hospital's profits (Becker's Hospital Review, 2014).

In order to successfully develop physician leaders for the future, the LG Health leadership team had to be committed to the long-term goal of developing these leaders. The leadership team had to make careful decisions about how they would invest their time, energy and resources to ensure that the health system could keep pace with the mindset shift they wanted to influence. Each step in the physician development journey built off of its predecessor, and each step built the confidence of the health system that the journey was a worthwhile investment. While the journey at the outset may not have specifically focused on the graduation of 21 Executive MBA graduates, the leadership team had to remain committed to the path throughout the process. Considering the many changes that healthcare endured through the course of the ten-year journey, visionary, consistent leadership helped to ensure that the system "stayed the course" rather than be distracted by the "tyranny of the urgent".

Competition, complications, and change are constants in any industry, country or county. Healthcare is not immune to these influences and will likely endure more of them in the future. The difference that leaders can make in their community depends upon their ability to establish a clear vision, balance their resources, and invest in their assets to the fullest extent of their ability. LG Health's physician leadership development journey is just one example of this type of leadership successfully executed, and it will continue to pay dividends to the Lancaster community for years to come.

REFERENCES

12 Statistics on hospital profit and revenue in 2012. (2014, January 21). Retrieved from https://www.beckershospitalreview.com/finance/12-statistics-on-hospital-profit-and-revenue-in-2012.html

Bodenheimer, T., & Sinsky, C. (2014). From triple to quadruple aim: Care of the patient requires care of the provider. *Annals of Family Medicine*, *12*(6), 573–576. doi:10.1370/afm.1713 PMID:25384822

Cochran, J., Kaplan, G. S., & Nesse, R. E. (2014). Physician leadership in changing times. *Health Care*, *2*(1), 19–21. PMID:26250084

Employer health benefits survey - Summary of findings. (2018, February 21). Retrieved from https://www.kff.org/report-section/ehbs-2017-summary-of-findings/

Griffith, J. R. (1998). *Designing 21st century healthcare: Leadership in hospitals and healthcare systems*. Chicago, IL: Health Administration Press.

Ibarra, H. (2016, April 18). *5 Misconceptions about networking*. Retrieved from https://hbr.org/2016/04/5-misconceptions-about-networking

National Health Accounts Historical. (2018). Retrieved from https://www.cms.gov/Research-Statistics-Data-and-Systems/Statistics-Trends-and-Reports/NationalHealthExpendData/NationalHealthAccountsHistorical.html

Rosenthal, E. (2014, December 16). *The odd math of medical tests: One scan, two prices, both high*. Retrieved from https://www.nytimes.com/2014/12/16/health/the-odd-math-of-medical-tests-one-echocardiogram-two-prices-both-high.html

Squires, D., & Anderson, C. (2015, October 08). *U.S. health care from a global perspective*. Retrieved from http://www.commonwealthfund.org/publications/issue-briefs/2015/oct/us-health-care-from-a-global-perspective

Taleb, N. (2010). *The black swan: The impact of the highly improbable*. New York: Random House.

Wingfield, N., Thomas, K., & Abelson, R. (2018, January 30). *Amazon, Berkshire Hathaway and JPMorgan team up to try to disrupt health care*. Retrieved from https://www.nytimes.com/2018/01/30/technology/amazon-berkshire-hathaway-jpmorgan-health-care.html

KEY TERMS AND DEFINITIONS

Care Connections: A special program designed to improve the access and care of medically indigent patients with complex medical problems and to coordinate and improve their care.

Interventional Care: Care delivered in reaction to a specific malady or set of diseases that is intended to improve the health of the individual.

Leader: Individual who is capable of managing risk and resources (finances, talent, goods and services, etc.) to improve the status of the individuals he/she serves.

Levinson Institute: A set of strategic leadership principles developed by Harry Levinson and taught at Harvard. Many physicians have benefitted from this training.

Network: A group of individuals connected to one another through a shared system, both literal (e.g., shared electronic platform) and figurative (e.g., shared experience).

Preventative Care: Care delivered proactively to prevent escalation or acquisition of a specific malady or set of diseases that is intended to maintain or improve the health of the individual.

Chapter 3
The Cohort Model:
From Theory to Practice

Terese Wallack Waldron
Saint Joseph's University, USA

Joe DiAngelo
Saint Joseph's University, USA

ABSTRACT

This chapter is written through the reflective and analytic lens of a Business School Dean with 35 years in higher education and focuses on the trends and future of the healthcare industry. Specifically, the chapter examines the planning, implementation, and identified outcomes of a cohort designed Executive MBA program. The issues highlighted in the first half of the chapter relate to 1) investing in individuals and the organizations they serve, 2) enhancing organizational capacity, and 3) implementation of pragmatic strategies to ensure an organizational leadership pipeline. The second half of the chapter suggests strategies as to how Chief Executive Officers, healthcare organizations, and partnering higher education institutions can develop both individualized MBA programs and professional training to ensure the development and retention of an energized healthcare leadership pipeline consisting of individual team leaders and change agents.

DOI: 10.4018/978-1-5225-7576-4.ch003

Reflection should be considered in a framework of self-awareness, context and in the perception of health and healthcare issues. (Craft, 2005)

INTRODUCTION

In order to grow and to achieve *enhanced capacity*, leaders need to be prepared for the future by investing in top individuals and in the organizations they serve. The days of "doing things the same way they have always been done" create their own compromises. Wall Street, Main Street and stakeholder groups have little patience for lackluster results.

To truly effect change, a commitment to investing in your organization's human capital – in this case – your top physicians and your high potential administrative talent -- is an imperative. Additionally, *retraining* your top physicians and emerging leaders may also factor into the *retaining* of top physicians and leaders.

From a Higher Education perspective and after planning for, producing and delivering five different healthcare "cohorts" in the past five years to Lancaster General Health (LG Health), the Pennsylvania College of Osteopathic Medicine and its alumni, Inspira Health Network, and most recently the American Osteopathic Association, I[1] have witnessed immeasurable intellectual growth, collaboration at its finest, the leveraging of best practices, innovative planning for the future that embraces today's and tomorrow's technology, impressive return on investment (ROI) for individuals and organizations, and a solid strategy that may be critical to future success.

Let me be clear by what I mean when I talk about the program's cohort. I am referring to a group of students who study with each other in the same academic model, starting and ending the model in a lock-step manner throughout the months needed to complete the required academic credits. The rationale for the development of this model is associated with higher student retention rates as well as the optimal shared educational experience of the cohort members. Research suggests that the cohort model develops mutual and intellectual stimulation, forms social ties, and enables the institutions to organize the programs in effective ways. Below are the benefits of developing a cohort based on the experience of our program, faculty, and the partner healthcare organization:

- Immeasurable intellectual growth;
- Collaboration at its finest;
- The leveraging of best practices;
- Innovative planning for the future that embraces today's and tomorrow's technology;
- Impressive return on investment (ROI) for individuals and organizations; and
- A solid retention strategy.

Saint Joseph's University's (SJU) business faculty has observed that in recent years, some of our very top Executive MBA students (concentrating in this healthcare curriculum) are physicians with 15, 20, and even 25+ years of clinical experience. Whilst they may have been attracted to the biology and biochemistry sciences as undergraduates, they have a remarkable commitment to excellence and learning. We have also collectively observed that many physicians who become MBA students tackle quantitative courses (Accounting, Finance, and Forecasting) with the same fever pitch as their medical school years or residencies.

As a result, the desire to earn an MBA degree in a specialization like healthcare is an ideal way to heighten the performance of a multi-talented physician. No doubt, the mettle and competency of physicians are well tested. Not surprisingly, however, the ability to connect healthcare to a business curriculum happens cohort after cohort. Any hesitation regarding the success that a physician may have in business school may be unwarranted. SJU faculty has witnessed excellence and award-winning submissions most recently at final Capstone presentations at Inspira Health Network especially in our Business Ethics, Health Policy, R&D/Innovation, Forecasting, Healthcare Systems Strategy, and Capstone courses (See Appendix for more details on 6 of 24 courses noted above).

By definition, graduate school and Executive MBA programs also foster a culture of immersed strategic and critical thinking, ideation and research and development, unbridled opportunity; improvement steps to enhance the status quo; and the emergence of true growth.

As a business school dean and because I am always committed to results, I would like these three interrelated issues to be at the very heart of this chapter:

Individual Investment + Organizational Investment = Enhanced Capacity

And I would like for these issues and the concepts that follow to be at the forefront of your mind as an outcome of reading this chapter. Imagine that we are having a conversation or a meeting about your organization, and its top physicians and administrators. Allow me to help you think about investing in individuals and investing in your organization to ensure enhanced capacity.

INVESTMENT IN THE INDIVIDUAL

Individual Investment + Organizational Investment = Enhanced Capacity

SJU, where I serve as Dean of the Erivan K. Haub School of Business, is a Jesuit institution. One of the most profound traditions within the Jesuit order, or the Society of Jesus, is *Cura Personalis*[2] – the care of the person. This aligns with the Hippocratic oath taken by doctors that include: "To prescribe only beneficial treatments, according to his/her abilities and judgment; to refrain from causing harm or hurt; and to live an exemplary personal and professional life" (Britannica, 2017). It is also consistent with Osteopathic medical schools that oeteopathic physicians are trained and encouraged to administer healing steps that impact the well being and health of the "whole person".

The "individual" not only fits well into this equation, but in my opinion, an individual is at the heart of most exemplary individual (and team) efforts and successes. If that is true – let's recognize the true need for investing in the individual. No doubt at your own organization, there are standout individual physicians and top administrators with distinctive strengths and capabilities to help lead, and to contribute to and improve your organization. Here is a series of questions to consider:

Q.1: How do you identify standout individuals?
Q.2: How can you help retrain standout individuals in the years following medical school, their respective residences and clinical rotations to ensure they are prepared for current and future challenges?
Q.3: How might you make it possible for standout individuals to become effective physician leaders and senior-level executives within your organization?

My short answers include:

A.1: Ask for nominations among your board. Meet with your Chief Talent Officer and get his or her feedback. Review all of those who have excelled at any earlier training. Reflect on committee meetings. Who is leading them and the organization on a more focused project level, as well as who is embracing those leadership roles and exhibiting contribution and glimpses of greatness?

A.2: This is really a question of opportunity and work-life-balance, as well as confidence and a desire to be advanced and to lead within an organization. Of course physicians have been in school for what may seemed like forever. However, the merger of healthcare experience, clinical practice and business acumen formulate a powerful combination for critical thinking and problem solving for the future.

A.3: Physicians and high potential administrators may have strong leadership competencies that are bolstered by an impactful cohort experience, team development beyond their previous norms, and a renewed energy in producing solutions for your healthcare enterprise.

If one was seeking to identify only a few individuals within his or her healthcare system there are several schools across the country that may be able to help a singular physician to become a physician leader. They will, however, be learning in isolation among other students from a plethora of disciplines.

INVESTMENT IN THE ORGANIZATION

Individual Investment + Organizational Investment = Enhanced Capacity

As we move to the second aspect of this equation, *Investment in the Organization,* I would like for you to critically consider the development and deployment of an exclusive Executive MBA cohort opportunity for your organization. A cohort model and platform represent an organizational investment that identifies top talent and challenges them to expand beyond their current capabilities. Ultimately this type of cohort construct showcases the aptitude and potential of your selected 20-25 participants. The "sponsorship" and approval of your executive leadership team and board members, board sponsors and board champions is an early recommendation and almost an imperative.

This singular leadership action on your part to support a cohort may help to re-set your organization for the future, as well as your leadership vision. It may also be an unparalleled opportunity for your organization.

If retaining key individuals is essential to your healthcare system's growth and continuation strategy, an Executive MBA cohort model like those developed at SJU may be invaluable. An exclusive cohort group creates an unparalleled organizational opportunity. An Executive MBA degree with a programmatic focus in healthcare like the one offered at SJU may also provide many individuals (up to 20-25 of your top performers), from the same organization, with an exceptional *second chance* to further develop their business acumen and individual, team and cohort leadership skills.

The cohort construct also allows the individual, the cohort teams, and the cohort itself to contribute more value to the organization. Additional strategic considerations should be made to identify career advancement opportunities for top participants with an imminent goal to engage and retain that very top talent. For example under the leadership of LG Health's CEO nearly half of the SJU-LGH Cohort-1 members advanced to new and expanding roles within the organization (see Table 1).

Table 1. A sampling of original titles to new titles

Original Title in 2013	Current Title
Medical Director Hospitalist Services	Chairman of Department of Medicine (Inpatient); Senior Physician Leader of Medical Specialties (outpatient) - LG Health
Care Transformation Manager (Population Health)	Director of Customer Engagement - LG Health
VP Operations - BGV	President - Horizon Healthcare Services
Medical Director	Director of Clinical Affairs - LG Health
Managing Physician	Physician Executive for Population Health - LG Health
Associate Deputy Director	Regional Medical Director - LG Health Physicians
Director, Nursing	Director of Operations – Medical Specialty, Urgent Care and Pediatrics - LG Health
Manager Lab Info System	IT Director of Ambulatory and Ancillary Application - LG Health
Chief Medical Information Officer	Chief Medical and Quality - LG Health
Senior Physician Leader	Managing Physician - LG Health
Director Physician Accounting & AP	Director, Budgeting and Forecasting - LG Health
Senior Physician Leader	Chief of Rheumatology - LG Health
Associate Director, Chair - Department of Family & Community Medicine	Medical Director - LG Health Physicians & LG Health Community Care

A singular anomaly, one physician, who participated in the first cohort, left the organization to become the Chief Medical Officer of a healthcare system in a neighboring state. Another administrative high potential colleague also shifted to a director role at the headquarters following a merger.

As stated earlier, in many cities and regions throughout the US and globally, healthcare systems represent some of the very largest employers in a city or region. So investment in your individual high potential physicians, in tandem with others in your organization, creates a powerful combination of investment in the individual plus investment in the organization.

Once you have the foresight and vision to invest in both of these key constituents – the individual and the organization – it becomes imperative to expand the scope of your investment. Your vision to investment in the organization truly requires board funding or a *Board Buy-In Process.*

Here are a few ways to consider approaching that board consensus to invest.

- You may seek out board members as *early adopters* and work with *assigned board members* who ultimately become the champions of this vision. This pre-work and board alignment are essential steps to secure the type of funding required for an exclusive Executive MBA cohort.
- You may also wish to reach out to others in the industry, within your informal cabinet, and within the healthcare vendor community (Equipment, the Pharmaceutical Industry and the Devices sector) to learn if others have taken on this type of initiative in their organizations.

When an organization makes a commitment to extensive training and development opportunities for physicians and high potential administrators, my suggestion is to stay focused on your goals and to achieve them. Also by optimizing the experience and by formulating an organization-specific cohort, you may be able to leverage a return on investment (ROI) formula that makes sense for this type of investment. Outside contractors, consultants and advisors also come with a price tag. Initiatives like an embedded cohort in your organization allow for your own selected physicians and administrative high potentials (your people) to tackle the tough challenges, to make their strategic recommendations, to help provide tactical plans, and ultimately to create value by having more internal buy-in to changes among their peers and those who report to them. It also helps to have your top leaders invested in the success of a cohort and its outcome. This leads to a cohort just for your people, your healthcare system, your board, and any other stakeholders.

An entire "Cohort" strategy and model starts with partnership between a healthcare organization and a higher education institution:

Healthcare Organization

- CEO and Senior Leadership's vision;
- Solid investment in individuals and an organization;
- Unyielding commitment from stakeholders that also includes: the Board of Trustees/Directors; and
- Ongoing support of the Sponsoring Department (in this case Human Resources), the physicians and high potential administrators who may become students.

Higher Education Institution

- Leadership team that will stretch its organization to deliver quality, value and relevance;
- Faculty who will teach, train, challenge, and most importantly inspire physicians and high potentials; and
- Administrative team who will make sense of all of the required variables, as well as pull all of these academic and healthcare system requirements together for a start-to-finish result.

Establishing your investment in the individual and investment in the organization vision also requires an *Investment/Buy in Process.* Here are some fundamental steps to bring your investors with you and to your goal:

1. As previously mentioned seek out early adopter board members who you anticipate will become champions of your vision. Also, seek out others in the industry, within your informal cabinet and the vendor community (Pharma and Devices) to learn if others have taken on this investment initiative in their organizations.

Once you have the support of your Board, consider an agile but effective Task Force or Cohort Committee, ideally led by your top Human Resource officer in the healthcare system. Begin to give shape to this vision by an informal identification of the top 20 to 25 candidates (develop the names of 30-35 for a group of 20-25, as not everyone will accept an invitation to participate) who may be tapped to participate in this investment in the *Individual + Organization = Enhanced Capacity* effort.

2. Develop a formalized *cohort framework* that will allow your board and leadership organization to have an improved way to understand the value of a cohort and its measurable outcomes.

As expected, it benefits an organization to be as inclusive as possible. In this case, the LG Health high potential student cohort consisted of two thirds from physician ranks, and one third from administrative departments. This "cultural" crossover proved to be an extraordinary opportunity to develop mutual respect, friendship and reliance that are not always organically developed or present in a healthcare system setting.

The measurable aspects of a cohort formation are also a top and early priority. With an eye on ROI, having a third-party administrator facilitate any benchmarking is preferred and serves as a best practice. Any verification of a cohort's progress both formal and informal may be valuable to board sponsors and stakeholders. Why would this benchmarking be necessary?

Let us be clear, even Healthcare System CEOs need to be accountable to their boards, and investments in the $1 to 1.5 million level for training, development, talent management and succession planning need to be vetted and valuable. Consequently, the healthcare system leaders should plan to provide specific data on the ongoing value of a MBA cohort program of this magnitude.

3. Another critical and early step from a multitude of perspectives is determining the size of your first and subsequent cohorts. Identifying the "cohort participation number" that is right for your organization impacts your organization, your investment total, the number of participants (those immediately eligible and those on a wait list) and any potential role and/or career advancements planned for a healthcare system.

As you amass, organize and evaluate the participants in a cohort, bear in mind the scale of your organization and the impact of career progression for those students that excel within a sponsored cohort. And most importantly be aware of where future talent may be found in your organization. If a physician with less experience presents himself or herself as extremely capable, do not overlook his or her participation based on age or life stage. A blend of skills, talents, generations, and aspirations adds to the dynamics of any cohort.

Selecting all the "same thinkers" will not necessarily be productive for your organization[3].

4. Create ownership for the cohort within your organization. Ideally, your Chief Medical Officer, your Chief Talent Officer and/or other Human Resource professionals will begin to "own" this investment in the individual and the investment in the organization vision and provide the internal support that is needed to interface with all possible candidates for the selection process. This process begins with selection of candidates and runs through the final vetting and approval stages. Once the selection of the 20-25-person cohort is complete, a new realm of details will be required. First and foremost the requirements include identifying issues that are important for the lifeblood of the organization. These issues and nuances can then be integrated into the curriculum with the buy-in and approval of your partner school's faculty who are teaching these MBA course. Other key considerations include:
   a. Program launch date (and plan to work backward from there);
   b. Enrollment deadlines and candidate interviews to meet application criteria;
   c. Third-party benchmarking, sourcing of a third-party research vendor and the development of a survey instrument that can be valuable and administered three times in the life of a cohort (at the beginning, middle and end of the experience);
   d. Collaboration with faculty to assure academic refinement steps and the integration of key issues and topics that impact your healthcare system; and
   c. Facilitation of IT training for online courses, and residency arrangements should you elect to have residencies for the kick-off and the final 24th course – the SJU's Capstone course.
5. The Healthcare Strategy course (course #23) and Capstone (course #24) work in final sequence to bring the greatest collective innovative opportunities, value and visibility to your sponsoring board.

The Capstone course is intentionally designed to be the pivotal and cumulative course that brings all of your investment back to the organization through the facilitation of "real" program-end projects and proposals suitable for submission and delivery to your sponsoring board.

Collaborative and early meetings with senior leadership allow SJU faculty and staff to orchestrate and to formulate the Capstone project concepts that may be studied at great length. In total – and throughout the four different cohorts that our faculty members have taught – student teams are asked to consider, select and vet one of five major Project options (1-5) that are detailed in Table 2.

Due to our reputation and core competency in industry-focused MBA programs, SJU has expanded its client base for this Executive MBA with a Healthcare concentration and propelled this cohort model. Since 2015, SJU has added four additional cohort groups. We were pleased to enroll our neighboring Philadelphia College of Osteopathic Medicine's physician alumni in its exclusive cohort. Their final Capstone projects included these invaluable topics that will be featured at the annual OMED18 conference in San Diego in Fall 2018 (see Table 3).

And finally and most recently, we worked with one healthcare system in New Jersey - Inspira Health Network - that elected to sponsor their high potential physicians and administrators in a six-course Advanced Graduate Certificate program. The April 30, 2018 presentations had its Board Members (the program sponsors) on the edge of their seats during four hours of presentations.

Table 2. Project option 4 and 5

Project Option 4 INNOVATION COMPANY at LGH: Would creating a $10 million Venture Fund to monetize LGH intellectual capital enable deployment of new technologies, tools and business models (Examples: therapies, personalized medicine, apps etc.)? Key Questions: • How to create a new venture that would bring innovative products and services for LGH? • Disruptive Innovation: What innovative business models could disrupt the primary care space? • Surgery/Efficiencies: Example: Taking a look at national and global models, how to cut the cost of cardiovascular surgery in half? • How would use of data analytics and Lifetime Value (LTV) of patients improve risk stratification and population health outcomes? • Consider future generations (value) when supporting indigent health cases now. • A case for disruption/risk that would net new opportunities. (i.e., a case for focusing on High-Risk, Medium-Risk and Low-Risk patient scheduling)
Project Option 5 Competition: The competitors in your market have evolved over time and now include both traditional and non-traditional competitors. Key Questions: • How will the evolving competition in your market with your top competitors reshape the market for your healthcare system? • What impact could this have on current market shares?

Table 3.

***PCOM-1* POSTER 1** -- Scenario Planning for Primary Care Practice Project Description: What will the primary care practice look like in 10 years with artificial intelligence (analytics), Telehealth (alternate care delivery) population health (reimbursement models) and what are the implications for the projected number of medical students, residents and practicing physicians needed for this delivery model of the future? **PCOM-1 POSTER 2** -- Privatizing Graduate Medical Education (GME) – A Stakeholder Analysis Project Description: How to privatize graduate medical education (GME), breaking free of dependence on Federal funding? What would be the response of the different stakeholders in the medical education communities and how to design a plan to get the buy-in from the stakeholders?

The operative word among the board members that day was:

WOW. So much had been realized even within six courses over eight months of time.

The investment in the individual and investment in the Inspira organization netted the network's leaders with four impressive and actionable plans for immediate consideration and deployment. These plans, too, followed the SJU faculty outlines of options to help drive their topics and the course outcomes.

The key Human Resource sponsors at Inspira also were pivotal in helping to frame the four final projects and the appropriate board sponsors for each.

- **Project 1:** Employee Health
- **Project 2:** Telehealth
- **Project 3:** Non-Urgent Medical Transport
- **Project 4:** Wearable Technology

As we conclude the investment in the organization topic, allow me to make a few more suggestions:

1. Seek out others you respect (and even those you do not) and ask their opinions. In my experience, it often proves helpful to have board members, key opinion leaders, and others within your healthcare space as unofficial ambassadors and advisors. Seek out opinion and process it to be certain that you are not blind sighted. I have mentioned project "sponsors" in the information above. This may be an ideal way to engage your board and leadership team more actively.
2. Make the investment matter with a solid Request for Proposal (RFP).

It is my view that selecting the right Higher Education partner to deliver a quality Executive MBA cohort experience is even more essential than selecting the physician and senior staff participants. A RFP process, based on purchasing practices above $1 million, may be required within your organization. If so, the due diligence of selecting a partner for a cohort begins with that first RFP distribution of the most basic facts, the timetable of partner selection and program deployment. The anticipated RFP budget, details on who has decision making authority, who is the key point person(s) and who will have the role of liaison and interface with the organization are all key to a successful RFP. Remember that it is likely to be a complex and slow process to make extreme changes to a chosen program that goes through an RFP-process.

Also, once a school or institution is selected, it's critical to be certain that the curriculum, the plan, the cohort, the timing, the investment, the scheduled payment(s), the benchmarking and more are all reviewed and mutually agreed upon. My advice: Be an active part of the concept development, as well as the planning and ownership of this process. If your board, your VPs, your Continuous Improvement Committee and others have some perspective on a cohort and its benefits to your organization, by all means collect that data and integrate it into the RFP as soon as possible. Conversely after an Executive MBA program and its curriculum are in place, be sure to work with the academic institution and your point person. Create a schedule of check-in meetings and calls so that the promise of quality and the integration of content will be delivered.

Make no mistake. This up-to-a-million-dollar investment and the scope of initiatives of this type require an RFP process. It can be time consuming. In fact, it can take several weeks, months, seasons, or in my world, semesters to be completed. But if selected as a health system's higher education provider, it's a true validation of your school's competence and a measure of its enhanced capacity too.

3. In your healthcare system team, you will need a point person who is focused, tenacious and willing to stay on task with the RFP process within your organization. You will also need to add into the RFP that your healthcare system requires a point person at a university who is focused, tenacious and willing to stay on task. It is also imperative for these two people to keep their respective groups engaged on a daily, weekly or monthly basis, and as needed. Again, the scheduling of

prescribed weekly and monthly meetings and check-ins are invaluable to win the business and to move it forward.

Some key steps in the delivery of a cohort include:

- Identifying the Administrative Team(s) and point person(s) from the healthcare system and the university that will make all of this happen.
- Creating familiarity and a code of collaboration. This is a win-win game. Be sure there is compatibility and trust that you are witnessing early in the process.
- Helping to promote the program within your healthcare system so that vetted and capable candidates can be interviewed and admitted to a cohort. Meeting the admission standards of your selected university will be a program cohort requirement.
- Aligning the industry-focused curriculum and faculty, as well as course sequencing and final project discussions (the earlier the better on this to establish a long-term view, board engagement and Executive-level commitment).
- Pre-planning and orchestrating a dynamic Orientation Session and possible once-a-year residencies. Arranging for complete online ZOOM training and technology support to go along with new laptops and other software. Be prepared to bring your healthcare system experts into the online classrooms occasionally.
- Sustaining a long-term view of how courses in the MBA program and the organizational objectives are coming together, especially for the final courses dedicated to real value, a ROI metric and organizational improvement.

ENHANCED CAPACITY

Individual Investment + Organizational Investment = Enhanced Capacity

As a dean, here are the times when I witness true value that certainly leads to enhanced capacity:

- When board members ask mid-way through the program if they can be a part of the next cohort.
- When a CEO, upon seeing the final Capstone presentations, puts $1 million in innovation funds into immediate play to have several projects further reviewed and mobilized by the healthcare organization
- When I witness students—like physicians – whose skill set is so driven by science and medicine – truly excel at business concepts, strategic planning, solid execution and team/organizational collaboration
- When a second client hears about the good work that is being done elsewhere and wants in on the MBA magic at SJU that can help refocus and redirect the talents and potential of both physicians and high potential administrators alike.
- Students from our PCOM D.O. MBA programs will be presenting their Capstone projects in a poster format in the SJU booth at the osteopathic physician premier conference – OMED. According to PCOM's CEO – this level of business acumen is instrumental to offering enhanced growth and third-act leadership, consulting and innovative career options for his alumni.

CONCLUSION

Individual Investment + Organizational Investment = Enhanced Capacity

This past spring, I was privileged to view four presentations at Inspira Health Network, as a result of impressive outcomes of the Healthcare Strategy and Capstone courses that completed this cohort experience. I was in the company of the network's senior leadership. Of the four presentations, with their concepts reviewed and endorsed by senior leadership, two of the concepts and strategic and tactical plans were further reviewed and deployed. Now that's what I call: *Enhanced Capacity*.

REFERENCES

Britannica, T. E. (2017, November 15). *Hippocratic oath*. Retrieved from https://www.britannica.com/topic/Hippocratic-oath

Craft, M. (2005). Reflective writing and nursing education. *The Journal of Nursing Education*, *44*(2), 53–57. PMID:15719711

Saint Joseph's University's course catalog 2018. (n.d.). Retrieved from https://sites.sju.edu/catalog/

KEY TERMS AND DEFINITIONS

Experience in Action: Real-life decision making in the leadership arena with accountability for decisions and outcomes.

Experiential Learning: Experiential learning theory (ELT) provides a holistic model of the learning process and a multilinear model of adult development, both of which are consistent with what we know about how people learn, grow, and develop. The theory is called "experiential learning" to emphasize the central role that experience rather than cognition or behavioral plays in the learning process.

Facilitator's Role: Guides and manages a group event to ensure that the group's objectives are met effectively, with clear thinking, good participation, and full buy-in from everyone who is involved.

High Fidelity Simulation: Provides participants with a learning environment in which to develop non-technical skills, that is safe and controlled so that the participants are able to make mistakes, correct those mistakes in real time and learn from them, without fear of compromising patient safety. Participants in simulation are also able to rehearse the clinical management of rare, complex or crisis situations in a valid representation of clinical practice, before practicing on patients.

Pedagogic Practice: Forms of social practice that shape and form the cognitive, affective, and moral development of individuals. Pedagogic practices influence the formation of identity as well as learning outcomes.

Reflexive Praxis: A learned skill that facilitates exploration of our personal context in order to identify our assumptions, biases, and the way we think. Understanding how we think and the sources of our individual way of thinking allows us to be more mindful of the way we communicate with others and make decisions.

ENDNOTES

1 This chapter is written in the first person singular from the desk of the Dean of St. Joseph's University, Haub School of Business perspective.

2 Society of Jesus is *Cura Personalis* – the care of the person. Cura Personalis. Retrieved from https://en.wikipedia.org/wiki/Cura_personalis

3 At SJU, we suggest a number between 20-25, and with 20, 24 or 25 being perfect numbers. The learning environment is dynamic, but it is not so large as to create classrooms that are overwhelming. Cohorts of 20, 24 and 25 participants are also divisible by 4 or 5 for eventual team assignments.

APPENDIX: COURSE DESCRIPTIONS

BUS 582 Business Ethics

The course examines competing ethical claims upon the healthcare industry in a market driven, profit seeking economy. The course begins with a discussion of a theoretical framework for moral analysis and proceeds to practical applications in healthcare delivery.

MPE 781 Health Policy

This course is an introduction to various components of the U.S. healthcare system. It examines the multiple facets of the healthcare system including key stakeholders (Payers, Providers, and Patients), private and public financing mechanisms for medical care, and the effects of both market competition and government regulation. The main objective of the course is for students to learn to be able to critically examine how to assess policy and coverage decisions and the tradeoffs (cost, quality, access) associated with various healthcare decisions or treatment alternatives.

MPE 650 Competitive Analysis

While examining the various strategies and strategic frameworks with evaluations about the advantages and shortcomings of each, the course will explore the range of competition from other healthcare networks as well as from the other "p" stakeholders in US healthcare delivery, including patients, payers, product sources (drug, devices, diagnostics), policy makers and other non-hospital providers. The explicit purpose of the course lies in developing a strategic perspective to solve problems encountered by hospitals rather than employing a tactical approach.

DSS 593 Forecasting for Healthcare

A comprehensive survey of the commonly used techniques in forecasting will be presented along with the major categories of forecasting approaches for hospitals and healthcare networks. The course includes presentation of case studies and forecasting with data sets. Computers will be used extensively throughout the course, primarily with available programs to perform the calculations after the problem has been correctly formulated. Emphasis will be placed on the interpretation and implementation of results.

MPE 720 Healthcare Systems Strategy

This course focuses on the development of corporate-level strategy by healthcare stakeholders. After providing an understanding about the types of strategies, students will craft strategies that enable hospital systems to adapt to ongoing policy changes/regulations, such as Accountable Care Organizations (ACOs) and to succeed as one of the key providers within US healthcare delivery to position themselves for success. Student teams will be tasked with crafting strategies to deal with specific issues facing the healthcare network.

MPE 795 Capstone

This course is a learning experience that reinforces knowledge gained throughout the program. Students will be asked to convert their findings from earlier courses, especially Corporate Strategy and Competitive Analysis, into plausible strategies that will address strategic issues facing the healthcare network. Student will present their findings to their senior management team when possible.

Chapter 4

Preparing the Right Physicians to be Exceptional Leaders in the 21st Century:

How to Maximize Their Success Most Cost-Effectively and Efficiently

Kenneth R. Cohen
The Synergy Organization, USA

Kenneth Hanover
The Synergy Organization, USA

ABSTRACT

This chapter describes evidence-based strategies found to most effectively maximize the Return On Investment (ROI) of physicians' formal leadership training programs. Recognizing that no two prospective physician leaders are exactly the same, formal leadership training programs cannot be most effective if these do not allow for organizational and situational differences as well as critical differences among physicians' demonstrated personalities and leadership styles. When selecting prospective physician leaders, the authors advocate for an individualized process which requires "Diagnosis Before Treatment," "Three Dimensional Screening," and the application of "More Effective Alternative Strategies" in order to avoid committing the "12 Deadly Sins."

DOI: 10.4018/978-1-5225-7576-4.ch004

INTRODUCTION

This chapter's authors recognize the significant potential value of providing physicians with formal leadership training in cohort forums, educating them about value-based decision making and alternative healthcare delivery models, and how graduates of such well-designed programs contribute to an organizations' learning climates. Clearly, the training content and milieu must be designed and delivered with due consideration for the desired outcomes; their diverse and related experiences indicate that leadership and teamwork training will enhance the skills of some, but not all, physicians. Even those with appropriate skills can be confused by the lack of clarity of a typical job description. Current realities and resource constraints demand that health care systems judiciously invest their limited resources in those physicians who will generate the best returns on investment and who will benefit key stakeholders the most. What should be screened for in prospective physician leadership development program participants must be based on the same attributes required of all successful physician leaders and senior executives.

This chapter identifies some critical, yet often overlooked, elements that warrant serious consideration to generate optimal results for everyone involved. It is anticipated that taking a guided "step back" to understand the factors affecting successful selection and placement of physician leaders will help broaden perspectives while simultaneously enhancing focus on those critical factors that significantly impact the ultimate success of physician leadership cohort training forums.

THE CHALLENGE

Effective physician leadership is more critical than ever before for hospitals as well as for health systems, clinics, clinically integrated networks, and others. A physician leader on the senior team, who demonstrates both an innate understanding of the care process and the provider's role in that process, has proven to be key to accomplishing goals. Capital decisions, service line management and supply chain management are just a few examples in which the roles of Chief Medical Officer (CMO), Medical Director, Vice President of Medical Affairs (VPMA) and service line lead brought value to many organizations. However, problems in selecting those key contributors are frequent, predictable and yet, avoidable.

Gordon L. Alexander, Jr., MD, former chief executive officer (CEO) of the University of Minnesota Medical Center and University of Minnesota Children's Hospital, notes that physicians frequently enter their health care administration roles without the benefit of years of experience managing aspects of a complex organization. While clinical experience is valuable, it does not always translate to success in broader leadership roles. All too often, the rules of the administrative road can be anathema to even a seasoned physician. In fact, the American College of Physician Executives reported that the competencies required to be an effective physician leader often contradict those of a good practitioner. For example, a good CMO must be persuasive, effective in delegating to others, and hold them accountable for their performance. Conversely, the solo practitioner primarily needs to be self-sufficient. While a general master of business administration degree or focused leadership training is helpful, it rarely changes the ingrained characteristics of a physician or predicts the type of performance he/she will display in a new role.

In addition, great variation is seen amongst VPMA, Medical Director, Department Chair, and Chief Medical Officer roles across organizations. Purposeful dialogue to define the uniqueness of these roles to that particular organization along with clear job expectations is often lacking, serving up the avoidable recipe for failure and unhappiness. Many physician executives have radically different ideas than their senior team colleagues about what is expected of the physician in a leadership position. Candid conversations are rare, and the physician typically does not have a predecessor to tap for insights. Being a presence in the doctors' lounge is giving way to managing service lines, taking responsibility for population health management and care transformation, monitoring value-based contracting, and many more activities. Furthermore, these responsibilities are now critical to an organization's success. With the challenges organizations now face, the perception is that there is no room for error—operationally or financially—at this level. The importance of setting the stage for physician leadership success cannot be understated. Author Lewis Carroll's (1865) observation applies well here: "If you don't know where you're going, any road will get you there."

A practical, proven and cost-effective solution to the challenges of critical and high-risk physician leadership positions is available. Traditional recruitment and selection processes often do not work and, in fact, can expose the organization to needless risks. Even those with appropriate skills can be flummoxed by the lack of clarity of a typical job description.

21ST CENTURY RECRUITMENT APPROACH

Healthcare organizations in the 21st century require an evidence-based, rigorous, scientific approach to job analysis, leadership assessment, and recruitment in order to ensure that the right decisions are made the first time. The evidence is obtained via a proprietary series of structured interviews and carefully crafted, standardized assessment instruments.

Diagnosis Before Treatment

This approach requires that incumbents and other potential candidates be assessed against previously agreed upon objective, empirically based standards. In the process, prospective leaders are measured and scientifically matched to their positions along those dimensions that matter most to their mutual, long-term success.

Synergy Screening System®

The Synergy Screening System® (also known as S^3) mitigates organizational risks and provides a clear road map for both the organization and the physician leader to achieve success. Deliberately identifying and addressing the developmental needs of high-potential physician executives provides the most efficient way to maximize these valuable resources to mutual advantage.

Just as evidence-based medicine recognizes that it always costs less to do the *right things right the first time*, progressive health care executives now understand that they need to assess the specific criteria for success and identify physician leader candidates who are natural fits. This evidence-based approach significantly increases their confidence and their selected physician leaders' odds (>95 percent) for success.

STEPPING BACK TO LEAP FORWARD

The importance of making informed decisions about the physician leaders we depend on every day cannot be overstated, because it is these decisions that separate the most successful leaders from the rest. The best leaders in the most successful health care organizations demand better-than-average results and know they need to rely on others' talents to achieve them. They deliberately surround themselves with people whose skills best complement their own toward attaining the organization's goals. They refuse to settle for "best under the circumstances", are far more rigorous in their selection and hiring practices than most others, and set realistic expectations of their physician leaders based on objective data.

However, most employers and their applicants find it difficult to articulate "up front" and with any degree of accuracy what they *really* want or need. An unfortunate result of this lack of clarity is poor productivity and a staggeringly high rate of job dissatisfaction. Yet, in retrospect, these same individuals typically have no difficulty stating with great clarity, confidence, and considerable emotion what they did not like about their previous organization, immediate supervisor, peers, and subordinates.

To reinforce this point, think about how many people you know who are unhappy with their careers and complain about having to go back to work on Monday, view

Table 1. Selection best practice

Hire in Haste, Repent at Your Leisure	
Evidence based selection is the systematic process of surrounding oneself with talented individuals and applying their strengths to promote measurable gains towards established goals. *The most effective leaders form synergistic relationships with those around them. They constantly strive to:*	
• Get the right people on the bus and in the right seats (Collins, 2001). • Build on their own strengths and those of others.	• Build on what is working instead of focusing on what is not. • Recognize they are not going to be great at everything they do.
Selection Best Practices were identified by The Synergy Organization, as one of the Six Building Blocks of lasting leadership.	

Source: www.synergyorg.com

Wednesday as "Hump Day" and breathe a sigh of relief and excitement as they say, "Thank God It's Friday." Now, consider 1) the elevated level of acute care hospital CEO turnover (at 18 percent in 2014); 2) employee job dissatisfaction rates; and 3) the fact that the majority of heart attacks occur on Sunday nights and Monday mornings. What all of this means is that we need to be very careful in whom we *choose* to depend on, because the quality of our selection decisions can easily affect our personal happiness, career success, and health as well (see Table 1).

THE 6P'S OF PHYSICIAN PRODUCTIVITY

What the best leaders know is that to thrive in a competitive market, they cannot afford to keep doing what has not worked. They expect to invest their limited time, organizational resources, and emotional energy on those people who will give them the most positive returns on their investment.

"Precisely Positioned Physician Personalities Propel Performance."

The good and bad news about effective leaders is that they tend to be optimistic and to look for the good in others. However, eternal optimists must accept a harsh truth in leadership selection and development, which is that not everyone can "accomplish anything you want if you just put your mind to it." US healthcare organizations have wasted billions of dollars trying to train and encourage staff and leaders to perform in ways they were incapable of or unwilling to over the long term.

Moreover, The Synergy Organization's national Best Practices in Healthcare Leadership research studies found that as much as 40 percent of senior executives' time is spent dealing with unnecessary conflict and problematic employees! Think about physicians and overall workforce this way: When the CEO steps back and takes an honest look at how poor performers negatively affect operations and the bottom line, he/she will begin to appreciate why the most successful organizations are adamant about conducting valid and meaningful assessments and performance appraisals of their leaders on an ongoing basis. The best leaders understand that they cannot allow anyone a free ride and need to be systematic in how they fill the limited seats on their bus.

Bus drivers

Superstars who push themselves and others to perform at their best every day

Bus riders

Generally good-performing, loyal staff and leaders who are dependable

Bus stops

Chronic malcontents who find ways to do "less with more," do not take responsibility for their actions and failures, and make our buses more pleasant when they exit

The Synergy Organization's research studies and consulting work have found that to be a consistent top performer, one needs to be fully engaged and passionate about one's work. This does not minimize the importance of training, such as that provided in physician academies but not every physician can be trained to be a leader! Just as we cannot train others to be taller, we cannot train every person to be motivated, empathetic, passionate, or honest.

Physicians bring their own extraordinary talents with them when they enter our organizations, and along with them, their core personalities. As hundreds of progressive healthcare executives have shared with The Synergy Organization since 1989, "I can teach others the finer technical aspects of their jobs, but I can't teach them their personalities." Training only enhances talent; it doesn't create talent.

Nevertheless, organizations still rely primarily on a candidate's prior experience, even when he/she has stopped developing his/her skills long ago. For example, think of the person whose CV suggests that he/she has 20 years of related experience. In reality, that experience may be the equivalent of about one year of marginal performance repeated 20 times over. Rather than hiring fresh new talent for their key leadership roles, organizations often hire each other's experienced failures and trade their problem performers back and forth. Therefore, one of the best ways to increase the effectiveness of our training programs is to better identify the most critical attributes of the "right people" we want to be trained, *right from the start.*

One critical, yet often overlooked, factor is money. Effective recruitment, selection, development and retention practices place considerable demand on increasingly limited resources and, given the current labor market, will become even more expensive for the next several years. But we also know that investment in increasing per person productivity and lowering turnover leads to better use of leaders' time and supports the company's bottom line. One key point worth making again is one that the most successful leaders have learned: It costs far less to do the right things right the *first* time.

As part of another national leadership research study involving direct interviews with 80 highly successful healthcare senior executives across the US, The Synergy Organization asked the question, "What does it cost an organization to hire the wrong person for a $100,000 or higher salary leadership level position?" In response to this pointed question, many of these CEOs paused, sighed, and shifted in their chairs. Then, they offered significant numbers to reinforce their experiences. They shared that the direct and indirect costs of a bad hire at this level had to be at least 6 to 10 times that person's annual earnings! Moreover, they stressed that the direct costs paled in comparison to the indirect costs. Indirect costs include the emotional toll on the organization, the failed leader's subordinates, and immediate co-workers. As one CEO succinctly stated, "It could cost you your job." When was the last time you heard someone admit, "I should have held onto that poor performer longer than I did"? Not often. Instead, in the vast majority of cases, most leaders tend to keep poor performers in a leadership role much longer than they should, and they come to realize with experience that a bad hire rarely gets any better.

If we take an honest look at traditional interviews, we will realize that at the precise moment when an applicant begins to feel like the right person, most managers stop interviewing._They start selling and closing on that individual. Few people have the ability to change course once all of this momentum has built up, leading to many hiring mistakes. That's why the use of objective second opinions and validated leadership assessments can prove especially valuable to the organization and the hiring manager. The best time to incorporate outside feedback about the candidate's overall fit and appropriateness for the position is before the hiring manager has fallen in love with the person and is waiting at the altar with all eyes, and momentum, upon them.

Consider this question: Whom do you spend most of your time with, your best performers, or your worst?

Consistent with the Pareto Principal (or 80/20 Rule), research has found that most managers invest the vast majority of their time, emotional energy, and material resources with those people who are least likely to benefit from this investment. A vicious cycle ensues for everyone involved, because those who are most likely to demonstrate the greatest improvements do not get what they need; instead, they get frustrated as their performance suffers and often quit, while the poor performers suck the life and resources right out of the organization.

One major way that top performers differ from poor performers is that the highest performers are consistently engaged with and committed to their work. Following is a quick way to validate this concept from your own experiences. Think about those people you have met who have impressed you as being absolutely extraordinary in their careers. How do those people feel about their work?

Identifying, early on, those physicians with the ideal characteristics and making suitable investments in them can pay rich dividends. Top performers stand out from their lesser-performing peers because the high-quality work gives them the opportunity to do what they do best, they love to do it and they become energized by it. They "do not have to leave their hearts and minds" at the hospital's front door and they view their work as a natural extension of themselves. It is almost impossible for them not to do their job with great care and high quality, and they show this enthusiasm in all aspects of their work. Now, imagine how much better off everyone in the organization would be if they could honestly approach each week with real enthusiasm.

The Synergy Organization's Four Factor Theory helps executives make those distinctions (see Figure 1). The graphic below contains two columns and two rows. In the first row, the left column considers content: Can the candidate perform the duties of the job? Does the candidate know what to do? The right column considers process: Will the candidate do the job? How will the candidate behave? Thus, the model considers not only if candidates have the capacity to do the job but also, equally and perhaps more importantly, whether they will be a good fit for the job.

Figure 1. The Synergy Organization's Four Factor Theory
Source: www.synergyorg.com

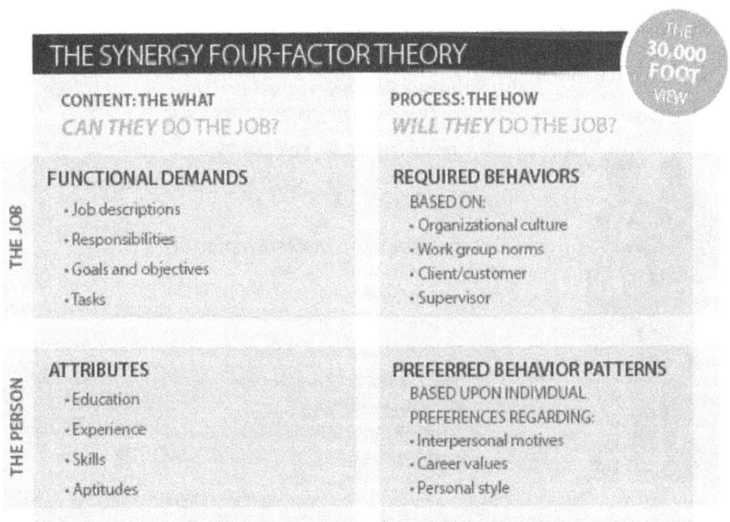

The left column also reveals some inherent weaknesses of traditional "paper matches" between generic job descriptions and professionally prepared résumés. At best, narrative-style job postings typically explain only what the employee will be required to do; similarly, résumés summarize only what the candidate has done. In contrast, the right column of the four-factor model stresses the importance of identifying *how* the job needs to be done and *how* the candidate is likely to behave.

Interviewers must also focus on those make-or-break variables for leader success: style, personality and the relative fit for the job. To get an accurate picture of a candidate, Synergy recommends evaluating their "heads," "hearts" and "feet" (see Figure 2). The head represents what they know; the heart, their passions (how driven they are to help other people); and their feet, their actions (how they have developed productive relationships, generated new business, etc.). Interviewers can use this three-dimensional model in many ways to help select the right people and avoid costly hiring mistakes.

Many health care professionals have witnessed the "revolving-door syndrome" occurring in key leadership positions. Positions with the highest turnover typically result from unclear or conflicting expectations. These expectations predispose organizations and employees to needless difficulties and failure. In addition, "snipers" or "Monday-morning quarterbacks" take potshots at others' hiring decisions. These people, who are reluctant to be pinned down in advance about their expectations of candidates, are exactly the same ones who say, "Well, I can't really tell you what I think about this person right now, but I'll know the right one when I see them."

Figure 2. The Synergy Screening System®
Source: www.synergyorg.com

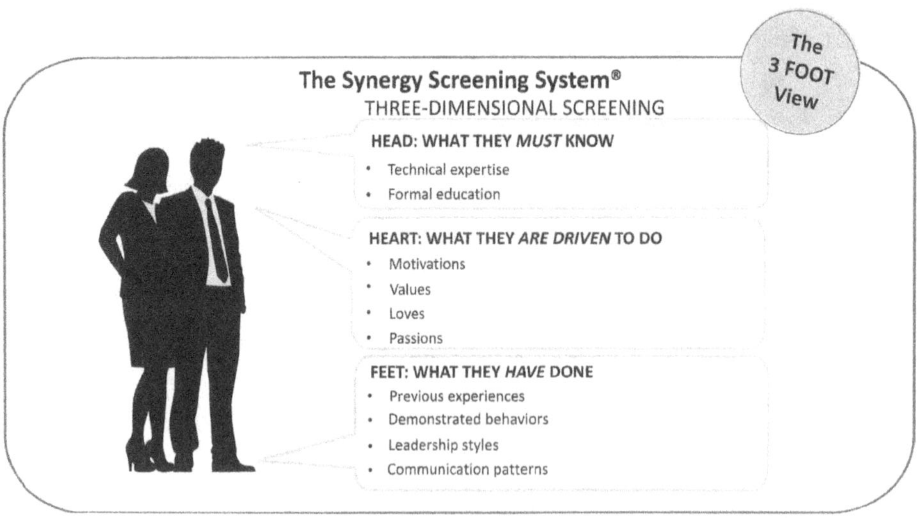

Using The Synergy Organization's validated assessment instruments and processes helps to identify the unique needs of the position more accurately and cost-effectively by getting buy-in from the position's major constituents on the front end—before you advertise, interview, hire and get second-guessed when that new leader doesn't work out. These objective profiles are also valuable for determining whether to promote from within the organization.

THE DIRTY DOZEN: 12 DEADLY SINS OF SELECTION

Diagnoses and Treatments for Effective Physician Selection

Selection failures should be viewed through the lens of "diagnosis and treatment". The following errors in physician leader selection are the twelve most dangerous and common mistakes healthcare executives make when hiring physicians for their leadership team.

1. The Employer Oversells the Job

In this scenario, employers start out an interview by exaggerating the job's positive aspects, describing only its good points and hiding many of its challenges. Instead, give candidates a realistic job preview, outlining real expectations of the position. Share with candidates the key aspects of the position—including those less-than-desirable activities. Introduce the candidates to people who work there (preparing these co-workers in advance), and give them a chance to ask questions; this is especially important considering candidates are reluctant to ask certain questions of their potential boss. In addition to preparing the candidate, this best practice demonstrates that you value your staff 's opinions and gives them the chance to let others know what they like about, and why they came to, your organization. Although they may not be accustomed to hearing honesty in interviews, most candidates appreciate being told the truth. Many have told us that they accepted a position because of this quality.

2. The Candidate Oversells Him/Herself

Applicants have become much more clever and sophisticated in recent years. Candidates now have plenty of resources available to them to learn how to say what they think the interviewer wants to hear. They tell you they have a great deal of experience and loves doing everything the job requires-only complicating further your task of making effective hiring decisions. To break through this oversell, ask the candidate and his/her references specific questions to help verify the truth. The questions must focus on specific descriptions of what they did and how they carried out the job, what issues they encountered, how they addressed them, and what results they achieved.

3. A Good Paper Match Overrules Evidence-Based Considerations

Too much emphasis is placed on the paper match between the curriculum vitae (CV) and the job description. Focus tends to be more on the candidate's educational training and experience than on what the candidate will do for you. Looking good on paper does not necessarily mean fitting in with you, the staff, other physicians or the organization. Instead, focus not on what they *can* do but on what they *will* do and, more importantly, what they *have already done and how they did this.* Ask candidates behaviorally based questions and require them to give you specific examples of what they have done that is most related to your needs.

4. Generic Job Descriptions Are Overly Relied On

Job descriptions often do not differentiate between the unique needs of similarly titled jobs within or across organizations. It is essential that an organization communicate clearly both to the candidate and to staff so that everyone shares a clear and common understanding of the job.

5. CVs Are Deceptive

CVs are neither an independent nor an objective appraisal of the candidate, and as such, they cannot be relied on as fact. Instead, the most effective way to avoid unpleasant surprises is to ask candidates, and their references, for specific examples of what related experiences they have and how they accomplished these.

6. Hiring Decisions Are Made at the Gut Level

Hiring decisions often are based on the hiring authority's subjective reactions to the physician candidate without sufficient regard for other valuable evidence about this prospect. To significantly boost your hiring quotient and return on investment (ROI), consult objective and accurate sources of data, such as validated leadership assessments, behaviorally based interview questions, and highly targeted professional reference questions.

7. Hiring Decisions Are Made on First (and Lasting) Impressions

Candidates who do not make good initial impressions in the interview might as well stand up quickly, graciously thank the interviewers for their time and go home. Instead of making snap judgments, employers should wait at least 20 to 30 minutes into the interview before allowing themselves to start forming conclusions. Remain open and seek out information that might contradict your initial impressions. For example, probe the unbecoming candidates for specific examples of their related activities, and probe those candidates who impress you initially for additional information to get more balanced information about both their strengths and weaknesses. The deadly sin of adhering to the first impression brings us to the next deadly sin.

8. Hiring Decisions Are Made Within the First Four Minutes of the Interview

Most hiring decisions are made within the first four minutes of the interview. Interviewers then spend the remaining 56 minutes trying to gather information to support the decision they already made. Initial impressions are formed, interviewers stop thinking, and sometimes their egos prevent their brains from making good business decisions.

Exacerbating the situation is that senior executives experience cognitive dissonance when they feel anxiety between what they want and what they perceive they are experiencing. If they suspect they have made a bad decision, they often try to find evidence to justify it. People do not like to feel anxious or be second-guessed in their decisions, so they rationalize to themselves what they have done.

9. Interviewers Hire People They Like

Certainly, it is important to like the people with whom you will be working. However, by the time the initial honeymoon period ends, unpleasant problems usually begin to surface. To avoid this trap, remember not to just hire a candidate because he appears to be a nice person. We frequently have to remind clients that although certain people might make wonderful "neighbors," they are not well matched to the needs of a given position. Selecting the seemingly nice interviewee who really is not appropriate for the job backfires even further when that physician becomes toxic to everyone she encounters. Senior executives often feel guilty, anxious, experience various forms of denial (e.g. "they just need more time to improve" and "their references swore that they walked on water"), and are concerned about how hiring these mismatches will reflect negatively on their own performance, so they delay having the difficult, yet inevitable conversations.

10. Interviewers Hire People Like Themselves

Favoring candidates with whom they share attributes or experiences (attended the same prestigious university, grew up in the same area, enjoys golfing, etc.) is a common yet dangerous tendency for interviewers. Clearly, what people say they *want* in a potential hire may not necessarily be what they *need*. The people you hire should complement your personal style and should not be exact clones of you. Instead, check with others who know you and the job well enough to make sure you are pursuing the right people for the job. Also, use behavioral profiles and other types of structured behavioral interviews to increase objectivity and accuracy in making these very important and expensive hiring decisions.

11. Interviewers "Hang Hats" on Candidates

Even the most seasoned executives attribute certain characteristics to their prospective physician leaders that are not necessarily based in reality. Candidates may remind interviewers of someone they know regarding physical appearance, speech patterns, or other characteristics. Guard against the tendency to "judge a book by its cover" by asking the same questions to all candidates, listening carefully and making sure to remain open to who the person in front of you really is.

12. The "Warm Body Will Suffice" Syndrome

Time is short. You needed the physician leader to be in place a month ago, so the first available candidate gets hired. Instead, avoid settling for less, because the price you will pay for lowering your standards can be your own downfall.

CONCLUSION

How to Avoid the Downward Spiral

Hiring the wrong physician for a leadership position can launch your organization into an increasingly tight downward spiral. Valued and reliable long-term employees complain and quit, productivity suffers, and the organization is worse off than before the new leader was hired.

Health care leaders do not have to fall victim to these common traps. Hiring effectiveness can improve significantly through the use of structured, behaviorally based questions and cost-effective pre-employment testing. Many progressive healthcare leaders who previously feared they could not afford to spend more time and money on these strategies said they learned two very important lessons:

1. They couldn't afford *not* to try them out. After testing them initially on a limited trial basis, they discovered that the direct and indirect costs of bad hires, turnover and aggravation were *much higher* than the relatively small investment of time and resources.
2. These strategies have enabled them to protect their most valuable assets: their human capital. Healthcare organizations came to regard these approaches as sound investments that provided them with immediate and significant returns.

ACKNOWLEDGMENT

Please note that this chapter was adapted from one of the authors' previous publications. Cohen, K. R. (2015). *Promoting physician alignment through evidence-based selection practices: Getting your docs in a row*. White paper. American Hospital Association, Health Forum, Chicago, IL.

REFERENCES

Carroll, L. (1865). *Alice's adventures in wonderland*. New York: MacMillan.

Cohen, K. R. (2008). *Best practices for developing effective and enduring board/CEO relationships*. American Hospital Association's Center for Healthcare Governance.

Collins, J. (2001). *Good to great*. New York, NY: HarperCollins Inc.

Synergy. (n.d.). Retrieved from: www.synergyorg.com

KEY TERMS AND DEFINITIONS

Developmental Assessments: Create individualized strategies to facilitate employees' growth and increase their productivity.

Evidence-Based: The deliberate, explicit, and judicious use of current best evidence in making decisions. It means integrating expertise with the best available external empirical evidence from systematic research.

Poor Performers: People who are unhappy with their positions and inflexible. Usually they do not change themselves to fit their job requirements. Instead, they try to change their job responsibilities to suit their own preferences.

Return on Investment (ROI): Measures gain/loss generated on an investment relative to the amount of money invested. ROI is usually expressed as a percentage and is typically used for personal financial decisions, to compare an organization's profitability or to compare the efficiency of different investments. The return on investment formula is ROI = (Net Profit / Cost of Investment) x 100.

Synergy Screening System®: An evidence-based, three-step scientific approach to hiring the right healthcare leaders the first time.

Top Performers: People who love their jobs and have a real passion for them because they encourage them to be who they really are.

Chapter 5
Developing Clinical Leaders:
The Impact of a Pharmaceutical and Healthcare Marketing MBA

Valerie A. Storey
University of Central Florida, USA

ABSTRACT

Complex 21st century healthcare systems require leaders capable of making strategic decisions grounded on sound medical and healthcare knowledge and practices. Traditionally, these two domains have been viewed through a binary lens. In the 21st century, these domains are best viewed through a unitary lens. Consequently, several medical and business schools have developed joint programs to train physician leaders who receive both medical (MD) and master of business administration (MBA) degrees. St. Joseph's University in partnership with Lancaster General Health (LG Health) system developed an Executive MBA program for aspiring healthcare system leaders who previously trained for only one domain. This chapter examines the impact of the Executive MBA on clinical leaders and the organization they serve.

DOI: 10.4018/978-1-5225-7576-4.ch005

INTRODUCTION

Program impact is an outcome measurement, "a systematic way to assess the extent to which a program has achieved its intended results" (The Evaluation Forum, 2000, p.9).

Performance, value and impact are important for all involved in planning, designing, implementing and delivering a new program. Any individual or organization investing resources such as time and money in their personnel expect to receive a positive return in today's financial and political economy. Shrinking budgets and rising expenses place an emphasis on gathering data, which documents program impact. Examining impact serves as a way to build and maintain program credibility as well as justify use of limited resources.

A variety of methods and techniques can be used for program evaluation. This chapter describes how program graduates of a bespoke (personalized to organizational needs) Pharmaceutical and Healthcare Marketing MBA for Executives developed by St. Joseph's University (SJU), Erivan K. Haub School of Business in partnership with Lancaster General Health (LG Health) reflected on their change in skill, competencies, knowledge, and attitudes toward leadership, collegiality, and organizational strategic planning.

COMPLEMENTING CLINICAL ACUMEN WITH BUSINESS KNOWLEDGE

An essential requirement of today's complex healthcare system is that clinicians, administrators, policymakers, and insurance companies work together to ensure adequate health care access and quality at a reasonable cost. As the system evolves in complexity, there is a growing need for physician leaders who can bring a clinical perspective to managerial challenges (Stoller, 2009). Insightful healthcare systems and independent physicians seek to address this need through the completion of a professional development course, often online, from one of the plethora of courses currently offered in the market place. One increasingly popular option is to complete a Master of Business Administration (MBA) degree or a MD/MBA.

MBA PROGRAM

In order to address contemporary challenges facing healthcare delivery—variable clinical quality, high costs, and poor patient experience—it is argued that skilled physician leaders are required who can blend clinical knowledge with management acumen (Ljuboja, Powers, Robbins, Huckman, Yeshwant, & Jain, 2016). A healthcare leader with these combined skills will have the ability to link the financial results of the organization to clinical outcomes. Although management education is slowly being integrated into medical school curricula, the prevailing approach for teaching these skills remains in Master of Business Administration (MBA) programs (Goyal, Aung, Oh, Hwang Besancon & Jain, 2015). An increasing number of physicians are also returning to business school after completing their clinical training through full- or part-time MBA programs (Hilsenrath, 2012).

MD/MBA PROGRAM

Combined MD/MBA programs is a relatively new but growing phenomena in the US. Currently, 40% of US medical schools have established a medical doctorate (MD) and master of business administration (MBA) dual-degree program, a fivefold increase since the mid-1990s (Patel, Arora, Patel, Kinney, Pauly, & Asch, 2014), and approximately 500 medical students graduate with this dual degree each year (Viswanathan, 2014). Rather than adding two more years of education, these programs integrate the medical and administration curriculum into five years. Typically, students completing a dual degree program take a year off between the second and third years of medical school to complete their MBA requirements (Lemon, 2018), completing the MD/MBA program in one extra year on top of medical school.

Dual degree physicians earn approximately $100,000 more than their MD counterparts in their first job after residency because they take on multiple roles in addition to direct patient care (Lemon, 2018). Critics of the MD/MBA argue that program graduates are drawn away from medicine into administrative fields. However, findings from a recent empirical study conducted by Krupat, Dienstag, Kester, & Finkelstein (2017) examining five years of data from students studying in the joint MD/MBA program at Harvard Medical School (HMS) and Harvard Business School (HBS) found that the vast majority embraced careers involving extensive postgraduate medical training, with long-term plans that leveraged their new perspectives. Patel *et al.,* (2014) found that many graduates with an MD/MBA pursue leadership and primarily nonclinical roles later in their careers. Nearly half of respondents in their study felt their MBA helped to inform their overall business and medical perspectives, supply multidisciplinary experience, and improve communication between the medical and business worlds.

Many physicians practicing today did not have the option of completing a MD/MBA although they appreciate that having a MBA credential on their resume could make them a stronger candidate when applying for positions in administration, policy, and industry. Therefor when the opportunity to complete an MBA at no financial cost to them arises, it is viewed as an appealing prospect by motivated, aspiring clinical leaders and administrators.

LEADERSHIP PATHWAYS

Typically there are two discrete paths into healthcare leadership, which reflect the degree path taken: as clinicians trained in healthcare delivery discipline, and as non clinicians trained in management including economics, finance, human resources, law, marketing, and technology. Both pathways have their own strengths and weaknesses. But the potential applications of the MD/MBA degree are vast (Lemon, 2018) from bringing medical innovations to market, to being a positive force for change in American medicine.

Combining the two pathways increases the capacity of both the individual and the healthcare organization. Physicians are capable of strategic planning through a variety of lenses and perspectives, are able to complete holistic cost benefit analyses, and make high-level business strategy decisions all while upholding a hospital or hospital system's core commitment to patient care. Thereby, creating a transparent organizational culture grounded on horizontal and vertical trust.

PERFORMANCE, VALUE, AND IMPACT

Performance and Value

As previously mentioned the MD/MBA program is a relatively new phenomenon although for some time a fairly small group of farsighted physicians have chosen to independently pursue an MBA program in the belief that the knowledge and skills gained will enhance their professional capital. This is costly for the individual and the program curriculum does not always meet either individual or organizational need. The ideal model is for a healthcare system to develop a "bespoke" program in partnership with an academic institution and then pick up the cost for employees to complete the credential. This requires a healthcare board that is willing to take a financial risk; and understands the substantial benefits of investing in developing clinical leadership capacity. The organization's board must make:

1. Ideological commitments to two practices-succession planning and leadership.
2. Pragmatic commitment to two actions-substantial financial investment and program evaluation.

This chapter is focused on a healthcare system where leadership was committed to engaging their primary care physicians and administrators in professional development, which addressed individual and organizational need. Not surprisingly the CEO and the system's board are keen to know of the benefits (or otherwise) of their financial investment.

Program Impact

Measuring program impact requires a program to change attitudes or behavior, or benefit society (Diem, 1997). Identifying program impact is important for four reasons: 1) to justify the investment of funding; 2) to earn and build professional, organizational, and political credibility and support; 3) to yield tangible data (quantitative and qualitative) that enable an institution to show the quality of their program(s); and 4) to satisfy the requirements of political bodies and funding agencies. Measuring impact is part of both the summative evaluation component, which judges the quality and worth of a program, and the formative evaluation component, which provides feedback to help improve and modify a program (Storey & Asadoorian III, 2014). In trying to identify appropriate program impact it is useful to be cognizant of Bennett's hierarchy of program cause and effect. Bennett (1975) developed a seven-step hierarchy that shows the causal links between the steps from inputs to outcomes. Program impact increases as you move through the hierarchy (Adapted from Bennett's Hierarchy of program cause and effect, 1975):

1. **Inputs:** Costs, time, and personnel.
2. **Activities:** Workshops, field days, seminars, awareness-raising campaigns.
3. **Participants:** Number of people, their characteristics.
4. **Reactions of Participants:** Degree of interest, likes and dislikes.
5. **Changes:** In knowledge, attitudes, skills, and aspirations.
6. **Practice Change:** Adoption and application of knowledge and skills.
7. **End Results:** Range of outcomes that might be desired in program delivery.

Bennett pointed out that program designers must be able to answer the question: "How do you know this program was responsible for these impacts?" Bennett stated that the data required to measure program impact on clients (e.g., program graduates, organizations) could be gathered in only three ways: ask them, test them, or observe them.

An effective, impactful program must be informed by horizontal and vertical communication meaning that program design and desired outcomes should be grounded on the input of all involved stakeholders, specifically program graduates. The development of a collaborative partnership in program delivery places a moral imperative on partners and stakeholders to help in the gathering of program data (Storey & Asadoorian III, 2014).

CREATING "SAVVY" HEALTHCARE PROFESSIONALS WITH BOTH CLINICAL ACUMEN AND BUSINESS KNOWLEDGE

Contextual Background

A cohort of twenty-one Lancaster General Health (LG Health) employees and Lancaster General Hospital Medical and Dental Staff members completed a bespoke (personalized to organizational needs) Pharmaceutical and Healthcare Marketing MBA for Executives through Saint Joseph's University's (SJU), Erivan K. Haub School of Business developed in partnership with LG Health. Fifteen physicians and six administrators began the program in Spring 2013 and finished in 2015. Students took one course per month, with breaks in August and December. Most of the two-year MBA program was completed online, including a weekly-synchronized class although occasionally, SJU's professors delivered lectures off campus at LG Health. Classwork included essays, reading assignments, group projects, online discussions and capstone team assignment (Duke, 2015). Classes were not scheduled during the summer semester. The program required an overall investment by LG Health of approximately $1 million, which included tuition as well as an overseas experience.

THE VOICE OF PROGRAM GRADUATES AND SENIOR LEADERSHIP AT LANCASTER GENERAL HEALTH

Program graduates were asked to reflect on the degree of change in their leadership knowledge, skills, attitude, and organizational awareness. Additionally, LG Health CEO and the Senior VP: HR/Chief Leadership Officer were also interviewed. Questions were sent to participants via email prior to a phone interview to facilitate self-reflection. The act of reflection required interviewees to process their thoughts and experience of the Executive MBA program they had recently experienced, more accurately assess their degree of change as a result of the program and overall provide more meaningful data.

For this evaluation of program impact, a three section questionnaire was developed that contained 15 questions designed to collect basic data from program graduates. In Section A questions focused on how candidates were selected for the program; how participants and the organization benefitted from the program; and perceptions of the cohort model, delivery format, and the capstone project. In Section B program graduates were asked questions focused on the development of their leadership skills and organizational knowledge. Questions in Section C focused on increasing organizational capacity (see Appendix 1). A second set of question, fourteen in total were sent to the CEO and Senior VP: HR/Chief Leadership Officer to gather contextual and descriptive data (see Appendix 2).

The author of this chapter conducted the phone interviews. Interviewees first reflected on their feelings on being invited to participate in the program and how they decided to allocate their own resources (primarily time) into the program. The questions acted as a catalyst for reflective thought rather than being systematically addressed.

SECTION A

Candidate Selection

Under the CEO's leadership LG Health's medical staff had been restructured and as a result there was a renewed emphasis on leadership and the responsibilities that come with being a Chair or Chief. There was a need to fast track able physicians into leadership roles but at the same time it was imperative that they were not overwhelmed by the new administrative knowledge and skills that they would require to be successful in the position. According to the CEO invited participants experienced mixed emotions of both anxiety and motivation:

Physicians and administrators were invited to participate in the program. The overwhelming majority accepted although personal and professional obligations prevented a few from accepting (as this was a considerable time commitment on top of their general practice). The cohort finally consisted of 15 physicians and 6 administrators. This was intentional as there was a need to ensure diversity of thought within the cohort.

One respondent commented:

I was apprehensive when I viewed the names of the people in the cohort as I seemed to have very little in common with some of them, and I wondered how worthwhile the experience would be. I was flattered and grateful for the opportunity of course, particularly when there was no financial cost to me.

A senior member of the leadership team at LG Health, and a community leader explained how he reached the decision to accept the invitation to complete the MBA program:

I was serving as President of the medical staff and I was asked to take a new role as President of our medical group, which was not in my plans. After reflection I accepted the new role. I was then encouraged to participate in the newly designed MBA program. My initial response was that I got the job without an MBA so why should I submit myself to additional pressure. I was not keen to go back to school. But as I looked at the knowledge and skills I needed to do the job well, I realized that the MBA curriculum was going to cover what I would be reading about any way in order to be successful. Also, folks already accepted into the program would be reporting to me so this program seemed a good way to go about building a team.

Whilst an influencing factor for this respondent was to keep ahead of his team a more junior respondent believes he was invited to complete the program based on:

Our talent development process with the organization, I believe our senior leaders selected physicians and administrators judged on their current performance, future potential, and likelihood to stay within the organization long after the program completed.

Another cohort member observed that:

The MBA program at Saint Joseph's was a natural next step for us and a critical one in achieving LG Health's goals to provide the best care and keep up with the changes in the healthcare industry.

Several interviewees made reference to their steep learning curve in becoming technologically competent. Undoubtedly, a 21st century healthcare organization seeks physician leaders who will embrace the role of change agent and have the skills to assist with information technology (IT) implementation, particularly electronic medical records (EMRs) and systems that link clinical and financial data. So gaining technology skills was a valuable if unintended outcome of the program:

The biggest adjustment for me wasn't being back in the classroom – it was the technology.

Completing assignments was initially stressful as my computer skills were extremely limited and I had little incentive to learn Excel, Powerpoint etc. But this program pushed me so not only have my computer skills improved but I also have an understanding of the time and effort that those reporting to me have put into producing a report or analyzing data.

Participant Benefits

When asked whether the program had benefitted them as an individual the issue of time and the impact on family was the first identified.

I think I benefitted from the program but during the program I regretted it when doing a paper on a Sunday afternoon. It was a lot of work. Content knowledge has helped a lot. I had never read about leadership theory; and also some of the harder sciences like finance and accounting. As a member of the finance committee it gave me more confidence to ask questions.

For some members of the cohort the experience was life changing in that personal trait and characteristics both of leadership and healthcare managers became more evident leading to changes in perception of some colleagues. This change in relationship status became evident in their daily work.

As program graduates remain in leadership positions. It made us aware of the theory and practice of successful change management. It made us better able to develop embracing vision and effective strategic plans. It also helped to create shared organizational cultural beliefs and values.

Another interviewee identified four specific ways in which he had benefitted from the program:

1. *I developed an understanding and appreciation for strategic and business planning, finance/accounting principles, performing projections and analysis.*
2. *I learned to adapt my leadership style for different situations and different teams.*
3. *I developed skills, collaboration techniques to lead teams of teams working to a common vision.*
4. *I appreciate the business ethics principles necessary to drive organizational performance improvement.*

One interviewee gave a practical example of how the program had helped him work through a complex change initiative.

Getting medical group doctor to change their schedules is challenging but we were able to take a step back and rather than transition into a confrontational situation which we would have done prior to the program we were able to take a more strategic but successful approach.

Organizational Benefits

One interviewee described how he believed the organization had benefitted from their financial investment:

Over the subsequent years, I worked with operational, service-line and information technology teams to create multidisciplinary clinical pathways directed to improve quality/safety and the patient experience with smarter spending. As a team, we leverage data-driven decision-making and continuous improvement to achieve our mission to advance the health and well-being of the communities we serve.

Reflecting on program impact and organizational benefit, one interviewee stated:

I now have a better understanding as to how I fit into the overall vision for the organization, and I believe I have become a little more empathetic and a little less cynical. I am better able to understand why certain managerial decisions are made and to be honest it has made me more committed to the profession.

Program Design and Delivery Model: Benefits

Most physicians are used to working independently, but through the cohort students formed close bonds during group projects.

The online delivery was particularly appreciated by practitioners:

The ability to access a class remotely from wherever I was using a laptop was a very new experience and challenging experience for me.

Since I had never completed online classes previously, I appreciated the chance to use the new tools and learn in a new way.

I absolutely appreciated the benefits of online learning and not having to travel for a long class after the end of a full workday.

In order to develop trust between cohort members the program schedule built in a number of face-to-face meetings:

During the two and half years, since we were all simultaneously experiencing the same courses, we could rely on each for support (i.e. mutual celebration of misery/challenges of the month).

I appreciated the ability to occasionally gather in person for classes as we could all teach and learn from each other's perspectives and experiences.

The outcome of the program's cohort design was perceived as pivotal to the program's success as program participants' transitioned from working as an individual to a team:

By having only LG Health leaders in the cohort it was overwhelmingly beneficial on a collegial, personal and professional level. It moved individuals into a team. Through the cohort they learnt about the role of other areas in the organization and gained a greater understanding of different expertise. They became respectful of other people's expertise, thought and points of view. This trickled over into their day job.

The program's culminating capstone required students to travel to Argentina and Brazil to observe varying healthcare delivery systems. Interviewees identified this activity as impactful for both LG Health and themselves as they were required to work collegially in order to successfully complete team projects. As the CEO observed:

In participating in the capstone presentations delivered by all students, the leadership team was astounded with the changes seen in the cohort – from the camaraderie developed to the new perspective on business issues healthcare is facing… Program graduates will be an important part of LG Health's future for many years to come.

SECTION B

Leadership

In relation to leadership style one interviewee referenced the influence of the CEO's leadership style, which he identified as "servant leadership."

I guess my leadership style is servant leader which is appropriate for a not for profit organization. Actually the program made me realize the responsibilities that a not for profit organization has. Now I really take our mission, vision, and values to heart. We come back to this in decision-making. What is the effect on the community? What is the effect on the patient? I understood this before but I now have a better understanding of our organizational culture. We are committed to providing professional development opportunities for all employees but in return we have certain expectation above and beyond medicine.

The following personal insights came from several interviewees:

I have developed the ability to recognize different learning and leadership styles and strengths, then align team members' preferences with our goals, so together we can accomplish more.

I now understand that leadership style needs to vary depending on the situation and the expertise of the individual. Previously I had always thought you needed to deal with everyone in the same way.

Organizational Knowledge

Overall the general consensus from interviewees is that LG Health has and will benefit considerably from the financial investment made.

I now take a broader approach in decision-making based on understanding the potential impact to multiple areas of the organization.

I can better balance the time to gather feedback and make decisions by consensus vs. communicate with the team that certain decisions are made by the leader based on the organization's mission, strategies, and goals.

I understand that decisions made are not personal and I am better able to put forward a viewpoint supported with data that leadership understand.

SECTION C

Developing Organizational Capacity

Several interviewees referred to the fact that they now saw a broader perspective of the organization and would consider the impact on others when making decisions. All interviewees identified the role of the program in developing their understanding of areas of the organization that they had never previously considered and their interconnections:

The program and the required assignments exposed me to different areas of the organization. I have a greater appreciation of how the system runs.

I now have an appreciation and understanding of the work across different departments in the organization like operations, finance, marketing, accounting, strategy, and business planning. This has helped me to create the balanced scorecard that we now use to monitor operations through our continuous improvement journey.

By working together in the program with a cohort of physicians, we can rely on each other to generate ideas and implement programs to reduce burnout.

We have a better understanding to assess current state contributing to burnout, to perform a cultural inventory contributing to burnout, and implement changes to improve personal resilience.

My team has noted that I tend to facilitate and engage them in decision-making. I also try to tie my comments to teams to our mission and vision to inspire them to align goals, engage in our work for a greater purpose.

DISCUSSION

The analyzed data revealed that participants experienced a positive change in leadership knowledge, skills, attitude, and organizational awareness (see Table 1).

Despite the fact that there was no student attrition and that over a third of students graduated with honors the MBA program has not been sustained. LG Health has now partnered with the Pennsylvanian Medical Society to deliver shorter professional leadership courses. This is less financially impactful to the organization and also the cohort is smaller (usually 10). Several interviewees pointed out that pragmatically this approach makes sense. "While we wouldn't hold this every three years, I could see us holding another cohort in a few years to grow new leaders and prepare them for the future." "At the end of the program there needs to be leadership roles to plug them into. Maybe in 5 years there needs to be another cohort when there are internal opportunities."

Table 1. Program impact

Factors contributing to applying to the MBA program	Applicability of the curriculum Team building Identified by senior leadership
Individual benefit	Increased awareness of organizational culture
	Increased empathy with colleagues in different areas within the organization
	Increased ability think strategically & holistically
	Increased technology skills Greater understanding of the responsibilities of a not for profit organization
Organizational benefit	Leadership pipeline-Individuals prepared to take on a collegial leadership role
	Physicians & administrators prepared to raise their voice as change agents for the good of the system
	Aspiring system leaders who understand the special role of a not for profit organization
	Strong communal sense of vision, values, and mission.
	Developing pipeline of young administrator/leaders
	Development of trust-vertically & horizontally.

CONCLUSION

Irrespective of the current growth of MD/MBA programs there is a scarcity of physician leaders in healthcare systems. A study by Gunderman and Kanter, (2009) found that amongst 6,500 hospitals in the US, physicians ran only 235. A later study by Goodall (2011), found that physicians in each of three specialty areas disproportionately lead the best-performing hospitals: cancer; digestive disorders; and heart and heart surgery. Furthermore, in 2013 (U.S. News and World Report, Honor Roll) reported that physicians lead the top five US hospitals, and 10 of the 18 hospitals on their "Honor Roll" are physician-led.

Physicians at LG Health understand that by accepting an organizational leadership role they will be better able to shape organizational decisions around what is best for patients, physicians, and the organization as a whole. Physician MBA graduates can provide critical clinical insight into management decision-making. Accordingly, one possible solution is to develop exponentially MD/MBA programs so that graduates may potentially fill a growing need within the workforce (Patel et al., 2014).

This chapter has focused on the SJU's bespoke Executive MBA program, which was specifically designed to meet the needs of LG Health. Whilst there had been a general expectation by LG Health leadership team that the program would develop leadership skills, and enhance organizational understanding, team building efforts, and administrator skills, it is evident from the interviewees highlighted in this chapter that there were unexpected consequences focused on softer skills such as trust, empathy, organizational holistic knowledge and of course increased technology skill and understanding. As the CEO pointed out, "in effect we created an in-house consulting group."

Hearing our aspiring physician leaders talk about corporate finance and understanding how that fits into the bigger picture is a game changer when coupled with their clinical expertise. These are the future leaders of this organization.

The curriculum covered concepts not taught in medical school. Subsequently, completion of the MBA will set program graduates apart from other candidates and allow them to find the management positions they may seek in addition to/or instead of their medical practice.

At the moment there is no known method that allows programs to establish irrefutable causal relationships between various program features and specific program outcomes (Storey & Asadoorian, 2014). At best, analytic evaluation methods provide only estimates and approximations. This chapter has presented the dynamic voice of program graduates of a bespoke Executive MBA program and argued that the program has impacted individual behavior and attitude, and proved value for money from the organization's perspective.

REFERENCES

Bennett, C. (1975). Up the hierarchy. *Journal of Extension*, *13*(2). Retrieved from http://www.joe.org/joe/1975march/1975-2-a1.pdf

Diem, K. (1997). *Measuring impact of educational programs. Rutgers Cooperative Extension. Fact sheet #869*. New Brunswick, NJ: Rutgers University.

Duke, L. M. (2015). *Penn Medicine: Lancaster General Health.* Progress Notes. Retrieved from http://www.lancastergeneralHealth.org/LG HEALTH/Healthcare-Professionals/Progress-Notes/Staff-Transitions/Meet-David-Polin,-MD-%E2%80%93-and-newly-minted-MBA.aspx

Evaluation Forum. (2000). *How to manage and analyze data for outcome-based evaluation*. Seattle, WA: Organizational Research Services Inc.

Goodall, A. H. (2011). Physician-leaders and hospital performance: Is there an association? *Social Science & Medicine*, *73*(4), 535–539. doi:10.1016/j.socscimed.2011.06.025 PMID:21802184

Goyal, R., Aung, K. K., Oh, B., Hwang, T. J., Besancon, E., & Jain, S. (2015). Survey of MD/MBA programs: Opportunities for physician management education. *Academic Medicine*, *90*(1), 121. doi:10.1097/ACM.0000000000000517 PMID:25229193

Gunderman, R., & Kanter, S. L. (2009). Perspective: Educating physicians to lead hospitals. *Academic Medicine*, *84*(10), 1348–1351. doi:10.1097/ACM.0b013e3181b6eb42 PMID:19881420

Hilsenrath, P. E. (2012). Healthcare management education settings in the United States: History and perspective. *Journal of Management History*, *18*(4), 386–401. doi:10.1108/17511341211258738

Krupat, E., Dienstag, J. L., Kester, W. C., & Finkelstein, S. N. (2017). Medical students who pursue a joint MD/MBA degree: Who are they and where are they heading? *Evaluation & the Health Professions*, *40*(2), 203–218. doi:10.1177/0163278715620831 PMID:26801747

Lemon, J. D. (2018). The MD/MBA: An emerging dual degree in healthcare. *The Journal of Lancaster General Hospital*, *13*(2), 52–55.

Ljuboja, D., Powers, B. W., Robbins, B., Huckman, R., Yeshwant, K., & Jain, S. H. (2016). When doctors go to business school: Career choices of physician-MBAs. *The American Journal of Managed Care*, *22*(6), 196–198. PMID:27355906

Patel, M. P., Arora, V., Patel, M. S., Kinney, J. M., Pauly, M. V., & Asch, D. A. (2014). The role of MD and MBA training in the professional development of a physician: A survey of 30 years of graduates from the Wharton Health Care Management program. *Academic Medicine*, *89*(9), 1282–1286. doi:10.1097/ACM.0000000000000366 PMID:24979286

Storey, V. A., & Asadoorian, M. O. III. (2014, March 24). The political sense of urgency for educational leadership preparation programs to show impact data: The case of Florida. *The International Journal of Educational Leadership Preparation*, *1*(9). Retrieved from files.eric.ed.gov/fulltext/EJ1024106.pdf

U.S. News and World Report. (2013). Retrieved from http://health.usnews.com/health-news/best-hospitals/articies/2013/07/16/besthospitals-

Viswanathan, V. (2014). *The rise of the MD/MBA degree*. Retrieved from https://www.theatlantic.com/education/archive/2014/09/the-rise-of-the-mdmba-degree/380683/

KEY TERMS AND DEFINITIONS

Clinical Leadership: Individual skills, knowledge, and competencies required to effectively balance the needs of patients and team members within resource constraints and management.

Innovative Program: The deliberate development of a program to develop and enhance clinical leadership.

Lancaster General Health: Is a comprehensive healthcare delivery system with an earned reputation for excellence, compassion, quality, and cost effectiveness. Located in Lancaster, Pennsylvania.

Leadership Development: The development of the capacity of groups and organizations for leadership as a shared and collective process balancing individual skill-enhancement and organizational capacity building.

Leadership Style: Manner and approach of providing direction, implementing plans, and motivating people.

Program Impact: Examines the effects of the program in achieving specific goals.

Team Leadership: Practices and values exhibited by leaders, governing a specific group of individuals who are working towards achieving a particular goal or objective.

APPENDIX 1

Table 2. Self- reflective questions

Section A
I was selected/volunteered for the program- Explain your response.
I have benefitted from the program in a variety of ways- Explain your response.
My organization has benefitted from me completing the program- Explain your response.
I appreciated the fact that I was a member of a cohort- Explain your response.
I appreciated the hybrid delivery of the program- Explain your response.
I benefitted from the capstone project- Explain your response.
My organization benefitted from the capstone project- Explain your response.
Section B
I now have the skills necessary to facilitate a strategic planning process- Explain your response.
I now have holistic understanding of my organization- Explain your response.
My leadership style has changed as a result of completing the program- Explain your response.
My team has noticed a difference in my professional approach to individuals and the organization- Explain your response.
Section C
Completing the program increased my organizational engagement-Explain your response.
Completing the program increased my capacity to reduce physician team members' burnout-Explain your response.
I recommend that SJU & LG HEALTH run the program again? Explain your response.
Do you think the program has ongoing value for not only the medical staff, but for the organization as well? Explain your response.

Please add any other thoughts and comments that you feel are relevant to reviewing program development & impact which have not been covered in these questions

APPENDIX 2

Table 3. Self- reflective questions

Section A
How did LG Health assess the need for a "bespoke" MBA program for physicians and other LG Health personnel? Was there a specific identified organizational problem?
Do you think the "bespoke" MBA program addressed the identified organizational need?
Can you give an example of how an organizational problem was solved by a program graduate grounded on their experience and learning in the program?
What were the underlying assumptions of the "bespoke" MBA program?
Section B
How were the program candidates identified?
Did any of your target candidates say no to the opportunity?
If a target candidate did say no to the opportunity what was the reason given?
Did all LG Health candidates graduate from the MBA "bespoke" program?
Section C
Have you noticed or been able to measure changed leadership behavior/quality patient outcomes of program graduates? Is the cost of the "bespoke" MBA program reasonable in relation to the organizational benefits? How has LG HEALTH benefitted from its financial investment? Is the program sustainable? Having now had a cohort graduate from the program is there anything you would have done differently?

Please add any other thoughts and comments that you feel are relevant to reviewing program development & impact which have not been covered in these questions.

Section 2
Curriculum Design

Chapter 6
Design and Program Elements of a Clinical Leadership Program:
The Saint Joseph's University Haub School of Business Experience

Anthony DelConte
Saint Joseph's University, USA

Michael J. Gast
Saint Joseph's University, USA

ABSTRACT

Healthcare delivery in the United States is an ever-evolving field that is changing across multiple economic and cultural levels. Healthcare delivery systems are being affected not just by emerging technological capabilities but by ongoing changes in the structure and role of health systems themselves, as well as in the diversity of the communities they service. The older model of physician-provider is likewise evolving, and today's clinician requires the skill set necessary to navigate this new healthcare delivery environment. This chapter describes the development and implementation of a clinical leadership MBA curriculum designed to provide physician-leaders with a strategic perspective on healthcare decision making that encompasses a broad range of structural, technological, financial, cultural, and ethical considerations.

DOI: 10.4018/978-1-5225-7576-4.ch006

INTRODUCTION

To address the evolving educational needs of future leaders in the healthcare field, St. Joseph's University (SJU) and Lancaster General Health (LG Health) collaborated to develop a comprehensive advanced degree program to train a physician and senior administrator cohort in topics ranging from the ethical, legal, and community implications of healthcare decision-making to the development, marketing, and structure of service provision for diverse patient populations. In addition to standard courses that would be present in any accredited MBA program, the program was also heavily focused on ethics so that the participants would be better able to recognize moral issues in healthcare and to distinguish these issues from questions of management, strategy, economics, psychology, law, and/or politics. Furthermore, physicians would have the tools to take the moral point of view toward these issues and to think of healthcare as not only affecting individuals, but also understanding the impact of healthcare delivery on entire communities and the institutions that support these communities.

For example, part of the program included an "immersion residency" trip abroad to study public hospitals in Latin America that are serving an increasing number of underinsured and chronically ill patients. The solutions employed by these hospitals made a deep impression on the students, who were inspired by the sense of mission among the hospital staff—to deliver equitable care to all patients—in spite of the sometimes inadequate resources available to accomplish that goal. The students were also able to readily see both the physical and quality-of-care differences between the public and private hospitals in healthcare systems that were functioning in an environment of political instability, social stratification, and economic hyperinflation, conditions that further exacerbate the disparities in healthcare delivery. In a final reflection paper, students could not help but comment on the endless marble construction inside one of the wealthiest hospitals in São Paulo, in contrast to the endless concrete inside São Paulo's public Hospital das Clinicas. In observing the ways healthcare was delivered in Latin America, the students gained insights into issues of disparity within a tiered system and reflected on how they may take these insights back to the debate about healthcare access, quality, and cost in the US.

The objective of this chapter is to describe the development and implementation of the LGH-SJU MBA program for physicians who were already involved in leadership roles. The question of whether to train future physician leaders during medical school or to wait until they have already attained leadership roles within their organizations before initiating management training, while relevant, will not be explored here. This chapter will focus on the development process, selection of the educational institution and student cohort for the program, and the elements that are educationally appropriate for such a program. Two courses offered as part of the MBA program will be selected to describe in more detail. The authors will also discuss standard and novel mechanisms for evaluating the performance of the students and educators in the program and ways to coordinate the students' educational experience with their real-life activities in the healthcare system. Program design, program content, composition of the graduate student group receiving the training, qualifications and range of expertise for the educators providing the coursework in the program, and the keys to successful completion of the program will be discussed.

Differing options for presenting required program information and conducting coursework will be defined and discussed. Training students in an environment where they may not be geographically proximate and where they are likely to be employed in full-time positions can be a challenge, and thus current modalities for facilitating instruction and allowing the widest range of student participation in the programs will also be discussed. Coordination with sponsoring commercial or healthcare organizations is a critical part of optimizing these types of graduate programs, as is crafting them to best fill the needs of the students and the organizations in which they will be working. Finally, philosophies of education that best suit this unique form of graduate education will be identified and discussed by the educators who have put them in place.

BACKGROUND: RATIONALE

The landscape of healthcare provision is changing at a rapid pace. To meet the challenges of the new paradigms for healthcare organizations, the leaders of healthcare systems, hospitals, and third-party payer organizations will increasingly need to be equipped to meet the changing demands of a complex and evolving healthcare environment. The skills required for the provision of healthcare have also been changing rapidly, and healthcare provider leaders in the 21st century need to be educated and practiced in the fields of finance, organization, and team-oriented management skills, among others. Meeting this challenge will require a focused and increasingly sophisticated education for these future leaders.

Many physicians who are currently in leadership positions tend to be older and male. According to Caryl Hess, physicians in leadership positions today were often trained in an era when "autonomy was rewarded, quality was an individual standard, and costs were ignored in favor of patient care" (Hess, 2013). In the past, the practice of medicine and the delivery of healthcare were viewed as a different set of realities from the business and operational aspects of healthcare. Physicians who embraced principles of business schools were often seen as "selling out" of their sworn responsibilities and duties around the delivery of healthcare. Many physicians would learn basic accounting skills in order to maintain their private practice in a limited capacity of bookkeeping and payroll. Some physicians would play the role of "managing partner" for their practice. Other physicians or groups would hire spouses or family members for accounting, scheduling, and office management activities. Other larger multi-physician practices would employ an office manager who might be credentialed with an MBA.

Although physician-in-management programs have been around for some time, their popularity has grown more recently. In 1993 there were 6 medical schools in the US that offered an MBA concurrent with earning a medical degree. Today more than 40% of the medical schools in the country have MBA programs offered along with a medical degree (Butcher, 2011; Goyal et al., 2015; Larson, Chandler, & Foreman, 2003). As physicians begin to understand the advantages of completing an MBA program, there is a realization that the value of a business education goes well beyond quantitative skills in finance, economics, and accounting. While medical education focuses on solving problems on an individual and independent level, business education focuses on populations and collaborative problem solving in a team environment. Achieving the balance of quality, cost, and access is not uniquely an American issue as it has been a focus for MD/MBA programs in Canada, which has had business education programs for medical students at McGill University starting in 1996 (Chen 2006).

An ongoing debate within educational institutions revolves around the degree to which educational training tends to focus on knowledge and scholarly pursuit at the expense of more practical professional skills. " Real-world" has become a veritable buzzword, particularly in academic medicine. As this debate continues, many medical schools are hiring faculty as professors of practice to emphasize those skills needed to become a successful real-world practitioner. Buckholz and Rosenthal have gone as far as to state that, although business schools have gained academic respectability by introducing scientific and scholarly methodologies, they have lost touch with those "complex social and human factors that are involved in business decisions" (Buchholz & Rosenthal, 2007). They further state that scholars tend to focus on narrow subjects that may be of interest to other academics but not necessarily to practitioners.

In the search for an educational institution well suited to their physician MBA trainees, the LG Health system leadership considered a number of research-focused universities. Because a future merger with an academic medical center was a possibility, they were particularly cognizant of the need for an emphasis on practical strategic knowledge and financial/administrative skills. To use the thinking attributed to hockey legend Wayne Gretzky, they wanted to skate to where the puck was going to be, not to where it was now.

PHYSICIAN MBA CLINICAL LEADERSHIP PROGRAM: DEVELOPMENT AND IMPLEMENTATION

Identifying the Educational Institution

The Erivan K. Haub School of Business at SJU is an international AACSB-accredited institution that offers both campus-based and online MBA programs. LG Health (now a member of the University of Pennsylvania Health System i.e. Penn Medicine) is a 663-licensed bed, not-for-profit health system that provides comprehensive health services to the Lancaster, Pennsylvania region. The LG Health system is the largest employer in the county of Lancaster, Pennsylvania and is regionally and nationally recognized for its outstanding clinical programs.

In 2012, the executive leadership of LG Health was seeking a strategic partner for the purpose of enhancing the educational experience of high-potential physician leaders within its organization and providing them with an opportunity to earn an MBA. The LG Health physician leadership had already had a taste of executive education in other programs, and in fact some physicians were finishing up a Wharton Leadership program that year. During the summer of 2012, the leadership of LG Health met with the faculty and staff of SJU to explore the possibility of collaborating on this project. To be successful, this type of program requires a large and varied faculty to execute the courses. Those involved with planning included deans and associate deans of the business school, director of the MBA program, additional MBA program staff aside, in addition to the faculty who would be instructors in the courses.

During the discussions with the LG Health leadership and SJU, a number of potential issues arose surrounding the possibility of enrolling healthcare providers, particularly those who grew up in an era of autonomy and self-determination. The group anticipated challenges in offering traditional business education where students must work in teams and collaborate more intensively. There were also discussions about healthcare professionals having to deal with uncertainty and ambiguity in the business world in a way they had seldom encountered in scientific and clinical situations. It was also discussed and decided during these meetings that LG Health would be seriously committed to developing the next set of leaders and, ultimately, that they wished to rely on internal expertise and be less dependent on outside consultants.

After several meetings, SJU was selected as the educational partner and preparations were begun to initiate a cohort of 20 LG Health physician and senior leaders into the Haub MBA program. The full-time faculty at SJU at that time included a physician, pharmacist, psychologist, and attorney, all of whom had significant experience in the healthcare industry. The MBA office was experienced in developing successful industry-specific cohort programs for healthcare institutions and was already at work on logistical and operational considerations. There was an immediate connection made between the leadership of LG Health and the faculty and staff at SJU. Soon afterwards, letters of invitation went out to high-potential physician leaders and other key individuals within the health system. A course schedule was planned to account for not only core content requirements, but also the flexibility necessary to accommodate busy physicians with night call and clinical responsibilities. After a thoughtful discussion, it was agreed that online class time would involve weekly synchronous sessions every Wednesday evening at 9:00PM EST. Throughout the 2-year period from 2013-2015, this time slot was an established routine, along with the cohort's other clinical, administrative, and personal commitments and responsibilities.

The University had promised a customized program geared towards the needs of physician executives and senior administrators. SJU was not going to deliver a generic, shrink-wrapped, off-the-shelf MBA program. The educational model chosen was primarily focused on online interactions, but included courses requiring face-to-face meetings. An immersion experience including an international course was also proposed and will be discussed later in the chapter.

Selection of the Student Cohort

As invitation letters were sent to high-potential applicants, the enthusiasm for the new program began to grow. Students were invited to attend and view ongoing MBA classes at the Ace Conference Center in Lafayette Hill, Pennsylvania. This conference center was then home to SJU executive education programs, including the Pharmaceutical and Healthcare marketing MBA program at the Haub School of Business. Student transcripts and applications were completed and SJU faculty members held personal interviews on the Lancaster campus. One of the chapter author's participated in a number of interviews and saw great anticipation for the program and gained thoughtful insights about course content from these potential students. No physician expressed any doubt that intense concentration on business skills, including managerial and leadership skills, would detract from their clinical responsibilities or care of their patients. Overall, the prospective cohort saw the program as an opportunity to develop leadership and management skills that would translate into a benefit to improve patient care on a population level. After vetting and discussion with the management team at LG Health, the final cohort accepted their offers to participate and continue through to graduation.

Program Formation and Objectives, Refinement and Customization of the Curriculum

In December of 2012, collaborative formal meetings were again held with LG Health senior leadership and representatives of SJU to define and customize courses and logistics leading to the MBA degree. The program was designed to extend just over 2 years and to be a hybrid of in-person and online courses. Onsite facilities at LG Health were an ideal venue for in-person classes and would function as the site of the inaugural leadership and ethics course in the spring of 2013. In parallel with course development and logistics, the legal departments of both institutions ironed out final agreement details. Because of the need for customization of the courses, the SJU faculty met regularly, often weekly, to discuss curriculum design and to assure integration and suitability of courses and materials. Table 1 lists courses offered in the LG Health_SJU MBA program and Table 2 lists options for learning formats.

The use of different learning formats was expected to be effective in allowing students to attend courses with minimal disruption in their already busy day-to-day responsibilities. Traditional classroom instruction was thought to be most useful for ethics and leadership courses, while the online format was thought to be suitable for many of the other course topics. Students would have access to instructors outside of the classroom time through email or office hour consultations.

Students would be expected to complete the usual courses of an accredited MBA program, including accounting, finance, and economics. In addition to these foundational courses, students would take courses covering health policy, competitive analysis, market research, forecasting, healthcare supply chain management, leadership, and development. The immersion residency experience was designed to be uniquely experiential in that students and instructors would spend most of their time visiting health centers and other medical institutions, with ample time for discussion and reflection over meals and bus rides. A brief description of two key courses follows, along with a description of the immersion residency.

Competitive Analysis (MPE650)

In February 2014, the LG Health student cohort embarked on its first journey of introspection and self-reflection through a course on competitive analysis. Prior to the course, the instructors met with senior leadership of LG Health,

Table 1. MBA program courses

Course Title	Course Number
Brand Management	MPE710
Business Ethics	MGT582
Business Statistics	DSS592
Capstone Hospital Strategy	MPE795
Competitive Analysis	MPE650
Corporate Strategy	MPE720
Data Analytics/Information Technology	DSS591
Economics Foundation	FIN501
Empowering Individuals & Groups	MGT520
Finance Foundation	FIN504
Healthcare Economics	MPE640
Healthcare Management	MPE660
Healthcare Regulation/Liability	MPE610
Healthcare Systems Integration	MPE 660
Leadership & Development	MGT581
Managerial Accounting	ACC561
Managerial Finance	FIN551
Marketing Foundation	MPE530
Marketing Research	MPE630
Pharmacoeconomics/Pricing	MPE670
Strategies for Managed Markets	MPE700
Supply Chain Management	MPE620

Table 2. Options for student learning formats

Traditional classroom instruction
Online instruction
Condensed, concentrated coursework
Threaded discussions
Immersion residency courses allowing students to experience healthcare and business practices outside of the United States.

including the SVP, Business Development & Ambulatory Services and SVP, Human Resources and Chief Learning Officer to discuss specifics of the services and programs offered at LG Health. The intent was to gain an in-depth understanding of the health system offerings to customize and feature these services in the course on competitive analysis. With an understanding of the proprietary programs offered, students could better identify specific services and efficient practices that impact the community's healthcare options and healthcare delivery, with the ultimate goal of improving healthcare services, developing additional components of those services that would expand and improve overall patient care, and raising public awareness of the services offered.

The course was designed to introduce students to basic paradigms and tools that underlie the establishment of market-based strategies to maintain, grow, and compete in the modern medical marketplace. As a major component of the course, students organized into brand teams to collaborate on specific deliverables. Some of these teams worked on the provision of specialty services such as cardiology, dermatology, and comprehensive orthopedic care. Each student was able to participate in a number of exercises designed to help them understand how medical practitioners and hospital systems adapt to changes in practice environments. One of the first steps in the process of the learning experience was to explore the concepts underlying the market components, customers, and stakeholders within their own hospital system.

The student cohort was then divided into teams of 4-5 students each. Team structure was important. The authors paid attention not just to organizing the teams, but also to fostering proper team behaviors. Among those behaviors were problem solving, decision-making, interpersonal abilities, teamwork, and leadership skills, as has been described by Katzenbach and Smith (1993). The authors believe the most important learning format involved team structure. This is the paradigm that many businesses and organizations use. Structural components and appropriate team behaviors were instilled in the teams to assure success. Each team selected an existing LG Health service (e.g., Cardiology, Orthopedic Care, Extended Care) on which to focus their study and their presentations. Through a series of presentations and discussions, students were then able to achieve a better understanding of their own hospital system's efforts to identify and foster the development of specific services and efficient practices that improve community healthcare.

To achieve these insights and goals, students were introduced to a disciplined process for assessing the competitive environment of their healthcare system. They began by identifying the customers and stakeholders of the products and services that are offered at LG Health. They then defined alternatives to the offerings, whether they be in adjacent geographic areas or services in a different setting within the county (e.g., Retail Drug Store clinics). During the second online session students developed a set of conceptual tools for completing an internal and external analysis of their services, which were then used to focus on specific areas that would differentiate LG Health from its competition. They were asked to grade the components of their selected services that would apply to the quality, quantity, and scope of patient care and compare those components to competing services in the community as well as in adjacent medical care spheres. Applying those tools and theories to a specific competitive analysis plan was the focus of the second part of the course. Students made final presentations during the last synchronous session at the end of the month and submitted final written descriptions of their findings.

As previously noted, the course was accomplished to a large extent in an online format that emphasized student participation. Participation was also enhanced through a series of threaded discussions that were selected by the instructors, which focused on aspects of competitive healthcare marketing that had not been discussed in class.

Upon the successful completion of the course, students were able to demonstrate proficiency in a number of areas. First, they were better able to recognize and understand branding of hospital and clinical care practices. What might now seem obvious to those working in sectors outside of healthcare may not be readily apparent to those who have largely focused on the clinical delivery of services. After completing this, and other courses, the need to market and communicate a differentiated product became understood as a key prerequisite to success. Furthermore, the students were better equipped to contribute to competitive analyses of key services and systems of importance to the LGH system. To achieve this analysis, they had to identify critical components of strategic marketing of healthcare services, such as market components, identification of customers and stakeholders, and assets for competitive marketing of those services.

Again, the goal of MPE650 was to perform a deep service analysis, with the goal of equipping physician leaders to improve community healthcare delivery. The students had to recognize and understand key customers and stakeholders and identify the competitive forces at play. They were to understand internal and external competitive analysis and communicate this in a form of a business staple, the SWOT (Strengths, Weaknesses, Opportunities, Threats) analysis. Finally, they were required to articulate their strategy to build and market their selected services in a final presentation of an integrated communication strategy using the competitive analysis tools they were provided and had mastered.

Specifics of the Competitive Analysis Content

The types of physician executive education programs available are as varied as the number of schools and institutions that provide them. Some programs train physicians to be executive managers, to run various types of healthcare systems, and to understand the healthcare financing and supply chain. Others focus on leadership qualities, including skills and behaviors that tend to cut across the different roles executive leaders will have in healthcare systems. The LG Health-SJU program was designed to provide a broad experience, focusing not just on specific knowledge or skills but on developing a mindset, a different way of thinking that would shape a new and innovative approach to problems and issues that do not yet exist. The Competitive Analysis course was based on this philosophical approach, to instill not just knowledge but a way of thinking.

Roughly 100 different services have been offered by the LG Health system, ranging from accountable care to x-ray and radiology services. Several of these key services have been designated "signature services" and are listed on the health center's website. Among these signature services are the Ann B. Barshinger Cancer Institute, Healthy Weight Management and Bariatric Surgery Center, Heart and Vascular Institute, Neuroscience Center, Orthopedic Center, and Women's health. It was these signature services that formed the basis for the student team project selections within the Competitive Analysis Course.

An example of one group's Competitive Analysis Plan incorporated a critical analysis of the health system's Orthopedic Center and joint replacement program. The Orthopedic Center has a reputation for world-class care and for creating exceptional patient experiences. As a result, the center attracts patients and referrals from outside the local geographic area and has been recognized and ranked by professional societies and accreditation centers. These include rankings in *US News and World Report*, certification by the Joint Commission for Joint Replacement, and in the highest levels of certification from the International Geriatric Fracture Society, and "Magnet" recognition by the American Nurses Credentialing Center.

There are a number of local competitors for the provision of orthopedic care, however, including the Lancaster Regional Medical Center (LRMC), which is LGH's highest volume local competitor. Students in the course considered the strengths and weaknesses of competitive centers, looking at a number of specific categories, including the culture, affordability, technical expertise, experience, patient outcomes, and regional reputation of the competitor. Developing such analyses required the students not only to have a strong working knowledge about how healthcare is delivered in their region, but also an understanding of how patients are entered into the system and how patients make the decision to seek care within the system and centers.

For example, as a part of the project students researched website metrics as to how long users stay on individual webpages, how they navigate and interact, and how they ultimately make a decision to enter into the healthcare system. By working in teams, students were able to conduct internal and external analyses. They used proprietary and publicly available data to evaluate the experience in terms of the number of cases and the recovery programs in place to reduce complications, readmissions, and lengths of stay. They looked at critical elements of differentiation, such as how the culture of their own and competing institutions has focused on the total patient experience through the collaborative team-based approach to care, quality, efficiency, and safety. They charted the patients' journey through preoperative home visits to arriving at the hospital, parking, registration, pre-op, operating room, recovery, nursing unit, and rehabilitation.

All of this was done with a patient-focused mentality. The authors believe that it is more difficult to conduct such an in-depth analysis without having a scientific, clinical, or medical background. Participants in a regular finance or marketing MBA program, while able to conduct overviews of these systems, cannot provide the insights that physicians and working hospital administrators can bring to the table. After conducting a careful analysis, student teams were able to develop strategic priorities based on future opportunities in the changing healthcare environment.

A few examples of these include expanding target markets to include the possibility of medical tourism. Other strategic initiatives involved in creating joint Health and Wellness programs to also include weight management, diabetes, exercise, sports medicine, and rehabilitation services, to not only correct patients' existing joint problems but to encourage long-term health behaviors. Other examples include addressing affordability of the services, improving staffing and communications both inside of and between services, creating measures to eliminate waste, and targeting payers and employers to become preferred centers based both on patient experiences and outcomes. Although creating a positive experience for customers has long been an accepted as part of the business world, applying this concept to medical practice is a relatively new phenomenon.

Healthcare Systems Integration (MPE 660)

A second course, taught by the authors in March 2015, centered on the concept of healthcare system integration and was focused on healthcare system mergers, acquisitions, and partnerships. Prior to the course (as was done in many of the courses), a survey was taken of the students' attitudes and experiences with the topics. Surprisingly, some of the senior physician executives had large amounts of experience in these areas. One in particular was involved in the formation of the LG Medical Group and was instrumental in the consolidation of multiple independent medical practices into a combined integrated medical specialty group.

Aside from the dichotomy of students with clinically focused backgrounds versus those with an administrative and business focus, there was also a generational dichotomy. As previously noted, some older physicians were trained at a time where autonomy allowed for greater levels of self-direction. Younger physicians recruited into existing practices had no such expectations but instead anticipated an employee-oriented business structure. These younger physicians also more readily embraced emerging technologies and change, including the use of electronic health records. In fact, during the course of the MBA program at LG Health, a major integration of an electronic health records (EHR) system was underway. As outsiders, the authors were able to characterize this rollout using a rocket launch metaphor and to understand that effective intra- and interdepartmental communications were a key element to assuring successful rollout of the program.

Healthcare Systems Integration was also conducted as an online course and included elements of healthcare system financing (including capital expenditure processes, bond issue and public/private financing initiatives, differences in the structure and culture of private versus public systems, religious versus secular systems, and conflict resolution for issues that might arise during the integration process following general agreement to execute the merger or acquisition). A number of case studies were evaluated and discussed, and guest speakers who had led or participated in healthcare system integrations were utilized. A wide range of online discussions and threaded discussions were assigned to students in preparation or follow-up to each class session and included expansion of topics discussed in class or subject areas of interest which were not discussed fully during the online sessions.

As in course MPE650, students were assigned to teams of 4-5 participants each. Each team selected a hypothetical merger or integration situation to use as a framework for a series of working sessions and presentations on specific areas of the process, including organizational and management schema, streamlining and duplication of services and personnel, financial and capital expenditure, decision-making, and issues of cultural integration. At the conclusion of the course, a final presentation by the team members and a final written paper were used to evaluate students' overall performance.

As things worked out, the course focusing on mergers and acquisitions was very timely for this cohort, as the LG Health system was about to embark on a merger itself, with the much larger University of Pennsylvania health system.

Assessment and Evaluation

Students were evaluated on their participation both in the online synchronous sessions and in a series of threaded discussions that invited them to take an in-depth approach to a number of issues. Aside from these individual evaluations, students were also assessed on team performance through team presentations and final papers. Ultimately, the instructors were also evaluated through surveys and other mechanisms of real-time feedback. This systematic approach to formative and summative assessment enabled instructors to review and modify the design of future programs. Standard assurance of learning practices was followed.

At the conclusion of the program and the end of the 650 Course, LG Health students met with senior management to recommend solutions to real-world issues regarding the marketing of healthcare services. These recommendations included which services should be continued, improved, or de-emphasized.

Global Immersion Experience in Brazil and Argentina

As the final course in the program, LG Health cohort accompanied by SJU instructors traveled to San Paulo, Brazil and Buenos Aries, Argentina in June 2015. The experience went beyond expectations for both the students and instructors. Each day began with a series of tours of healthcare institutions and centers, providing insights about healthcare delivery tiered to the rich and the poor, at extremes that go beyond those seen in the US. One student group summed up the experience in a final reflection paper below. The experience of the other groups was similar, and it is not an overstatement to characterize the experience as transformational. Upon the return to LG Health, the group was clearly changed and somehow developed more of a shared vision. As one physician-student eloquently put it, we did not all know each other well before earning our MBA, but after this experience somehow at meetings "we had each other's backs." There was a sense of trust and camaraderie upon emerging with the MBA that went beyond the simple skills and knowledge of the individual courses.

Here is one of the final reflections of one of the student teams (Duke M, et al., 2015):

Our visit to Hospital Garrahan in Buenos Aires, Argentina was an incredibly rewarding and inspirational experience. Hospital Garrahan's primary objective of creating a culture of quality in providing care that is equitable, accessible, patient-centered, and rational was evident in our discussions with staff, indicating strong leadership in the system... The ability to adapt and flourish, despite more significant restrictions than we face in the US, was a life-changing experience that will assist us as we transform healthcare at Lancaster General.

Garrahan's leadership structure provides the foundation to support their mission, vision, and values. Physicians make up the senior leadership of the organization and there is a clear line of sight for the medical staff in the leadership structure. The board is a four-physician group, and directly reporting to the board are several medical directors, all of whom are physicians as well. With physician leaders, the quality of patient care is accounted for in the decisions that guide the institution. They have a matrix organization and strive for multidisciplinary care of patients to create the highest quality and safest care for the patient. Quality is an institutional priority, with interdisciplinary training of all staff in the quality mindset...

...Despite being 5,000 miles from home and on the other side of the equator, the similarities in the challenges that we face in providing healthcare were strikingly similar for Garrahan, Brazil, and the US. Garrahan has more demand for their services than they can meet. They have developed innovative solutions such as telemedicine as a means of triage more out of necessity, rather than convenience, as we are doing in the US. Similar to the US, they focus on bed turnover and outpatient access as other ways to meet the demand. The public Brazilian hospital was also burdened with long waiting times for services and provided "pre-consult" triage visits with physicians to determine if a patient was in need of the services prior to the appointment. Despite long wait times, patients in Brazil and Argentina are content with receiving care and do not appear as unhappy about waiting as we see in the US...

...Even though there are multiple complex issues with which they have to struggle, Garrahan is clearly dedicated to their mission of providing high-quality care to complex illnesses in children in a compassionate, patient-centered way. Their senior leadership, being all physicians, has instilled a culture that was evident in the employees' strong desire to fulfill that mission. The resilience of the people of Argentina to deal with their multiple challenges and still provide high-quality care was commendable. They will be a source of inspiration for us at Lancaster General as we deal with many of the same issues with significantly more resources than the population of Argentina.

SUMMARY AND CONCLUSION

Working with the 21 students from LG Health has been one of the authors' most rewarding experiences at SJU. Both physicians and hospital administrators have been among the most outstanding and highly motivated students that the authors have encountered. In the Competitive Analysis course, the students critically evaluated their service offerings against the unmet medical needs of the communities that they serve. In the Healthcare Systems Integration course, students looked at hospital joint ventures and studied the pros and cons of hospital mergers and acquisitions. They observed how mergers sometimes worked and how many failed miserably (one of the most cataclysmic was the failed integration of UCSF and Stanford Medical Center in the San Francisco Bay area). This was incredibly timely for this cohort because the LG Health system was going through its own merger activities with the University of Pennsylvania.

The final summer immersion course concluded with an international residency in South America. During this São Paulo-Buenos Aires study tour, students visited a multitude of private/public hospitals in order to gain a broader perspective of the managerial and operational challenges facing healthcare organizations beyond US borders. The international residency provided a unique exposure to global healthcare. Students observed not just the business of medicine but how to create a better patient experience despite scarce resources and outdated technologies. They gained insights to provide this experience for patients, the healthcare professionals caring for them, and ultimately the communities they serve. The student's personal growth created a culture of unprecedented trust that allowed these visionary leaders to achieve possibilities they could not have reached before they started as a cohort.

ACKNOWLEDGMENT

Dr. D. would like to thank Dr. G. for being a co-teacher of these remarkable students. He brought his own dimension and professional perspective to the classroom. Also having guest speaker Eileen Cardile, CEO of another healthcare system that had just undergone its own merger activity, was incredibly valuable to all. The authors would like to thank Dean Joseph DiAngelo for considering the possibilities that this project and future educational programs would bring. We would also like to thank Terese Waldron, Jonathan Dart, and Kathy Klarich from the office of executive education.

The authors also thank MedVal Scientific Information Services (Princeton, NJ) for editorial assistance in preparing this manuscript, which was provided free of charge. This research received no specific grant from any funding agency in the public, commercial, or not-for-profit sectors.

REFERENCES

Buchholz, R., & Rosenthal, S. (2008). The unholy alliance of business and science. *Journal of Business Ethics*, *78*(1-2), 199–206. doi:10.100710551-006-9329-5

Butcher, L. (2011). The rapid growth of MD/MBA programs: Are they worth it. *Physician Executive*, *37*(1), 22–26. PMID:21302745

Chen, S. H. (2006). The merging of medicine and management--McGill University's MD-MBA degree. *McGill Journal of Medicine*, *9*(1), 3–4. PMID:19529800

Duke, M., Foley, R., Lauter, S., & Young, B. (2015). *Hospital Garrahan reflection paper*. Academic Press.

Goyal, R., Aung, K. K., Oh, B., Hwang, T. J., Besancon, E., & Jain, S. H. (2015). Survey of MD/MBA programs: Opportunities for physician management education. *Academic Medicine*, *90*(1), 121. doi:10.1097/ACM.0000000000000517 PMID:25229193

Hess, C. (2013). Health care educators: New directions in leadership development. *The Journal of Leadership Studies*, *6*(4). doi:10.1002/jls.21269

Katzenbach, J. R., & Smith, D. K. (1993). *The wisdom of teams: Creating the high-performance organization*. Cambridge, MA: Harvard Business School Press.

Larson, D. B., Chandler, M., & Forman, H. P. (2003). MD/MBA programs in the United States: Evidence of a change in healthcare leadership. *Academic Medicine*, *78*(3), 335–341. doi:10.1097/00001888-200303000-00021 PMID:12634220

ADDITIONAL READING

Gunderman, R., & Kanter, S. L. (2009). Perspective: Educating physicians to lead hospitals. *Academic Medicine*, *84*(10), 1348–1351. doi:10.1097/ACM.0b013e3181b6eb42 PMID:19881420

Lazarus, A. (2010). Physicians with MBA degrees: Change agents for healthcare improvement. *The Journal of Medical Practice Management*, *26*(3), 188–190. PMID:21243893

Patel, M. P., Arora, V., Patel, M. S., Kinney, J. M., Pauly, M. V., & Asch, D. A. (2014). The role of MD and MBA training in the professional development of a physician: A survey of 30 years of graduates from the Wharton Health Care Management Program. *Academic Medicine*, *89*(9), 1282–1286. doi:10.1097/ACM.0000000000000366 PMID:24979286

Sherrill, W. W. (2000). Dual-degree MD-MBA students: A look at the future of medical leadership. *Academic Medicine*, *75*(10Suppl), S37–S39. doi:10.1097/00001888-200010001-00012 PMID:11031168

Sherrill, W. W. (2001). Tolerance of ambiguity among MD/MBA students: Implications for management potential. *The Journal of Continuing Education in the Health Professions*, *21*(2), 117–122. doi:10.1002/chp.1340210209 PMID:11420866

KEY TERMS AND DEFINITIONS

Accreditation: The process of credentialing an institution for its intended mission especially in healthcare or education. Accreditation involves quality and safety and has financial considerations. Hospitals should be accredited to operate.

Cohort: A group of students who initiate and complete the MBA program at the same time. They attend the same classes and generally work on projects in groups.

Immersion Residency: A course taken outside of the usual classroom or online setting in which the students travel to a different location (usually outside of the United States). The experience involves visits to a number of companies, institutions, and centers where participants tour and meet with key stakeholders in relevant industries.

Real World: Drawn from actual events or situations.

SWOT Analysis: An analysis framework to assess a product, service, or company's strengths, weaknesses, opportunities, and threats. This analysis is frequently used in developing strategy, marketing, and planning.

Synchronous Sessions: Online classroom sessions which are held in real time using a video conferencing platform which allows for interactive conversation and sharing of media including slides, word documents, and videos. Sessions can be recorded and archived for those who may be unable to participate in real time.

Threaded Discussions: A useful tool to encourage engagement and discussion in online courses. The course instructor posts a topic or thread and students comment, answer, and contribute to the discourse. This tool works well to augment discussions occurring in synchronous sessions or as a replacement to those discussions.

Chapter 7
A Capstone Course Linking Business Knowledge and Strategic Initiative

George P. Sillup
Saint Joseph's University, USA

Stephen J. Porth
Saint Joseph's University, USA

ABSTRACT

This chapter describes the capstone course in which students act as internal consultants and apply the knowledge they acquired from previous courses in the MBA curriculum (e.g., strategic thinking, competitive analysis, statistics, forecasting, financial analysis). Students form teams of complementary backgrounds and expertise (e.g., president physician services, director of nursing, community medicine physician, rheumatologist) to develop and write a strategic plan, demonstrating a comprehensive understanding of business knowledge and the competitive environment. Uniquely, in this capstone, the instructors collaborated with top management of Lancaster General Health (LG Health) to identify a set of strategic priorities focused on five issues: standardization, innovation, competition, growth/scale, and interaction with the University of Pennsylvania. Each of these became a project assigned to a team of students who concluded the course and the MBA program with a presentation of their strategic recommendations to top management of LG Health.

DOI: 10.4018/978-1-5225-7576-4.ch007

INTRODUCTION

In March of 2013, Lancaster General Health (LG Health) and Saint Joseph's University (SJU) formed a partnership to better prepare physicians and healthcare professionals for managing in an increasingly complex and volatile healthcare sector. The partnership resulted in the launch of an online MBA program for a cohort of LG Health physicians and healthcare professionals. The cohort consisted of 21 top physicians, nurses and managers from LG Health enrolled in an MBA Program custom-designed and delivered by business faculty at SJU. The program, which continues to be offered to healthcare professionals, is unique in that it is delivered primarily online and is designed specifically to address the unique strategic and operational complexities of healthcare institutions. Furthermore, the program culminated with an innovative capstone experience that afforded students the opportunity to act as internal consultants to LG Health senior executives on a series of strategic priorities identified by the LG Health senior management team in collaboration with the authors of this chapter. The purpose of this chapter is to describe the capstone experience.

The healthcare sector and healthcare organizations have grown increasingly complex with advances in technology, regulatory and compliance pressures and the volatility and uncertainty of insurance markets. Medical and nursing schools provide physicians and nurses with rigorous training in science and medicine but doctors and healthcare professionals are typically not prepared to manage the business side of medicine and deal with the strategic, financial and operational complexities of their healthcare institutions. Recognizing the gap in the experience and education of healthcare professionals and the needs of today's healthcare institutions, LG Health's CEO, envisioned a solution to bridge the gap.

After careful evaluation, LG Health decided to partner with SJU and the Haub School of Business because SJU has a long history of graduate business study that is focused specifically on the pharmaceutical and healthcare sectors. Collectively, Haub School faculty members have decades of industry-relevant experience, including expertise in legal, regulatory, sales, financial, marketing, management, strategy and healthcare provider positions. When the LG Health-SJU partnership was formed, SJU had already had more than a dozen years of experience in delivering the MBA with a healthcare focus. Additionally, SJU uses an innovative hybrid learning approach, incorporating online and in-class courses, specifically crafted for a sophisticated and time-pressed healthcare professional.

Cohort learning has some special advantages. It can offer an intensive, collaborative and experimental learning environment that not only fosters in-depth individual business knowledge but also enhances organizational awareness and builds institutional culture (Prouty Project, 2017). For example, doctors in rheumatologic medicine gain greater appreciation for the challenges of doctors in emergency room medicine and vice versa. Cross-departmental teams begin to form within the culture, breaking down institutional silos and building teamwork.

Additionally, the learning experience accompanying course work increases students' strategic awareness about issues facing their organization. This is especially important in healthcare due to the dynamically changing and volatile environment as Congress ponders alternatives for the Affordable Care Act (Sternberg, 2017). Such was the vision of LG Health's CEO, who foresaw the favorable impact to the organization despite today's trend for companies not to invest in graduate study for employees (Marotti, 2016). This vision resulted in the development of the MBA program with SJU and ultimately yielded 21 MBA graduates (Duke, 2015).

The integrated cohort of LG Health's professionals included with both physicians and healthcare professionals, including nurses and managers (see Appendix A for list of the cohort's members' backgrounds). The schedule for the two-year MBA curriculum was designed to accommodate the students' professional responsibilities and allow for time to balance the demands of both professional and personal lives. Breaks were built into the program in August and December to allow students to "catch their breath" (see Appendix B for the curriculum). As students progressed through the curriculum, they gained greater knowledge of the business functions (e.g., Accounting, Marketing Research, Finance, Legal) and began to acquire new strategic skills and insights. This background was critical preparation for the custom-designed capstone course scheduled for the conclusion of the MBA program.

PLANNING THE CAPSTONE LEARNING EXPERIENCE

After considering the students' new business knowledge capabilities from completing the previous individually selected courses, several steps were taken to develop the capstone learning experience. First, it was determined that the last two courses, Corporate Strategy (MPE 720) and Capstone Hospital Strategy (MPE 795), would be taught in tandem by the same two faculty members. Each course was one month long, beginning on the first day of a month with pre-assignments and concluding on the last day of the month with the due date of final assignments. The two courses were designed to build on the knowledge acquired in previous coursework and to apply that knowledge to current issues or opportunities faced by LG Health. The second course would culminate in a set of team presentations to senior management and board members of the hospital. In effect, the students formed teams to serve as internal consultants of LG Health (see Appendix C for the guidelines for these projects and presentations).

The two key learning objectives of the courses were (1) to research and explore a strategic issue/challenge/opportunity faced by LG Health, and (2) to develop a set of recommendations that constitute a clear, comprehensive and forward-looking plan to address the issue or opportunity.

To identify and define the nature of the strategic projects, the faculty members reviewed LG Health's strategic plan and met with LG Health's top management to understand their perspectives and to identify their most prominent and pressing strategic initiatives. (Although LG Health has now merged with the Hospital of the University of Pennsylvania, the individual initiatives are considered proprietary and will not be disclosed.) Not surprisingly, the projects identified by LG Health management and the faculty were strategic initiatives that are relevant to many major medical centers.

The faculty reviewed individual student's work over the breadth of the MBA curriculum and met with them individually to identify areas of common interest and expertise to address the identified strategic issues. Referencing this information and with the input of LG Health senior management, five student teams with complementary expertise and gender balance were formed to address the five different strategic projects.

CAPSTONE IMPLEMENTATION

Per the course's syllabus, student teams were required to meet several milestones. Eight knowledge sessions emphasizing tenets of strategic planning and planning sessions were conducted online and in-person over the two months, culminating in the teams' final papers and presentations. A key session was an initial planning meeting among both faculty members and each of the five teams to discuss the strategic initiative to which their team was assigned, review the two capstone objectives and to talk about the guidelines for the team's final paper and presentation. This session was followed by a required draft of the final paper, reviewed by three faculty members. Following review of the team's draft paper an in-person meeting was scheduled with each team where feedback and coaching was provided. The extent of the team coaching ranged from the content and comprehensiveness of the teams' strategic recommendations to the depth of theory research and supporting resources.

A final in-person session focused on the teams' final draft papers and presentations, concentrating on fine tuning the project before the presentation to the board and senior management. Faculty also reviewed expectations about the length of team presentations (15-20 minutes followed by a 15-20 minute Q&A session). Teams were encouraged to create back-up slides that were not part of the presentation slide deck and to begin their presentations with an "executive summary" that identified the purpose of their project and linked the purpose with their strategic recommendations. Students were also made aware of the anticipated audience (LG Health's top management, LG Health board members, and SJU faculty). The order of team presentations was determined by random selection. During the Q&A session, team members were encouraged to respond based on their expertise and contributions to the team project.

Following these productive working sessions, the student teams delivered their presentations, all within the allotted time, and comprehensively addressed questions from the LG Health management and board and SJU faculty. Using a standardized assessment grid, SJU faculty evaluated the content and delivery of the team presentations, and the quality of the Q&A session.

Lastly, LG Health's senior management shared closing remarks about the benefit of the course and the insights generated by the students in addressing the strategic challenges and opportunities of LG Health. This experience along with the enhanced visibility of the cohort afforded by their participation in the MBA program, resulted in new opportunities for career advancement among the cohort members.

CONCLUSION

Most importantly, the MBA learning experience and the capstone courses in particular gave the students immediate and direct application of their newly acquired business skills to initiatives of strategic importance to LG Health. Furthermore, it demonstrated how people of diverse academic and professional backgrounds established common ground through their experience in the MBA program and broadened their perspective on the challenges of the overall organization. The capstone gave them a voice in the strategic initiatives of organization and a stake in its success. Several of the teams' recommendations were implemented within six months of the final presentations.

It is important to note that throughout the course, technical and administrative support was available for both faculty and cohort students. Similarly, LG Health supported the program's inception and implementation.

To evaluate the success of the program, Assurance of Learning (AOL) was conducted with each student to measure his or her business proficiency by comparing pre- and post-scores on an AOL exam. Additionally, to evaluate the technical support and customer service aspects of the program, an independent consultant from Better Decision Research (Quant Qual focus group research) was hired to conduct a survey with all the cohort students.

Leveraging their newly acquired knowledge, many of the cohort students have advanced to positions of higher responsibility with the Hospital of the University of Pennsylvania (HUP) HUP/LG Health and/or other hospital organizations. Following the cohort learning experience with LG Health, SJU continues to deliver cohort-based learning experiences to physicians and healthcare professionals through its Executive MBA Program.

REFERENCES

Duke, L. M. (2015). They're in business – 14 physicians earn MBAs. Retrieved from http://www.lancastergeneralhealth.org/LGH/Healthcare-Professionals/Progress-Notes/Staff-Transitions/They-re-in-business-14-physicians-earn-MBAs-Cap-an.aspx

Marotti, A. (2016). Company support for MBAs fell off a cliff, so schools are getting creative. *Chicago Tribune*. Retrieved from http://www.chicagotribune.com/bluesky/originals/ct-mba-sponsorship-from- employers-bsi-20160811-story.html

Prouty Project L3 Invest in Your Best. (2017). Retrieved from http://www.proutyproject.com/l3---cohort-based-leadership-development

Sternberg, S. (2017). Hospitals, doctors decry senate move toward Obamacare Repeal. *USA Today*. Retrieved from https://www.usnews.com/news/

KEY TERMS AND DEFINITIONS

Cross-Departmental Teams: Teams from different work areas of the hospital (e.g., emergency room and data analysis).

Hybrid Learning Approach: Learning approach that incorporates online and in-class sessions.

APPENDIX A: BACKGROUNDS OF COHORT'S MEMBERS (MANAGER OR PHYSICIAN)

1. Director of Nursing (Manager)
2. Chief of General Internal Medicine (Physician)
3. Health Physicians Care Transformation Manager (Manager)
4. President, Horizon Health Care Services and Affiliated Home Health (Manager)
5. Physicians Director of Clinical Affairs (Manager)
6. Chief of Staff (Manager)
7. Chief Physician Executive (Physician)
8. President, Physician Services, LG Health Physicians (Physician)
9. Physician Executive for Population Health Management and Care Transformation (Physician)
10. Associate Director, Family & Community Medicine (Physician)
11. Director, Special Projects (Manager)
12. Chair, LG Health Department of Medicine (Physician)
13. Director, Ambulatory & Ancillary Applications (Manager)
14. The EMG Group (Physician)
15. Chief Quality and Medical Information Officer and Physician Executive for Quality (Physician)
16. Managing Physician, LG Health Physicians Lititz Family Medicine (Physician)
17. Director, Budgeting and Forecasting (Manager)
18. LG Health Physicians Arthritis and Rheumatology (Physician)
19. Vice President, Academic Affairs (Physician)
20. Chair, Family & Community Medicine (Physician)
21. Managing Physician, LG Health Physicians Twin Rose Family Medicine (Physician)

APPENDIX B: CURRICULUM (ONLINE AND IN-CLASS)

MGT 582 Business Ethics Mar 2013 IC
ACC 511 Accounting Foundation Apr 2013 IC/OL
MGT 520 Empowering the Individual & Groups May 2013 OL
DSS 591 Contemporary Info Technology Jun 2013 OL
MPE 530 Marketing Foundation Jul 2013 OL
FIN 501 Economics Foundation Sep 2013 OL
MPE 625 Creating Effective R&D Oct 2013 IC
FIN 504 Finance Foundation Nov 2013 OL
MPE 610 Healthcare Regulations Jan 2014 OL
DSS 592 Business Statistics Feb 2014 IC/OL
MPE 650 Competitive Analysis Mar 2014 OL
MPE 630 Marketing Research Apr 2014 OL
DSS 593 Forecasting for Healthcare May 2014 OL
MPE 620 Supply Chain Management Jun 2014 OL
MGT 581 Leadership & Development @ LGH Jul 2014 OL
ACC 561 Managerial Accounting Sep 2014 OL
MPE 640 Healthcare Economics Oct 2014 OL
FIN 551 Managerial Finance Nov 2014 OL
MPE 710 Brand Management Jan 2015 OL
MPE 700 Strategies for Managed Care Feb 2015 OL
MPE 660 Healthcare Management Mar 2015 OL
MPE 720 Corporate Strategy Apr 2015 IC/OL
MPE 795 Capstone Hospital Strategy May 2015 IC
MPE 770 International Residency Jun 2015 Optional

APPENDIX C: PAPER/PRESENTATION GUIDELINES

Content

Preface and Executive Summary to include:

- Table of Contents with page numbers
- Executive Summary - state the purpose of your project, the strategic issues, questions and/or objectives you will address and summarize the strategies your team recommends

Background and Statement of Purpose

- Brief discussion of relevant background information about the challenge or opportunity
- Describe the purpose of the project and identify and describe the strategic decisions, issues, or questions that are being addressed

Research and Literature Review

- Describe your research methods and the relevant data, results and findings from your team's literature review and research

Recommendations

- Based on your research and supported by the research, identify your recommendations for the project including goals, strategies, resources required, timing, etc.
- Explain what should be done to foster successful implementation of your recommendations
- Identify next steps for successful implementation

Conclusion

- Provide a brief summary of your project

References

- Include all sources

Appendices

- Add any relevant supportive information

Style

- Report should be 20 pages max. (excluding appendices) and double spaced
- Submit two electronic copies via Blackboard; one for grading and one for LGH
- Sources need to cited within text and as a bibliography under References
    - Use consistent format for textual citations and bibliography
- Report must be well-written with a unified and consistent style of writing and presentation
- Incorporate graphs, charts, and tables within the text instead of in an appendix when possible

Chapter 8
Team Building and Function in a Physician Leadership Program

Anthony DelConte
Saint Joseph's University, USA

Michael J. Gast
Saint Joseph's University, USA

ABSTRACT

Among the critical skills to be developed in a physician leadership program are teamwork and collaboration. The team approach to the design, execution, and implementation of healthcare programs should be stressed. To encourage this approach in our physician leadership program, the authors use team structure as an essential component of classroom structure to encourage completion of real-world projects and assignments relevant outside of the classroom environment. This chapter demonstrates how teams were formed and evaluated in courses involving the marketing of healthcare systems services and healthcare system mergers and acquisitions. This chapter also describes components in the development and implementation of a clinical leadership MBA curriculum designed to provide physician-leaders with a strategic perspective on healthcare decision making that encompasses a broad range of structural, technological, financial, cultural, and ethical considerations.

DOI: 10.4018/978-1-5225-7576-4.ch008

INTRODUCTION

The evolution of the Lancaster General Health (LG Health)-Saint Joseph's University (SJU) MBA cohort and the development of a customized educational program have been previously described in detail. To implement a successful learning environment most executive and non-executive business programs rely heavily on the use of a team structure to create an experiential learning situation. While the team approach as an organizational structure has been ingrained in the corporate and business world for decades, in medicine the focus had traditionally been on individual responsibility and performance. Physicians had been seen as "captains of the ship" particularly in surgical suites where decisions made by committee, however efficient, cannot meet changing demands requiring split-second actions. The pharmaceutical industry had embraced the team approach, as drug development is complicated enough that no one individual can master all of its critical aspects. Today we see the need for a more collaborative team approach to medicine in both industry and in the provision of care within healthcare systems, as the complexity of providing care has also increased. Functioning as a member of a team can be a challenge for anyone, particularly one whose core values recognize individual achievement. Singular achievement and advancement have long been hallmarks of personal success for both medical practitioners and healthcare system managers, but it is clear that participation in and encouragement of team function is now a signature characteristic of the modern, successful executive. As healthcare systems embrace the concept of team delivery of healthcare, they are also looking toward ways to provide teams with the proper skill sets and training to function (Hughes, 2016). "Empowering" teams has become a buzzword and teams can only reach their true potential when they are both empowered and when their members and leaders hold a set of shared values important to them.

Once teams are selected, they typically pass through a series of stages. If successful, this results in high performing, highly functional teams. This process has been described frequently in the past and is often attributed to Tuckman (1965.) Among the challenges facing individual members of the teams in our courses were leadership of the team, coordination for the team's functions, and maintaining appropriate behaviors in meetings and other team interactions that would allow team processes to proceed smoothly. One of the goals of our work with students in the graduate programs is to allow them to practice these concepts in a team environment, classify them and to define them and discuss them openly in a 360° fashion with their teammates, instructors and other classmates.

COURSE DELIVERABLES AND CHALLENGES

Common to the courses taught by the authors in the LG Health-SJU cohort program were components of team deliverables requiring a very focused, cooperative, and collaborative approach. Although the content may have varied based on differing course objectives the process was similar across the course structures.

Generally, the teams had three major deliverables: First, they needed to develop a preliminary team presentation related to the components of their plan. Second, they were to develop final team presentations of their completed plans. Finally, the teams were required to submit a 10- page paper of their strategic plan based on what might be presented to a senior management team of a company or institution where they were engaged.

To perform these tasks, teams had to integrate their understanding of the course materials, threaded discussions and class readings into actual strategic plans.

Here are examples of courses in which the team process was used in our graduate program:

MPE 625: Fundamentals of Clinical Research

MPE 625 was a course designed to introduce our graduate students to the effective design of research and development activities in large pharmaceutical companies or within healthcare systems settings. The course addressed most of the significant aspects of the research and development process, including the role of the clinical research team, the regulatory affairs group, the safety organization, quality assurance, pharmacodynamics, bio statistics, and the larger pre-launch team activities. Topics covered ranged from discovery and pre-clinical activities all the way through phase four research and post launch safety screening. For this course, the teams were created by random selection, requiring students to select assignments that required the development of new skills and, thus, compromise on team responsibilities and time commitment. The teams were asked to take their products through the Investigational New Drug (IND) and New Drug Application (NDA) or other approval steps as well as theoretical advisory board meeting interactions with US or international health authorities.

The teams were asked to create clinical development plans for new pharmaceutical entities or medical devices. They were first asked to establish a product profile for their new entity, then to create a clinical trial plan, and finally to assess the timing, costs and regulatory milestones of their hypothetical development program. At the end of the course the teams were responsible for a written comprehensive summary of their development plan. Finally, the students were asked to review the activities of their product development team and to assess how each member contributed over the course of clinical development. Presentations and written summaries were performed as team activities but students were asked to provide individual evaluations as well.

In MPE 625 special attention was dedicated to aspects of clinical research that involved team function. Successful conference room strategies included techniques for listening and integrating information from other team members and understanding time-critical questions that needed to be answered within specific frameworks. Executing strategies, respecting the expertise of other teammates, and achieving team consensus before concluding any given meeting were emphasized and discussed both in class and on line between classes.

MPE 720: Global Corporate Strategy

In MPE 720 each team had three major responsibilities: Initially, a preliminary team presentation of selected components of a hypothetical International Strategic Plan (ISP). Secondly, creation of final team presentations of completed ISPs. Finally, a 10-page formal ISP submission, based upon what might be presented to management in one or multiple companies about integration activity that the team proposed. This course focused on the management of multinational corporations (MNCs) with particular emphasis on pharmaceutical companies operating across national borders. The international environment implies greater opportunities as MNCs have access to a wider variety of markets and resources. However, this environment also implies greater organizational and managerial challenges. The aim of this course was to investigate whether these challenges are worthwhile and how they can contribute to a company's "triple bottom line" – people, planet, profit. To accomplish this, the students were asked to evaluate hypothetical global opportunities for pharmaceutical/medical device companies from the following perspectives:

- Understanding the strategic imperatives that motivate companies to go global;
- Addressing organizational challenges in international markets;
- Understanding the managerial challenges in global environments; and
- Recognizing planning requirements for successful project implementation.

During the first session teams were assigned for the creation of an International Strategic Plan (ISP). Class sessions focused on understanding why and how pharmaceutical, medical diagnostic and device corporations can successfully enter global markets. Furthermore, we examined situations where strategic licensing and partnerships provide viable alternatives to global expansion. Students thus had an opportunity to work as teams and to reflect and integrate their understanding of the course materials and threaded discussions into an actual International Strategic Plan (ISP) for a pharmaceutical and/or medical device in a global market.

The purpose of this assignment was to integrate team knowledge, expertise and strengths and provide a synthesis applicable to understanding issues affecting the management of a Multi National Federation (MNF).

It is important to note that the ISP had to address the initial projects a MNF must do successfully to establish a sustainable presence in the global market. The ISP could also be about initiating a clinical trial program, a new production facility, a research alliance with a small biotech company within an international country or a program of corporate social responsibility in a developing country. Each team chose one from among these options.

To perform these tasks the teams had to integrate their understanding of the course materials and threaded discussions and class readings into an actual international strategic plan for a pharmaceutical and or a medical device in the global market the ISP had to follow certain established guidelines and include for critical components:

1. A business purpose and strategic imperative;
2. A summary of organizational goals and challenges;
3. A discussion for strategies for reaching those goals and meeting the challenges; and
4. Managerial action plans for implementing and monitoring progress in executing on the strategies of the ISP.

For the preliminary ISP the students were expected to provide an introduction and executive summary, an explanation of the product chosen, a proposed expansion option with rationale, a discussion of business goals, and most importantly, a blueprint of proposed organizational structure and how integrated teams could be created to most effectively execute the planning and integration of these international businesses, including discussions of culture and executive structure.

The ISP for each team was required to have 10 ISP components, including an analysis of strengths, weaknesses, opportunities and threats (SWOT), a global leadership chart, regulatory considerations, sales and marketing strategies, and a discussion of integration, currency issues across borders, and accounting harmonization. This clearly was a daunting task.

MPE 650: Competitive Analysis

MPE650 was a course that focused on the competitive marketing and development of specific services within a healthcare system. The team approach for the course was unique, in that the entire cohort consisted of executives and physician leaders from within the Lancaster General Hospital Healthcare system. Thus, the students in the course knew each other, had occasionally worked together in the past, and were developing marketing plans for real life services in the healthcare system (although not necessarily services with which they had been associated). Additionally, the students were geographically co-located, had similar intense work schedules, and had access to common resources for completion of their class projects.

The course was designed to introduce the students to the basic paradigms and tools underlying the establishment of market-based strategies to maintain, grow and compete in the modern medical marketplace. The exercises within the course were designed to help them understand how medical practitioners and hospital systems need to adapt to changes (and competition) within practice environments. We explored the concepts underlying the market components, customers and stakeholders in a hospital system, and the establishment of goals for medical care that would lead to continuous improvement of healthcare in a community. Specific areas of learning included definition of competitive analysis components and basic principles of the branding of medical care. Through a series of presentations, in class discussion, and inter-class online activities, the students strove to achieve a better understanding of their own hospital system's efforts to identify and foster the development of specific services and efficient practices that would improve community health care.

The course endeavored to introduce the students to a disciplined process for assessing the competitive environment of their healthcare system. First, by defining the components of an overall strategy. Next, by identifying the customers and stakeholders of the products and services offered by the system. Then we defined the alternatives to our offerings – be they geographic or in a different setting within our geography (e.g., a Retail Drug Store clinic) and developed a set of conceptual tools for completing an internal and external analysis to help focus on specific areas where the system might be able to differentiate itself from the competition. Finally, the teams began to apply those tools and theories to a specific competitive analysis plan which were the focus of the team's final presentations.

Final presentations and papers had to demonstrate the team's ability to:

- Recognize and understand key customers and stakeholders;
- Identify the competitive forces at play in the healthcare space;
- Understand internal and external competitive analysis;
- Make decisions regarding the offering of services and products that differentiate services from competitors; and
- Articulate a strategy for communicating their service using the tools for evaluating a competitive environment.

At the conclusion of MPE650, the students became a part of a large strategic initiative for the LG Health System to globally re-evaluate its services and its place within the larger healthcare community.

TEAM SELECTION PROCESS

Adjusting to Different Cohorts in the Instructional Process

We found that there were two basic types of cohorts within our graduate program. The first, which was typified by our competitive analysis course, involved a cohort where the students knew each other and had worked together within their healthcare system previously. Existing leadership had already been established. The pecking order based on experience and rank within the organization was well established within the cohort prior to the students entering the graduate program. In this case, team leadership and activity assignment within the team went more smoothly, as roles and responsibilities had been established prior to the class. The second type of cohort involved students who had no prior affiliation with each other and who often were separated on geographic location, time zone, and prior work experience. These courses, typified by MPE625 and MPE720, presented new challenges for the students. They had to work out assignments while simultaneously getting to know one another and evaluating the expertise and availability of their new teammates. This situation more closely reflected the real life experience of merger or integration activities or of the development of teams for clinical research in completely new areas of endeavor. Although team formation and execution of team activities were more challenging in cohorts where the students had no prior association, within our framework all of the teams seemed to function well, as the students were able to make appropriate adjustments and carry out their assignments over the duration of these courses.

In summary, selection of teams for the courses depended on the size of the cohort, nature of assignment, geography, common employers or occupations, desire for team balance by function or experience, and the need for team leadership. In our course structure, the team's purpose was not as study teams or test taking teams but as teams that would complete projects that mimicked a real-life situation in the world. This selection generally followed one of 3 different methodologies, which are described as follows:

Faculty Selection Based on Student Background and Experience

This method allows the faculty to distribute class members among the teams in a way that will create diversified teams based on instructor criteria for what constitutes diverse. For example, the authors have chosen teams in the past so that there will be no team members from the same company, department, or functional discipline on a team. In the author's experience, teams structured in this manner tend to become high performing once they begin working together and self-assign roles and responsibilities.

Student Self-Selection

In the LG Health cohort, some teams were self-selected, which allowed team members already familiar with one another to work together again. This structure has the advantage of avoiding some of the initial formative stage of teams when team members are still trying to get to know one another. Also, team members seem to select people that they already know and like which gives them something of an advantage in completing tasks and collaborating. The authors have witnessed self-selected teams who are able to "hit the ground running" and reduce the time spent in the forming component of team development. These teams tend to skip this phase or have a much-abbreviated forming phase on the path to become high performing teams. Much of the accelerated function of self-selected teams is grounded on the establishment of trust, which can be present if team members have a history of successfully working together. The importance of establishing trust has been characterized by Aki (2012) as a critical component of team building. Occasionally self-selected team members may have a shared preference for type of product, service, or activity they will be working on as a team (e.g., MPE650.). The down side of this type of structure is that they may already share some of the same ideas, so creativity and innovation are not stimulated in a team that has picked a group of individuals with many common shared experiences.

Random Selection

Allowing random team generation is a quick and easy way to organize teams. Most learning management software, including BlackBoard and Canvas, allow quick student team randomization. Random teams level the playing field and there can be no complaints of favoritism or “stacking the deck” to create super-teams since the process is truly random. Teams after random selection will generally have to go through a “getting to know you” phase, although if randomization is successful, they can produce a team with diverse backgrounds and ideas and lead to innovative and creative ideas. In contrast, rarely do teams formed by self-selection require readjustment due to incompatibility. It is preferred to make any such adjustments sooner rather than later.

TEAM ASSIGNMENTS

In general, the way the authors’ utilized teams followed an approach of requiring regular presentations which would build one upon the last until a final presentation was made to the instructors and the entire class.

The teams were given choices within certain boundaries to select the service or product or the type of integration that they would develop over the duration of the course. By having the freedom to choose, teams were able to develop a sense of ownership of the project from the very beginning through to completion.

The teams internally decided on the roles and responsibilities of each of the team members in completing the project. This was often a function of the experience and the prior training that the students individually brought to the project. Sometimes students were forced to research and develop new expertise if it did not exist among the team members. The students would then determine who would assume leadership roles and provide assignments, who would function as project managers, and who would provide communication amongst team members. They also had to determine appropriate work schedules to coincide with their own busy calendars and had to allocate the requisite time to assemble the information for the next steps in the process.

Finally, they had to develop a presentation plan that allowed all team members to participate in sharing the information they had assembled with the instructors and their classmates. Each week the process was repeated as the teams built, revised, and refined their projects working toward their final deliverable.

One example of this process occurred in course MPE 650, where students developed marketing plans for their selected healthcare system service in four steps. Each subsequent step required the use of different data sets, which forced the team to reorganize their presentations as the process moved forward. As this process unfolded, team members were also learning how to function as a team. They learned from what they did right, but more importantly, they learned from their mistakes. They learned what worked and what did not work in assembling their final deliverables. Beyond the content of their outputs, the secondary gain was what they learned about team function and what a successful team process would look and feel like.

EXPERIENCE WITH TEAM FUNCTION

Once selected, teams typically met (occasionally in person, but more often remotely) to get acquainted with other team members and to organize the core team functions needed to carry out their assignments. As in real world situations, the tasks before the team were fairly well defined (in this case by the course instructors) but the methods, by which they were to be carried out, and by whom, were matters for the team to decide.

The first task for the team was always to select their leaders, and project managers – sometimes, but not always the same person. Because our teams were small (usually 4 or 5 students) the team members were often asked to complete several tasks or fill several roles, and to switch areas of research, presentation or writing over the course of the activity. Often, due to time considerations within a given week (recall that the students almost always had real world job responsibilities) team leadership or distribution of presentation activities would be handed off to another team member temporarily. There was no clear pattern for leadership selection among our randomly selected teams, although the responsibility often fell to the oldest or most experienced member of the group.

Most commonly, the teams would assess their workload for the next presentation or document and internally negotiate who would accomplish each part. If constraints of time or expertise became a barrier for completion of one student's part, another student always stepped up to assist or complete that part of the team assignment. Almost always, the team member requiring assistance would provide compensatory activity in subsequent team assignments. If technical or time issues prevented a teammate from presenting their portion of an assignment in class, inevitably another teammate would step in and do an excellent job of delivering the information to the instructors and the class. This suggests that information sharing among team members was common practice. It was also true that a team member would often help another teammate with a particularly challenging aspect of their presentation or research – a characteristic practice among successful teams. Teams would always meet or communicate between class sessions to coordinate their work activities and prepare for their next tasks. Rarely in the author's experience in courses utilizing teams, was there an unprepared team or team member, or an apparent gap in team responsibility. This speaks highly of the quality of the students, their maturity, and of the manner in which the use of teams for task completion raised the level of performance of all students. Perhaps the habit of establishing good communication stems from working in a healthcare setting where communication skills are critical to patient safety and overall quality of care. Students seized the opportunity (in a rather intense environment) to build and practice the team skills required to form and lead successful teams in their real-life professional roles.

Another challenging task for the student teams was the assembly and submission of final written papers summarizing their projects. This required a high level of coordination of the writing, editing and compiling of material from multiple team members – usually across several time zones and busy schedules. Generally, this had to be performed by a single individual who took on the responsibility of project leader responsible for paper development and submission. The process generally seemed to function smoothly, with the project leader managing the advice, editing concerns of the individual authors and the cajoling required to achieve timely submission of the papers.

Finally, the students were asked, formally and informally, to assess the contributions of themselves, their teammates, and the team process to the successful completion of their course work. Their responses at this graduate level were overwhelmingly positive. They felt that utilizing a team approach to problem solving strengthened their efforts, providing support and additional perspective to their efforts. They also agreed that they gained valuable insight into the structure and function of teams through these efforts and the accompanying discussions and that it improved their ability to utilize all of the assets available to them in their real world jobs to plan and execute complex tasks and improve communication with both senior management and co-workers.

Course time included separate and integrated discussions of successful team techniques:

- Principles of meeting etiquette;
- Setting long and short term team goals;
- Setting goals and agendas within meetings; and
- Division of team responsibilities.

OPERATIONAL TEAM CONSIDERATIONS IN EXECUTING CLASS PROJECTS

After the students were organized into teams, they began the difficult work of selecting, researching and compiling the materials for their course learnings and presentations. Although the teams for these exercises were smaller than the multifunctional teams on which the students would be serving in their professional lives, the principles of team behavior and the processes leading to successful team deliverables would mimic those of their "real-life" team activities.

The first task for the teams was to select a leader (or leaders) for their course activities. Our students generally chose older, or more experienced members of their group to take control of work assignments and organization of team functions, such as meeting times and content, division of labor, and presentation structure. For the LG Health cohort teams, these leaders were often individuals who already held respected leadership positions within the healthcare system. Choosing team leaders in the heterogeneous teams in the other courses was more challenging. Stronger personalities, or those with more flexible time commitments were sometimes deciding factors in making those decisions. In several instances, teams chose to share leadership responsibilities, partition those leadership tasks, or change leaders as the focus of the team evolved from data collection, to presentation organization, to creating a written document at the conclusion of the course. This paradigm reflected the common business practice of shifting team leadership to accommodate the changing needs of project teams as the primary focus of such teams changes over the course of a longer-term project.

Once team leadership was established, the team's next task was to select an appropriate project to develop and complete for the subject of the course. These projects (as previously described) varied from evaluation and creation of a marketing plan for a particular service within a healthcare system, to simulation of a domestic or international integration of two healthcare entities, to development of an "end to end" development program for a new drug or medical device - from concept to launch. Teams generally approached this difficult task by selecting a project with which one (or more) of the team members had some familiarity. Often, leadership of the group would be modified to reflect the team members who had that expertise.

Research of the several aspects of the team's project was then partitioned among the team members, based upon their interests, expertise and the needs of the team for information. From a teaching perspective, it was less important that the work product of the team be 100% accurate, than that the team understood the concept that information needed to be gathered and that the team had to make decisions to identify what materials were needed and who would be responsible for that gathering. Although this sometimes led to students placed in the awkward position of de novo understanding of their assigned area, the realization that team needs and compromise were required components for successful completion of the team's project was the desired (and always achieved) outcome of this part of the team's activity.

Because the team assembled and presented their projects as a progressive build, the role of individual students in the presentation process changed over time. It was a team decision about who took the lead in each week's presentation, based on the emphasis for that portion of the project and the work that had been completed by the team during the week. The team members had to coordinate the content, order and preparation of these presentations between class sessions. In general, all team members contributed to the presentations and to their in-class discussion during the course.

At the conclusion of each course, each team was required to submit an appropriately referenced final document for final grading. Again, each team member contributed portions of these documents, but the coordination, assembly and review of the papers was a function in which all team members participated. Final assembly and submission of the work was coordinated by a team member, often, but not always a team leader. Working together, assessing and addressing team needs, and compromising on difficult team decisions were integral aspects of team behavior that the students encountered at every point in the exercise.

EVALUATION OF TEAM FUNCTION

In addition to being evaluated on the content, students are evaluated on how they performed as a team. Evaluating the team dynamic is not always an easy process, as it is sometimes difficult to observe and determine how the process developed. To aid in this determination, a survey of each individual can be done to assess the team dynamic. For example, students can rate their teammates' performance on a 10-point Likert scale (see Appendix). Team members can comment on whether or not their peers attended team meetings, whether or not they contributed to the project intellectually, supported team goals, and submitted their contributions in a timely manner. A more difficult competency to evaluate, but equally critical component of team dynamic is the communication behaviors between team members. Predictable communication is important in maintaining trust among team members, and irregular and unpredictable communication patterns tend to hinder trust (Jarvenpaa 1999.) In evaluating final presentations, the authors can generally gain a sense of how well the teams communicate both to their external audience and to each other. Along with the content of information presented, the students undergo assessment of the team process including how they handle responsibilities and how they communicate and make decisions.

CONCLUSION

Large, complex organizations often function with many working parts. Communication within the organization becomes difficult when multiple functions must work in parallel to achieve both short-term and long-term goals. This has consistently proven true in both the planning and execution phases of projects.

To combat the dysfunction of organizational components working at cross purposes or out of synchrony with one another, most organizations now utilize the concept of a project team to achieve their goals. Large project management groups have been designed and put in place to lead individual teams or to coordinate activities of the multiple functions that these teams must complete. Each of the various functions within the organization contributes one or more members to these project teams. The project team individuals are then allowed to focus on their particular special interests, while the project manager is responsible for assembling the team at regular intervals and enhancing communication between the different functions to achieve the final goals. In addition to project managers, most successful teams also appoint team leaders who focus on the strategies that must be employed by the team to complete their tasks, while the project managers handle coordination of the technical aspects of the team.

Team management as a tool to complete large, complex, often multinational, projects have been in place in the pharmaceutical industry for several decades. In the pharma paradigm, multiple sub-teams also need to be in place for geographic, functional, or special task considerations. The project managers are responsible for ensuring that multiple tasks with long, complicated timelines are completed and in place so that all of the other parallel tasks of the team may function appropriately and be completed in a timely fashion. Team composition is dictated by the nature of the task and will usually include components from the many disciplines that comprise a successful drug development program, including a core group made up of representatives from regulatory affairs, clinical development, and various aspects of the marketing team at a minimum. Pre-clinical, biostatistics, safety, and other members of the organization join these core members of the team on an ad hoc basis. During the initial planning phases teams are often larger and receive input from almost all of the disciplines that will eventually produce a marketed pharmaceutical product. Team members will join or temporarily drop out of the team as the projects continue, but generally rejoin the larger team as drug development nears its completion and pre-marketing, pre-launch activities consume more of the team's time.

The need for teams in the development and management of healthcare systems has been a more recent practice. As healthcare systems grow and subsume greater numbers of functions (e.g. more physical plants including hospitals, outpatient facilities, physician practices and free- standing activities) the need for coordination between services and wrap around communication with healthcare system management becomes even greater. The authors have also seen the need for large multifunctional teams during merger and integration functions as healthcare systems grow and take on newer components - especially when two similar functions, for example two hospitals, are involved in the integration. Then, in addition to determining which physical facilities will be used for which functions, the need to merge financial systems, operating cultures, and other aspects (such as capital expenditures and differing regulatory environments) requires teams which understand the functioning of each of the organizations to work on smoothing the integration process. Even for standard healthcare system function in the current healthcare environment, the need for CEOs and other senior managers in the healthcare system to understand the many diverse aspects of the system generally requires a team to assemble, compile and sift information in order to provide management with timely and condensed updates so that significant decisions may be made. The same need for team functioning also applies to academic and smaller hospital organizations.

With these considerations in mind, the authors felt that it was essential that students in a graduate program for pharmaceutical and healthcare marketing become familiar with the general principles and best practices of team composition, function and presentation of focused deliverables that they will need to utilize in their professional lives. The best way to accomplish this goal is to make team practice and decision making an integral part of the course work in the individual courses in which they participate.

REFERENCES

Aki, S., & Mila, H. (2012). Building trust in high-performing teams. *Technology Innovation Management Review*, *38*, 38–41.

Hughes, A. M., Gregory, M. E., Joseph, D. L., Sonesh, S. C., Marlow, S. L., Lacerenza, C. N., & Salas, E. (2016). Saving lives: A meta-analysis of team training in healthcare. *The Journal of Applied Psychology*, *101*(9), 1266–1304. doi:10.1037/apl0000120 PMID:27599089

Jarvenpaa, S., & Leidner, D. A. (1999). Communication and trust in global virtual teams. *Organization Science*, *10*(6), 791–815. doi:10.1287/orsc.10.6.791

Tuckman, B. W. (1965). Developmental sequence in small groups. *Psychological Bulletin*, *63*(6), 384–399. doi:10.1037/h0022100 PMID:14314073

KEY TERMS AND DEFINITIONS

Acquisition: Transaction in which one organization takes control of another organization's assets.

Cohort: Refers to a group of students who start and finish their degree program (in this case MBA) at the same time.

De Novo: From the beginning, new, from scratch.

Deliverables: The work product provided by the individual or the team to whom it was promised. (In the examples here, the deliverable is provided to the course instructor).

Forming: A group coming together with a shared goal or objective.

Investigational New Drug (IND) Application: The US Food and Drug Administration (FDA) requires a sponsor to submit an IND before they can conduct a clinical investigation with and new product. This requirement is based on the Code of Federal Regulations (CFR) 21.

Launch: The first step in the final delivery of a product or service that has been in development.

Likert Scale: A survey-measuring tool used to determine opinions or attitudes.

Mergers: Transaction in which the ownership of a company, organization, or institution are combined together to form a new entity.

Multinational Corporation: A legal entity that operates or has assets in more than one nation and that is distinct from its owners.

Multinational Federation: A collection of organizations formed to represent their common interests.

New Drug Application (NDA): Is the application or request for permission from the FDA to market a new drug.

Norming: The team makes progress on achieving their objective.

Performing: The team is effective in meeting their objective.

Phase IV Studies: Clinical research trials that are conducted after the approval of a pharmaceutical product.

Storming: A team struggles and may disagree on both the objective and the means of getting there. Sometime in this stage, the team is still trying to get to know one another and to discover roles, responsibilities, and how to communicate.

Team Stages: Typically teams will go through four stages during their existence: forming, storming, norming, and performing.

APPENDIX: TEAM MEMBER EVALUATION FORM

(Evaluation of your own team)
Team: ______________________________
Name: _______________________________
Please evaluate and rate the performance of your team members on the issues shown in Table 1. Use a Likert scale of 0 (worst) to 10 (best). Use only whole numbers and list the LAST names of your team's members. Do NOT include yourself.
Thank you for your participation in this exercise. Your responses will not be disclosed to other team members and will be used in aggregate to evaluate individual performance.

Table 1.

	1	2	3	4	5
Team Member's Names					
Rating Scale 0 = worst to 10 = best					
Attendance at team meetings through each period.					
Support of team efforts, i.e. cooperative.					
Aware of and met deadlines to complete each phase of the simulation.					
Understanding of team tasks and sharing of insights and knowledge.					
Overall contributions and value given to the team and its members.					
Include INDIVIDUAL TOTALS					
If you were to rate each of your group members in terms of their total contribution to the group, do you believe this individual has done his/her fair share of work? Circle one	Yes More Less	Yes More Less	Yes More Less	Yes More Less	Yes More Less
If you were a hiring manager, would you voluntarily choose her/him to be on your team again? Circle one	Yes No Unsure	Yes No Unsure	Yes No Unsure	Yes No Unsure	Yes No Unsure

Chapter 9
Reconceptualizing Medical Curriculum Design in Strategic Clinical Leadership Training for the 21st Century Physician

Catherine Hayes
University of Sunderland, UK

Kim Hinshaw
Sunderland Royal Hospital, UK & University of Sunderland, UK

Kevin Petrie
University of Sunderland, UK

ABSTRACT

This chapter provides an insight into the value of tacit knowledge and how this contributes directly to the concept of human factors in the context of multi-disciplinary teamwork. In considering the notion of implicit or intuitive knowledge and how this can be taught in practice, the authors draw on the field of creative praxis as a means of harnessing knowledge from other (often under-acknowledged) signature pedagogies of direct relevance to medical practice. The authors focus on the significance of situational awareness and context of medical and healthcare provision as a means of driving debate around the value of affective domain learning and its role in 21st century physician practice. These are bracketed under the category of non-technical skill acquisition, which is linked heavily, in the published literature to date, with holistically positive patient outcomes.

DOI: 10.4018/978-1-5225-7576-4.ch009

INTRODUCTION

The optimization of prognostic outcomes for all patients, are endpoints that all physicians have a moral and ethical obligation to provide in their daily practice. Medical and surgical curricula have traditionally emphasized the importance of functional psychomotor and underpinning cognitive skill and placed less significance on tacit knowledge as an integral part of the human factors influencing non-technical skills in applied practice. Within the context of this medical education and pedagogical praxis, the relative inseparability of the cognitive domain and the affective domain have long been debated, but in an environment where the recognition that leadership and multidisciplinary team-working is a fundamental key to the enhancement of prognostic outcomes then this must become a core focus of all medical curricula. Our shared authorship of this chapter originates from the tri-partite stance of pedagogic practice, emergency obstetrics and creative practice, all of which we value and believe have the potential to add credence to the concept of tacit knowledge. The core commonality in the epistemological basis of each of our professions is evident and we believe our deliberate transcendence of disciplinarity, in relation to how 21st Century Physicians ought to be prepared for the real world, reflects our own work in applied professional, clinical and creative professional praxis.

AFFECTIVE DOMAIN LEARNING IN MEDICAL EDUCATION

At the heart of successful affective domain learning lies the capacity for situational awareness and higher order critical thinking skills, which characterize the relative immediacy of advanced clinical decision making in medicine. Implicit within both these core critical thinking skills and decision making processes, is the concept of tacit knowledge, which harnesses the innate ability of surgical and medical practitioners to effectively communicate, lead, work as part of a team, use initiative, harbour resilience and be assertive at the front line of patient care. On a global level, these skills are critical to safe and efficient medical practice, regardless of the situational context of care delivery. The precedence they are given is commensurate with the concept of the safety critical environment, demonstrated, for example, in this chapter, on labour wards where the capacity to engage non-technical skills across the multidisciplinary maternity team can impact directly on patient outcomes in emergency obstetric practice.

IMPROVING PHYSICIAN NON-TECHNICAL SKILLS (NTS) IN MEDICAL AND SURGICAL PRACTICE

For the purposes of this chapter, we examine and situate non-technical skills gained during affective domain learning and consider the notion of the term 'Human Factors', which provides an operational definition for the interrelationships between 'systems' (i.e. the healthcare infrastructures within which care is delivered) and the human characteristics of those delivering care in everyday healthcare practice. This gives a broad overview for the understanding of structure and agency in medical practice. We use the experience of one of our authors as an emergency obstetrician to evidence our recommendations for the future development of medical education, in relation to Hinshaw's (2016) previously published work on the subject. We acknowledge that human factors and NTS knowledge and training are required for all members of the maternity team (midwives, anaesthetists, nurses and ancillary healthcare staff) but in this chapter will focus on the relevance to physician training. The critical interaction between team members and their use of non-technical skills in the context of near immediate decision making, hinges on the tacit and intuitively led response that characterizes human reaction in an emergency. A consideration of their relative impact on the health and safety of medical and surgical working environments is crucial if medical and surgical outcomes are to improve in practice by 21st century physicians.

MULTI-DISCIPLINARY TEAMWORK AND THE RELEVANCE OF CREATIVE PRACTICE

The functional dynamics of multidisciplinary teams, stems from the fact they are often constituted from individuals of diverse clinical and academic backgrounds; as a consequence the signature pedagogies represented within them, pose a challenge to medical educational curriculum developers in terms of providing learning opportunities which extend the reach of practitioners within and between healthcare disciplines.

LESSONS FROM CREATIVE ARTISTIC PRACTISE

Creative artistic practise is one discipline from where medical practise can learn much about the significance of tacit knowledge, ambiguity and the lack of a fixed cannon of knowledge. Consideration of tacit knowledge captures the notion of the 'art' of medical practice, which is so firmly rooted in applied creative practise. Whilst technical skill also features as an integral characteristic of the artist, the capacity to apply tacit knowledge lies at the heart of all creative endeavours. Tacit knowledge is knowledge that cannot be readily articulated verbally. It is a term often used in art and design in relation to knowledge of both materials and processes. For example, a ceramics artist is likely to have built up considerable levels of tacit knowledge in relation to clay, such as how firm it needs to be to join a handle onto a teapot without it falling off or how hard to squeeze clay between the fingers when throwing on a potter's wheel. This kind of knowledge is developed through the experience of working with materials and processes in a studio environment. Parallels exist in the context of emergency obstetrics, where an obstetrician uses intuition to determine whether a deliver necessitates surgical intervention. Each of these processes necessitates relative immediacy in decision making (Hickman et al, 2017).

THE THEORY-PRAXIS NEXUS

Theory might well be taught via more transmissive methods in lecture theatres but practical knowledge is more likely to be gained from demonstration and practice (including practise) in the studio and experiential learning in practice at the front line of patient care. This approach has some parallels with clinical practise in that one partly learns to be a practitioner by trying to be one 'on the job'. A nurse for example, learns to nurse partly on the ward (or a simulation of the ward). Similarly, an art student learns what it is to be an artist by trying to become an artist in the studio. It has been suggested that this can create a relative tension between practise and theory, in that the learning of 'know how' is focused very much on practise. This has been long debated in the context of health and medicine where issues of how to bridge the theory –praxis nexus have long pervaded the context of clinical and professional practice (Choy, Edwards-Groves & Grootenboer, 2017). Alongside this, in creative practice, Orr and Shreeve (2017) highlight that, across disparate disciplines, both art and design, and nursing students and staff question the need for theoretical study alongside creative and experiential practise, respectively.

THE SOCIAL NATURE OF CONTEXT AND SITUATION

Although an artist might develop their personal tacit skills by working individually, much of art and design learning is also situationally and contextually social in nature. This brings into play the idea of learning in 'a community of practice'. This is a terms coined by Wenger (1998) to describe how groups of people who share a concern or a passion learn as a group through regular iteration, for example in the workplace. This learning might not always be intentional but can develop tacitly through the social interactions or multi-disciplinary team working. This necessitates three core elements, namely, the place of learning, the community and the practice. In the context of the art studio, students learn via dialogue with the tutor, their peers and also with their own emerging artworks. The emerging artist predominantly learns by making something and then reflecting on their creation, for example a painting. They then build on the knowledge that they have gained by changing the painting or making another. They are also likely to be influenced, supported and facilitated in this process of learning via interactive dialogue with their tutors or peers. This is achieved by articulating opinions that can actively test the value or construct meaning for piece. Affective domain values have direct relevance in this context. The value of an artwork is discussed and negotiated through this active dialogue and potential for social interaction in the context of creative practice. Alongside this the process makes it possible for those learning to value the concept of ambiguity, which is fundamentally important to the learning process as the art student is unlikely to be developing a copy of something that is 'known' – they will be aiming to invent or re-invent what art 'might' or potentially 'could be' be through their practice. This needs curiosity and the ability to cope with risk and uncertainty, which is directly paralleled in the field of emergency obstetrics. Across both contexts there are no categorically 'correct' answers.

THE VALUE OF COLLABORATIVE THINKING

There have been some explorations around the value of collaboration between medical and creative practitioners. The 'sKINship' research project explored the parallels between plastic surgery and fashion pattern cutting to locate what each professional might learn from the other (Solomon, 2013). Casey (2009) has explored how creative practice might help trainee nurses to recognize and communicate what they know and feel about their professions. The potential generic transferability of knowledge from other disciplines is also evident in the context of oil/gas exploration, nuclear safety and aviation, whose disciplines are culturally and pragmatically associated with the term 'safety critical industries'. The lessons learned and which can be adapted to fit medical and surgical practice, are outlined in Table 1 to demonstrate the core operational definitions underpinning the concept of non-technical skill for affective domain learning in physician education and practice.

EVIDENCE OF EDUCATION AND TRAINING IN PRACTICE

Curriculum development and justification of curricula content is being modernized to incorporate a redress of this balance. This has necessitated the integration of change across whole organizational hierarchies with their interprofessional interactive dialogue and capacity for effective communication being central to a wholesale change. This has incorporated contributions of staff at every level of the organizational hierarchy from ancillary healthcare assistants and administrators to allied health professions nurses, midwives and physicians.

THE NOTION OF REFLEXIVE PRAXIS IN PHYSICIAN EDUCATION

The concept of Reflective Practice is now a globally accepted norm of the majority of physician training programs and is acknowledged to be an essential and integral part of what constitutes professional practise. Whereas though, reflection is advocated as a means of encouraging practitioners to 'slow down' and tentatively and deliberately explore their experiential learning from practise, much of the instant decision making in practise is rooted in

Table 1. Elements and definitions of non-technical skills for affective domain learning

Element	Definition
Cognitive Skills	
Situational Awareness	*The sensory perception of elements in the environment, the ability to understand their meaning, and the prediction of their status in the near future.*
Decision-making	*The process of reaching a conclusion and discerning a course of action to meet the needs of a given situation*
Social or Behavioural Skills	
Teamwork	*A collaborative and dynamic process involving two or more people, engaged in collective multiple activity, with the aim of completing a shared goal/task.*
Communication	*The exchange of knowledge of information, requests, ideas or suggestions and intuitive feelings (tacit knowledge) or concerns.*
Leadership	*A team leader has delegated authority to direct and coordinate the work of other team members. However, leadership skills (maintaining standards, planning, prioritizing, managing workload/resources) may be shared within the functional parameter of teams*
Followership	*The active ability of individual team members to perform delegated tasks, to co-operate, to support the leader and to offer constructive challenge when appropriate.*
Assertiveness	*The quality of being appropriately self-assured and able to express an opinion confidently without aggression.*
Personal Resource Skills	*The capacity to manage stress and demonstrate an awareness of the detrimental effects of stress and coping with fatigue and the ability to implement coping strategies in individual and collaborative practice (e.g. resilience)*

the concept of applied critical reflexivity, which advances the capacity of reflection to facilitate a conscious consideration of potential impact on future action. The process necessitates accessing both cognitive and affective domain reflection and applying both with the immediacy of what has become tacit knowledge.

From a methodological perspective in the context of pedagogical design it is possible to apply the concept of Situational Analysis (Clarke & Friese, 2007) to physician practise, where multifactorial variables combine to impact directly on how medical students can be taught to consider and prioritise as many as these of possible as an integral part of their applied practice at the front line of patient care, where the consequences of flawed decision making can be potentially devastating. In teaching 21st century physicians, it can be argued that critical reflexivity i.e. the application of reflection to practice is of greatest significance. However critical self-reflection can be a solitary and, dare we say, self-indulgent process, which being part of a team necessitates being cognisant of.

Situational analysis places emphasis firmly on the construction of reality but provides a degree of consideration for the unique situations, team dynamics and organizational hierarchies that frame patient care and management. What needs to be stressed is that tacit knowledge in practice transcends the reach of competency domains and must be firmly examined in the context of human factors analysis if reflexivity beyond tokenism is to be achieved in transformational educational practice.

There is presently no agreed or 'one size fits all' mechanism for teaching reflexivity in medical education and it has become a discipline specificity, which is the preserve of the few in the context of medical teaching. In curricula where cognitive and psychomotor skills are given precedence, it is understandable why reflective practice and reflexivity are often regarded as the additional extras that characterise a tokenistic approach to affective domain learning. Apparent within this, is the sense of physicians having a need to be taught not only course content but the mechanisms and processes by which they can best engage with curricula to understand not just what but how they learn. In the UK, the Royal College of Obstetricians and Gynaecologists (RCOG) conducted a critical review of the present seven year postgraduate training programme for physicians and confirmed a significant imbalance between time spent developing 'technical skills' [80%] compared to 'non-technical skills' [20%] (RCOG, 2015). The importance of this imbalance is most apparent when we look at clinical practice, where critical review confirms an uncomfortable reality *where non-technical skills and human factors errors account for 83% of cases of poor outcome in maternity care* (Coroyannakis, 2013). The triennial MBRRACE-UK report reviews all cases of maternal death and also describes human factors errors as highly relevant in many cases (Knight, 2014). Recurrent issues included: basic observations not recorded or responded to (ie poor situation awareness and communication), delayed involvement of senior staff by junior staff (poor situation awareness, communication, followership and team-working) and lack of involvement of specialist help when needed (poor leadership, decision-making and team-working). Based on this evidence the need for improved patient outcomes as a direct consequence of medical curricula that are fit for purpose, needs minimal justification (Kumagai, 2014). Here it can be posited that the only significant means of improving patient outcomes for physicians and surgeons is the redress of this balance via the reconceptualizing of the educational theoretical underpinnings of leadership and teamwork training (Hinshaw, 2016b).

Central to an understanding of how improving patient outcomes can be achieved via effective education and training programs involves the deconstruction of the pedagogic praxis informing the teaching and more importantly the learning of cognitive capacity, psychomotor competence and affective skill (Hayes, 2014). Embedded through all three must be the ethos of a safe and just culture, which shifts the focus of human error avoidance to one of a process of accountability which can delineate between a deliberate violation of protocol and a situation in which an intuitive and timely response could potentially be a matter of life and death for a women in the care of obstetrics and gynaecology teams across the world. The primary recommendation within the 2015 RCOG report was *"...to ensure that the revised core curriculum and assessments are orientated towards increased professionalism, particularly in the areas of leadership, team working, communication, human factors and awareness of health systems"*. The significant revision is now almost complete, with four newly-defined professional identities and 16 core 'Capabilities in Practice' [CiPs]. (RCOG, 2018). Under the generic professional identity 'Healthcare Professional' sit seven CiPs; CiP5 will ensure that: *"The doctor understands and applies basic Human Factors principles and practice at individual, team, organisational and system levels"*.

HIGH FIDELITY SIMULATION IN PEDAGOGIC PRACTICE

Conveying the complexities surrounding human interaction in relation to anatomical and physiological presentation and the reproduction of meaningful interaction is the fundamental basis of high fidelity simulation in healthcare practitioner education. This is one of several methodologies that will underpin the revised RCOG postgraduate curriculum. The levels of sophistication afforded to pedagogic practice now mean that the replication of these features can take place in an array of educational contexts and settings. This provides students and educators with the opportunity of extending knowledge by affording them to observe the implications of high-risk healthcare interventions. Couple this with the capacity to remove the reality of the consequences of inappropriate decision making and truly reflexive practice becomes a reality. Seminal work in human factors analysis has shaped a culture of learning that provides students with real life simulation. The commonest examples of this are the aviation and space industries whose reliability and validity in risk aversion and the safety records they routinely present have ensured their capacity to most credibly inform developments in healthcare education. Similarly, the 'gamification' of reality that has permitted the development of strategic thinking and higher order thinking skills for almost a thousand years, continues to provide sensory stimulation for students in extending their intellectual reach, where they can integrate knowledge and take responsibility for risk (Nevin et al, 2014).

Perhaps the best known and most historical example of this is playing chess, which gamified war strategy, focused higher order thinking and as part of the process increased the intellectual reach of its players. High fidelity simulation has identical aims and following Laerdal's seminal work in Gamification (with the original development of Rescusci Anne) the diversity and sophistication of available high fidelity models has exponentially increased. This has ensured that as a pedagogic 'norm' healthcare education now routinely incorporates high fidelity simulation into educational and training scenarios (Alinier et al, 2014).

Within the context of medical educational pathways, the physiological capacity of high fidelity simulation to exhibit a real time response to clinical interventions has become a fundamental mechanism by which social and interactive learning can incorporates and make possible the development of all three domains of learning. Consolidation of learning through de-briefing is a pivotal part of this process and the capacity of students to internalise and make meaning of experience from clinical practice through clinical practise is a hallmark of medical simulation in the context of training.

Recreating authentic academic learning environments is another key proponent driving progression and sustaining change around the concept of medical education (Foronda et al, 2014). By situating cognition in this manner, and by integrating the latest software packages, it is possible to change generic learning environments to represent reality and to deliberately objectify environments so that the student experience is framed by situational context as well as pedagogical underpinning. This highlights the capacity of simulated learning environments to enhance capacity for the transferability of theoretical knowledge into applied practice at the front line of patient care and interaction (Merriman, Stayt & Ricketts, 2014).

TACIT KNOWLEDGE AND SKILLS AS A CONSEQUENCE OF EPISTEMIC COGNITION IN REFLECTION AND REFLEXIVITY

- The relevance of epistemic cognition in the broader context of metacognition and cognition.
- The articulation of experience is fundamental to being able to express processes of critical reflective practice and critical reflexivity.
- Traditionally this has been hinged around processes of critical incident reflection. The key to critical synthesis is the capacity to deconstruct experience, challenge assumptions of personal and professional identity and then reconstruct experience that can provide insight and direction for the future of clinical practise.

CORE PRINCIPLES FOR AUTHENTIC PEDAGOGIC PRACTICE IN PHYSICIAN AND SURGEON EDUCATION AND TRAINING

- Consideration and development of facilitator roles
- Processing and articulating lived experience in action

CONCLUSION

Focus on the context of multi-disciplinary teamwork, experiential learning and capacity to adequately provide affective domain learning has characterized innovation and creativity in medical education for the last decade. This chapter has moved this debate to one that considers the capacity of future physicians to acknowledge the value of tacit, alongside cognate knowledge in the context of the quality of patient safety and the provision of compassionate care. The exemplars from emergency maternity care and creative practice demonstrate how learning from contrasting signature pedagogies can provide an insight into how best tacit thinking can be valued and acknowledged as part of formal training and highlight its relevance to values based recruitment. We posit that a medical education which values an inherent holistic approach to those who will provide front line care for generations of future patients will aid the development of leadership skills that facilitate the value and worth of all clinicians. The overarching and cross cutting themes highlighted in this chapter reflect a need to maintain quality frameworks in medical education for physicians but advocates the opportunity for the early promotion of the development of the independent, higher order critical thinking that characterises leadership at its best. By extending the reach and moving beyond disciplinarity for physicians of the 21st Century, we advocate creativity as a bridge to innovation in curriculum development for doctors that is both fulfilling and which potentially has a direct impact on the level of quality that patients receive in practise, both functionally and affectively.

REFERENCES

Alinier, G., Harwood, C., Harwood, P., Montague, S., Huish, E., Ruparelia, K., & Casey, B. (2009). Arts-based inquiry in nursing education. *Contemporary Nurse*, *32*(1-2), 69–82. doi:10.5172/conu.32.1-2.69 PMID:19697979

Choy, S., Edwards-Groves, C., & Grootenboer, P. (2017). Provoking a (re) newed frontier in theorising educational practice. In *Practice theory perspectives on pedagogy and education* (pp. 265–280). Singapore: Springer. doi:10.1007/978-981-10-3130-4_14

Clarke, A. E., & Friese, C. (2007). Situational analysis: Going beyond traditional grounded theory. Handbook of grounded theory, 694-743.

Coroyannakis, C., Chandraharan, E., & Matiluko, A. (2013). Comparative analysis of the human 'WORM': Role of human factors on adverse incidents in two adjacent obstetric units in London. *British Journal of Obstetrics and Gynaecology*, *120*(1), 413.

Foronda, C., Gattamorta, K., Snowden, K., & Bauman, E. B. (2014). Use of virtual clinical simulation to improve communication skills of baccalaureate nursing students: A pilot study. *Nurse Education Today*, *34*(6), e53–e57. doi:10.1016/j.nedt.2013.10.007 PMID:24231637

Hayes, C. (2014). *Professional practice for podiatric medicine*. M&K Publications.

Hickman, S. E., Hammes, B. J., Torke, A. M., Sudore, R. L., & Sachs, G. A. (2017). The quality of physician orders for life-sustaining treatment decisions: A pilot study. *Journal of Palliative Medicine*, *20*(2), 155–162. doi:10.1089/jpm.2016.0059 PMID:27802064

Hinshaw, K. (2016a). Non-technical skills to improve obstetric practice. In S. Arulkumaren (Ed.), *Best practice in labour and delivery* (2nd ed.; pp. 389–390). Cambridge, UK: Cambridge University Press. doi:10.1017/9781316144961.035

Hinshaw, K. (2016b). Human factors in obstetrics and gynaecology. *Obstetrics, Gynaecology and Reproductive Medicine*, *26*(12), 368–370. doi:10.1016/j.ogrm.2016.09.002

Knight, M., Kenyon, S., Brocklehurst, P., Neilson, J., Shakespeare, J., & Kurinczuk, J. J. (Eds.). (2014). *Saving lives, improving mothers' care: Lessons learned to inform future maternity care from the UK and Ireland.* Confidential Enquiries into Maternal Deaths and Morbidity 2009-12. Oxford: National Perinatal Epidemiology Unit, University of Oxford. Retrieved from https://www.npeu.ox.ac.uk/mbrrace-uk/reports/confidential-enquiry-into-maternal-deaths

Merriman, C. D., Stayt, L. C., & Ricketts, B. (2014). Comparing the effectiveness of clinical simulation versus didactic methods to teach undergraduate adult nursing students to recognize and assess the deteriorating patient. *Clinical Simulation in Nursing*, *10*(3), e119–e127. doi:10.1016/j.ecns.2013.09.004

Mitchell, P. (2017). *Safer care – Human factors in healthcare training manual*. Retrieved from http://teamstepps.ahrq.gov/taq_index.htm

National Academies Press (NAP). (2012). *Improving the decision making abilities of small unit leaders*. Washington, DC: The National Academies Press.

National Institute for Health and Care Excellence. (2017). Intrapartum care: Care of healthy women and their babies during childbirth. *NICE Guidelines*, *133*(6), 614-21.

Nevin, C. R., Westfall, A. O., Rodriguez, J. M., Dempsey, D. M., Cherrington, A., Roy, B., & Willig, J. H. (2014). Gamification as a tool for enhancing graduate medical education. *Postgraduate Medical Journal*, *106*(4), 189–198. PMID:25352673

Orr, S., & Shreeve, A. (2017). *Art and design pedagogy in higher education: Knowledge, values and ambiguity in the creative curriculum*. Abingdon, UK: Routledge. doi:10.4324/9781315415130

Royal College of Obstetricians and Gynaecologists. (2015). *Final report of the curriculum review group 2015*. RCOG. Retrieved from https://www.rcog.org.uk/globalassets/documents/careers-and-training/curriculum/curriculum2018/final-report-of-curriculum-review-working-group.pdf

Royal College of Obstetricians and Gynaecologists. (2018). *A new core curriculum for obstetrics & gynaecology – consultation document*. RCOG. Retrieved from https://www.rcog.org.uk/en/careers-training/specialty-training-curriculum/curriculum-2018/curriculum-2018-consultation.pdf

Solomon, R. (2013). Skinship: An exchange of material understanding between plastic surgery and pattern cutting. *Collaboration through Craft*, 114.

Wenger, E. (1998). *Communities of practice: Learning, meaning, and identity*. Cambridge, UK: Cambridge University Press. doi:10.1017/CBO9780511803932

KEY TERMS AND DEFINITIONS

Creative Practice: Refers to professional practice (usually in an arts-based discipline) or to processes usually used in professional practice that has the intention of producing work for a purpose beyond the deliberate acquisition of knowledge. In this sense, the term *professional practitioner* can refer directly to anyone who pursues professional/creative practice beyond the specific context of arts-based disciplines.

Human Factors: Refers to the environmental, organizational, and job factors, and human and individual characteristics that influence behavior at work and affect health and safety in the workplace.

Multi-Disciplinary Team: Multidisciplinary care is used to describe the contribution of all members of a healthcare team to ensure the highest standards of shared decision making resulting in the best quality care for individual patients. The MDT varies but can constitute medical and healthcare professionals and administrative and support workers who have the same goal of positively contributing and working together. Each member makes a fundamentally unique contribution to the management of patients in the context of their personal care pathway. This is undertaken in a situational context supporting active communication and dialogue between all parties, regardless of their individual level in the organizational hierarchy.

Obstetrics and Gynecology: An area in medical practice that specializes in the care of women during pregnancy and childbirth (obstetrics) and in the diagnosis and management of health issues relating specifically to women (gynecology).

Reflexivity: The degree of self-reflection on action that ensures experience can inform subsequent similar events or experiences in the light of knowledge gained. It is a prospective form of ensuring the experiential learning from reflective practice can be positively integrated in the future, regardless of the initial outcome or circumstances of any given scenario.

Safety Critical Environment: An environment comprising individuals, equipment, and organizational systems in which safety is of paramount importance and where the consequences of failure or malfunction in one of more elements can result in serious harm, including injury or loss of life and damage to property or the environment.

Signature Pedagogies: A term characterizing the disparate nature of different clinical and academic disciplines and the educational practice that underpins them. For example, the difference between humanities and empirically based science subjects or creative artistic practice.

Tacit Knowledge: In contrast to formal, codified, or explicit knowledge, tacit knowledge is an informal, intuitive, and often socially constructed "gut instinct" that can be inherently difficulty to articulate or verbalize.

Chapter 10
Developing a Clinical Leadership Pipeline:
Planning, Operation, and Sustainability

Valerie A. Storey
University of Central Florida, USA

Thomas E. Beeman
University of Pennsylvania Health System, USA

Karen Flaherty-Oxler
Atlantic Health System, USA

ABSTRACT

Healthcare systems are embarking on efforts to improve organizational leadership as a lever to promote organizational efficiency. Such efforts have a solid base of research attesting to their effectiveness, and some view them as particularly cost effective. This chapter fills an important gap in the literature on healthcare systems leadership by presenting (1) a rationale and approach from the perspective of a healthcare systems chief executive officer for understanding the strategic planning, resources, and expenditures associated with efforts to prepare, hire, evaluate, develop, and support clinical leaders; (2) a theoretical foundation and framework for a systems approach to an organizational healthcare leadership pipeline; and (3) a sample case study describing the observed outcomes of a strategically developed leadership pipeline. The case study highlights the resources required to put in place and operate clinical leadership pipelines—pipelines for preparing, hiring, supporting, and managing clinical leaders—based on one large healthcare system.

DOI: 10.4018/978-1-5225-7576-4.ch010

INTRODUCTION

The complexity of healthcare requires excellent leadership to address the challenges of access, quality, and cost of care. Creating a pipeline of effective healthcare leaders requires developing leadership competencies that differ from the usual criteria of clinical and scientific excellence by which physicians have traditionally been promoted to leadership positions (Stoller, 2013). Adopting a long-standing practice from successful corporations, some healthcare institutions, medical societies, and business schools now offer leadership programs that address contextual healthcare leadership competencies.

The authors of this chapter draw on experience with such a program through Lancaster General Health (LG Health) to provide recommendations for developing a healthcare leadership pipeline. Previous chapters have reported on the investment by LG Health in emerging physician leaders culminating in a cohort-based healthcare system executive leadership MBA developed in partnership with St. Joseph's University (SJU). During the past 10 years, LG Health's leadership has successfully created a pipeline of health care leaders to fill executive positions, search committees, board openings, and various other organizational leadership positions grounded on the belief that (1) healthcare leadership can be taught and learned; and (2) investment in a clinical leadership pipelines increases organizational value and capacity.

SECTION 1

In this section the authors present a rationale and approach from the perspective of a healthcare system's CEO for understanding the strategic planning, resources and expenditures associated with efforts to prepare, hire, evaluate, develop, and support clinical leaders.

Rationale

Healthcare much like the law, education and engineering requires esoteric knowledge. The cultures of these professions are well established and attempts to reform them must come from within or the resistance will be strong. Most of healthcare reform has come from the outside trying to use payment methodologies to change behavior, but fundamentally people want the same healthcare delivered, but they want it for less. Unless the model of delivery changes it is unlikely that sufficient change will occur to bend the cost curve. It seems that the most effective way to change a profession is to empower enough critical mass of providers to both create and embrace change.

Efficient healthcare delivery requires a multi disciplinary, well-coordinated clinical team in which each member has an important and orchestrated role in ensuring that patients are properly cared for. Some of the roles such as physician and nurse are historically synergistic, mostly complementary, and require a great deal of professional respect for the boundaries between them. Whereas newer relationships such as physician administrator - developed as a result of the complexities of modern healthcare and the business model - frequently lead to perceptions of turmoil amongst an organization's bureaucratic culture due to the focus on expertise rather than seniority.

Healthcare System's CEO Perspective

Strategic Planning

More recently, health systems have realized that since the core of healthcare is the clinical care revolving around the patient, then clinical leaders are essential to lead the changes that will be required in order to reinvent the way care is delivered. This is necessary due to the precipitous cost of healthcare delivery, which is approximating 20% of the GDP in 2018 and seems unsustainable. All efforts to change healthcare such as Obama care and the Budget Reconciliation and Finance Act 2015, have attempted to change the economic model, not the clinical model. Forward thinking organizations have recognized the necessity of having clinicians in top leadership roles such as the CEO. One such organization, arguably one of the most prominent in the United States (US) the Mayo Clinic, uses a dyad relationship model where the CEO is a physician and his dyad partner, the CFO is a well trained finance executive. This dyad model is proving to be very effective and in some cases a triad model has evolved using a physician, nurse and administrator in this leadership role.

Operational Process

If we accept healthcare is a clinical enterprise and a team undertaking then the dyad and triad model is one approach that may have the capacity to meet the needs of a complex system. But such a model does not develop by osmosis. Bringing talented individuals together does not create a team but educating team members to work both vertically and laterally, and to lead dynamically can be taught through relevant, and appropriate professional development.

More recently healthcare has recognized that service lines, the organization around disease or wellness such as cancer institutes, and women services, make more sense than merely around surgery, medicine or pediatrics, a more typical taxonomy. Service lines allow organizations to look at the patient and the patient experience as holistically as possible. To manage a service line for example such as cardiovascular care requires cardiologists, cardiac surgeons, radiologists, nurses, technicians and administrators to name a few.

It seems then a logical sequitur to educate dyads and triads as a cohort. Although the readiness of the cohort to lead has been evident, it will take further study to determine whether this method is cost effective. However, early indications around Population Health strategies at LG Health demonstrate initial success in changing the model and creating efficiencies that result in cost savings, better patient satisfaction and better outcomes.

SECTION 2

In this section the authors present a theoretical foundation and framework for a systems approach to a sustainable organizational healthcare leadership pipeline.

What Does the Research Reveal About Clinical Leadership?

In 2016, Sarto and Veronesi reviewed the case for clinical leadership and hospital performance. The authors assess physician leadership at the level of CEO, clinical director and participants on hospital governing boards and quality committees. The applied performance measures include financial and resource management, quality of care and hospital social performance, which is a multidimensional construct that captures the relationship between hospital expenditure and benefits to local communities. They concluded that their findings, based on 18 studies, support the case for physician leadership.

Additionally, the Theory of Expert Leadership (TEL) also supports physician leadership (Goodall, 2016). The theory suggests that a leader should have deep knowledge of the core business of the organization that they lead. For example, in healthcare, it was observed that the top 100 hospitals in the USA were statistically more likely to be led by physicians instead of non-medically trained managers.

In a study that includes random samples of 35,000 US and UK workers matched with their employers, the influence on job satisfaction of an employee's immediate boss is examined. The study found that expert supervisors are strongly associated with high levels of employee job satisfaction, and that supervisory competence is more important than pay (Artz, Goodall & Oswald, 2016). In a healthcare setting, the leadership qualities of physician supervisors have also been found to influence clinician job satisfaction and well-being (Shanafelt, Gorringe & Menaker, 2015).

Kearns et al., (2009) identified ten benefits to the healthcare organization when the CEO is also a physician:

1. Better understanding on nature of challenges & common knowledge base
2. Improved understanding of patient care operational issues
3. Unwilling to compromise quality/safety/labor for profit
4. Finance as a means not an end
5. Aligning differing values (RNs, PHAs, DOCs, etc.) & improved interactions
6. Greater value on physician leadership, compensate appropriately
7. Anticipate change within health care industry and selectively embrace new technologies/methods, e.g., new trends, governmental regulation
8. Better coordination with referral sources (private offices/clinics)
9. Less duplication of similar services within region, more collaboration among local hospitals
10. Greater insight into clinical/patient care activity on local and regional level

Yet, amongst the nearly 6,500 hospitals in the United States, only 235 are run by physicians (Academic Medicine, 2009),

Building an Organizational Leadership Pipeline

A competent leadership pipeline filled with those who are ready to assume pivotal leadership roles has never been more important as the demand for qualified and skilled leaders potentially exceeds the supply (Fibuch, Van Way, 2012). Yet, many healthcare systems have been slow to respond to the need to develop a leadership pipeline sometimes referred to as increasing "bench strength," i.e. the growth of new leaders who can ultimately replace key leaders.

Strauss, Soobiah, and Levinson (2013) noted that developing leaders in healthcare systems is a recent phenomenon. For example, in a systematic review of leadership training programs they concluded that there was a 'remarkable paucity of literature that presents the benefits of such leadership training.' A later study conducted by Collins, McKinnies, Lieneck, and Watts (2016) analyzed the perceptions of CEOs in US hospitals regarding leadership development trends and succession planning. Results of the study were compared to identical surveys delivered in previous years for the purposes of identifying possible trends and changing perspectives. They found that succession planning and the development of a leadership pipeline is a strategy that still has not been thoroughly adopted by health care organizations. Although it is encouraging that succession planning efforts and the development of organizational leadership pipelines have seemingly increased.

Conger and Fulmer (2003) suggest five guiding principles of best practice for building an organizational pipeline (see Table 1).

Leadership Development Programs

Based on a systematic review of best-in-class leadership development programs, Day and Halpin (2011) identified several general principles of effective leadership development (see Figure 1), which have been incorporated in notable leadership programs. Medical societies (e.g. American Thoracic Society, United States and Canadian Academy of Pathology, American College of Chest Physicians, American Association for Physician Leadership), medical schools and healthcare organizations (e.g., Cleveland Clinic, Mayo Clinic, Virginia Mason, McLeod Health, Hartford HealthCare, Drexel University College of Medicine, Aurora Healthcare, Emory University's Woodruff Health Sciences Center, etc.) and business schools–often in affiliation with healthcare organizations (e.g. Harvard Business School, The Wharton School

Table 1. Viewing the five guiding principles of best practice for building an organizational pipeline through an organizational and individual lens

Organizational Lens	Individual Lens
1. A development focus	On the job opportunities to apply & demonstrate new management knowledge & skill acquired as a result of professional development
2. Identify key assignments & positions that move talent through the pipeline	Awareness of learning needs, career potential & opportunities
3. Transparency	Awareness of the organization's talent management system & and the ability to assess own potential for advancement
4. Assessment of quality & quantity of the pipeline candidates on a regular basis	Awareness that all organization's personnel appointments are data driven. Awareness that for every leadership position the organization has prepared two internal employees ready to step into the position vacated
5. Continual improvement-flexibility to adapt to improve the strength of the pipeline	System must be used, trusted and flexible

Adapted from Conger & Fulmer, 2003. Developing your leadership pipeline

of the University of Pennsylvania, Weatherhead School of Management of Case-Western Reserve University and Cass Business School of City University of London) characterize these leadership development principles (Goodall & Stoller, 2017). Day and Halpin (2001) conclude that successful leadership programs need to be systematic and consistent rather than discrete or innovative (p.viii) and that the most important principle in successful leadership development efforts is the presence of an influential champion.

Healthcare Leadership Competencies

The identification and validation of healthcare leadership competencies provides a dynamic foundation for building a viable healthcare leadership pipeline (Clement, Hall, O'Connor, Qu, Stefl, & White, 2010). By definition, competencies are a set of skills, knowledge, and abilities within a particular knowledge base. Kouzes and Posner (2012) identify five leadership commitments: challenge the process; inspire a shared vision; enable others to act; model the way; and encourage the heart.

Several respected associations representing healthcare leadership groups provide guidance on specific competencies needed to be successful in healthcare management. These professional groups include the American College of Healthcare Executives (ACHE), the American College of Physician

Figure 1. Essential elements of an effective leadership development program
Adapted from Day & Halpin, 2001. Summary of Best Practice General Principles

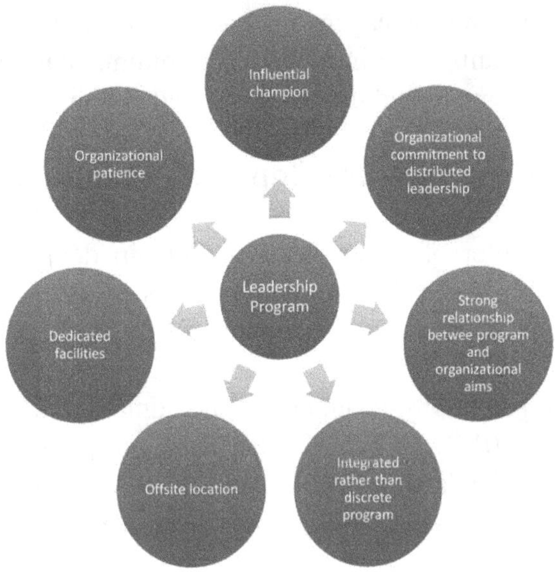

Executives, the American Organization of Nurse Executives, the Healthcare Information and Management Systems Society, the Healthcare Financial Management Association, and the Medical Group Management Association (Broom, Wood & Sampson, 2013).

According to ACHE (2015), leadership preparedness is identified as the principle element that interconnects all the other domains of focus. These domains include communication, relationship management, professionalism, knowledge of the healthcare environment, and business skills/knowledge. The most important competencies identified for healthcare leadership are leadership skills, behavior, understanding organizational climate/culture, communication of the vision, and managing change. These overriding themes help frame the ACHE's core curriculum for leadership self-assessment and development and provide guidance for other healthcare associations conducting self-assessments of their managers' proficiencies.

The Healthcare Leadership Alliance (HLA), identify five crucial domains for success: communication and relationship management, leadership, professionalism, knowledge of the healthcare environment, and business skills and knowledge (HLA, 2013).

Liang, Howard, Koh, and Leggat (2013) also identify five healthcare leadership competencies: evidence based decision-making; operations, administration, resource management; knowledge of the community, the system, and the organization; interpersonal, communication qualities, and relationship management; and the ability to lead and manage change.

Healthcare Leadership Development Programs

An early implementer of a healthcare leadership development program grounded on healthcare leadership competencies was the Cleveland Clinic (Stoller, Berkowitz, & Bailin, 2007). In September 2006, the Cleveland Clinic Academy (CCA) was launched as an integrated program to help establish a pipeline of competent physician, nurse, and administrative leaders (Hess, Barss, & Stoller, 2014). CCA grounded their program on the available literature regarding leadership competencies for health care (Stoller, 2009) (See Appendix A for CCA identified competencies needed to lead an effective healthcare system).

CCAs leadership model and curriculum is organized around four pillars: leading change; developing self and others; fostering teamwork; and demonstrating character and integrity (Stoller, 2017) with strong emphasis on the emotional intelligence model (Goleman, 2009). Some courses are lead by faculty dyads consisting of a Clinic faculty content expert paired with an external faculty member, largely from business schools. The goals of CCA are to offer a leadership and management curriculum for internal health care providers and to extend the existing leadership development offerings (Stoller et al., 2007) to a broad institutional audience.

A report published by Hess et al. (2014) focused on CCA courses designed to help develop a leadership pipeline for the Cleveland Clinic show that from 2006 – 2012, course attendance steadily increased with 6,050 attendees (staff, N = 2,440; nurses, N = 551; & other caregivers, N = 3,059). The authors draw attention to the fact that their data is unique in that it represents the largest attended health care institution leadership development program to date. Key findings are that the program has been well attended, highly rated by attendees, and that it aligns with an institutional strategy to develop leadership bench strength, enhance system integration, and to support global initiatives.

Noelke (2009) describes how Gundersen Lutheran Health System developed a multi step approach to developing the organization's leadership pipeline. Five essential steps in the leadership development process were identified over a period of two years (see Table 2).

Patel, Brennan, Metlay, Bellini, Shannon, and Myers (2015) explain an approach taken by University of Pennsylvania Health System in 2010 to address healthcare leadership training void, called the Healthcare Leadership in Quality (HLQ) track for their clinical residents. This longitudinal, two-

Table 2. Five essential steps in the leadership development process

1. Define leadership competency	Organizations needs to identify the critical knowledge, skills, experiences and traits required of their leaders i.e. build a tiered leadership competency model that includes criteria for executives, directors and managers to ensure well-defined profiles with the appropriate mix of skills, knowledge and attributes to address the challenges facing the organization e.g. nine areas: operations, finance, vision, strategic thinking, building partnerships & teams, staff development, change management, performance management, & leadership character. The competencies are integrated into HR processes including behavioral interview questions, position descriptions and development offerings. They form the bases for 360-degree feedback and talent assessments.
2. Identify high-potential talent	Four leadership levels: 1. Physician Executive pool 2. Physician Administrative leadership pool 3. Administrative Executive pool 4. High Potential Administrative leaders at the director level.
3. Assess talent	Individual development needs are discovered through use of many robust assessment tools and provide a summary of leadership strengths and development needs for each candidate. Organization determines an initial strategy for closing the gap between where the candidates are and where they would like to be from a leadership standpoint.
4. Develop individual plans	Individual development plans are developed based on organizational need and the candidates' growth needs. Plans can include individual coaching, onboarding, continuing education, national learning networks, mentoring, project assignments, committee appointments, cross-functional stretch assignments, role expansion or job rotations.
5. Track progress	Milestones and success measures identified to ensure that candidates build skills and experiences that apply to the leadership competencies and to future roles. The investment of time and resources creates an executive team that views its role as one of cultivating leaders and sustaining a long-term leadership pipeline for the future.

Adapted from Noelke (2009), Five core processes to help executives gain an accurate picture of leadership bench strength, capability and readiness.

year graduate medical education (GME) track aligns with the quality goals of the University of Pennsylvania Health System and is embedded within the residency program. The track includes a core curriculum, integration into an interprofessional health care leadership team that is accountable for quality and safety outcomes on a hospital unit, a capstone Quality Improvement (QI) project, and mentorship. To date empirical evaluation of the track has demonstrated impact on individual and organization outcomes (Patel et al., 2015).

Section 3 is focused on one health system where 40 physicians, nurses and other leaders went through an intensive Wharton Business School led leadership development, and mentorship program for six months. From that group of 40, 21 leaders, 16 of whom were physicians and 5 non physicians were then asked to participate in a 22 month long, cohort model, executive MBA program. The advantages of the cohort model is that it provides a supportive learning structure, promotes academic and social interaction (Mandzuk, Hasinoff, & Seifert, 2003), builds communities of practice (Wenger, 1998), fosters peer mentoring (Bagaka, Badillo, Bransteter, & Rispinto, 2015), and gives equity to individual's voice (Gutteridge, 2015; Wang, 2013). As cohort members get to know one another academically and personally, they can maximize learning opportunities with one another because of their shared learning experiences. The group becomes a vehicle to support learning. However, there are some known disadvantages such as the possibility of groupthink, and flawed thinking and decision-making due to group pressure (Sunstein & Hastie, 2015).

SECTION 3

In this section the authors present a sample case study of how a strategically developed leadership pipeline is implemented and observed outcomes. The sample case study describes the resources required to put in place and operate clinical leadership pipelines—pipelines for preparing, hiring, supporting, and managing clinical leaders—based on one large healthcare system.

Clinical Leadership Collaboration

As a result of the LG Health-SJU partnership, LG Health were confident that their clinician leaders were well positioned in the organization to work in collaborative partnerships (clinical team members, physicians, nurses, and other therapists). These partnerships forged by frequent and intentional discussions were the foundation for organizational change. Senior leadership now expected more from collaborative teams as they developed shared values, organizational insights, and a broad overview of the system in which they participated and contributed to. They were able to take strategic decisions that were always grounded on the organization's goal of improving care and outcomes at the right cost for the community. When other health care systems sought support for transformation from large consulting companies, LG Health had their own team of consultants ready to lead the changes needed.

Case Study: Improve Collaborative Care in Intensive Care Settings

Long length stays in the Intensive Care Units (ICU) do not always improve care and may lead to unplanned co-morbities for patients. We knew that collaborative communication by experts with clarity around the patient's plan of care was desired and vital to improve patient safety and reduce patient harm. Our clinical leaders had previously attempted to create an Intensivist model for our ICU, yet without success. The current practice model allowed any physician no matter their specialty or training to admit patients to the ICU and care for them during their stay. This model was not contemporary nor sustainable as it enabled physicians to order specialty consultations as needed yet many did not understand the fragility of the complex ICU patient and the rising risk with each days stay. With the rise of the Pulmonary and Critical Care Intensivist medical specialty, we knew we needed to embrace a higher level of coordinated care.

The existing model of care was not wrong, just not in pace with clinical training; new learnings and patient care needs. Our revised model was different as we now had clinical leaders, respected for their talent and clinical skills able to lead different conversations about change. They more clearly understood how creating this value for the organization, the patients and their families positioned this system as a destination for extraordinary care. Our clinical leaders, now armed with new insights and wisdom were able to champion to other Intensive Care admitting providers the timing and need to move this forward now. They spoke with passion about the quality imperative and need to set partisan politics and division aside to create what was needed to improve care.

Clinical leaders were persuasive in their conversations about external competitors and the growing "virtual" Intensivist models sweeping the country. These new threats appeared to galvanize the Medical Staff to create and support what was needed. Clinical leaders, with their administrative partners, created the Intensivist model and socialized the requirements, anticipated changes and improved quality and care. What they now knew was that one conversation is one conversation and that every constituent and partner needed insights as to the "What" and the "Why" for this change. As a result of their learnings, their conversations were more targeted and strategic and drove the changes for the system.

Clinical leaders also changed the process of clinical rounds to predictable, inclusive and outcomes driven rounds. The time of the rounds was standardized and occurred formally twice each day. All team members were now prepared to share their professional insights and track progress toward patient care goals during these rounds. The care was coordinated; deviations from the expected clinical pathways were realized quickly and changes made. Families were encouraged to be part of these rounds, resulting in improved communications and clearer understanding of the care transitions ahead. These rounds were in addition to regular patient care huddles that happened throughout the 24 hours each day.

The increased interdisciplinary dialogue and collaboration influenced the Leapfrog rating for the hospital to become an "A." Intensivist care was 24 hours each day and support to the non-ICU physician to collaborate care was created. Clinical leaders led the clinical rounds and conversations with new data about length of stay, ventilator days, infections, and the number of days that lines and drains were in place in a patient. This clarity and communication enhanced care transitions. Availability of ICU bed capacity for other patients resulted, providing more timely care to patients in the right care setting.

We learned that to achieve these results, the clinical leaders needed a learning environment built with trust and respect and one where collaboration was as important as outcomes. These clinical partners sustained this momentum and created new collaboratives in Surgical Services supply standardization, Telemetry reduction/improved outcomes work and new models for Advanced Practice providers.

CONCLUSION

Medicine requires a collection of highly trained and dedicated professionals. Like a symphony, physicians, nurses, and other professionals must work in concert to care for a single patient. This model has evolved over centuries. The entrenched system has been rewarded economically and reinforced by the payment system and payment changes alone will not change the system. As a consequence senior leadership at LG Health decided to take a different approach. Starting with a physician Leadership Academy which lasted for a year and has since trained close to 200 physicians, leading to a Wharton Program from coaching team leaders and ending in an Executive MBA Program for 21 clinicians has created a critical mass and agile cohort to lead change within the organization. The success of the organization has been well documented but the results must be monitored over time. The authors would argue that the organizational outcomes have more than paid for the $1M financial investment. However, the need to measure monumental success over time in relation to finance, patient satisfaction and outcome success has yet to be measured. Although signs look very promising, (e.g. significant savings for Medicaid patients with reduced admissions, length of stay and costs), it appears that leadership education for clinical leaders, particularly for physicians and leading to an MBA in a cohort is both efficacious and valued for all concerned. One of the biggest challenges for healthcare executives is around trust. Physicians and healthcare executives have long battled over resource issues and control. The blame lives on both side of the equation. Executives have to realize that the changes required in healthcare today are involved in the clinical model and how it must adapt to a new environment. Only caregivers, particularly physicians who are licensed can make this happen. Consequently it is the Executive that should break away from his/her paradigm and invite physicians to the Leadership table. By making this leap of faith, at least one organization has proven that physicians are willing partners and the measurement is operational and organizational success.

REFERENCES

American College of Healthcare Executives. (2015). *Healthcare executive competencies assessment tool.* Retrieved from https://www.ache.org/pdf/nonsecure/careers/competencies_booklet.pdf 201

Artz, B., Goodall, A. H., & Oswald, A. J. (2016). Boss competence and worker well being. *Industrial & Labor Relations Review*.

Bagaka's, J. G., Badillo, N., Bransteter, I., & Rispinto, S. (2015). Exploring student success in a doctoral program: The power of mentorship and research engagement. *International Journal of Doctoral Studies, 10*, 323–342. doi:10.28945/2291

Broom, K. D., Wood, S. J., & Sampson, C. J. (2013). Current trends in graduate-level healthcare management education: An examination of accreditation outcomes. *The Journal of Health Administration Education, 30*(3), 159–179.

Clement, D. G., Hall, R. S., O'Connor, S. J., Qu, H., Stefl, M. E., & White, A. W. (2010). Competency development and validation: A collaborative approach among four graduate programs. *The Journal of Health Administration Education, 27*(3), 151–173.

Collins, S. K., McKinnies, R., Lieneck, C., & Watts, S. (2016). A trend analysis of succession planning in health care as perceived by chief executive officers in US hospitals. *The Health Care Manager, 35*(4), 333–339. doi:10.1097/HCM.0000000000000126 PMID:27669428

Conger, J. A., & Fulmer, R. M. (2003). Developing your leadership pipeline. *Harvard Business Review, 81*(12), 76–84. PMID:14712546

Day, D. V., & Halpin, S. M. (2001). *Leadership development: A review of industry best practices. Review on corporate training*. Technical Report 1111. Retrieved from www.au.af.mil/au/awc/awcgate/army/tr1111.pdf

Fibuch, E., & Van Way, C. W. III. (2012). Succession planning in health care organizations. *Physician Executive, 38*(5), 44–54. PMID:23888663

Goleman, D. (2009). *Emotional intelligence: Why it can matter more than IQ*. London: Bloomsbury.

Goodall, A., & Stoller, J. K. (2017). The future of clinical leadership: Evidence for physician leadership and the educational pathway for new leaders. *BMJ Leader, 1*(2), 8–11. doi:10.1136/leader-2017-000010

Goodall, A. H. (2016). A theory of expert leadership (TEL) in psychiatry. *Australasian Psychiatry, 24*(3), 231–234. doi:10.1177/1039856215609760 PMID:26460332

Gutteridge, D. (2015). Chronicle of a novice researcher: The Challenges and rewards. *International Journal of Training Research, 13*(2), 159–170. doi:10.1080/14480220.2015.1077723

Health Leadership Alliance. (2013). *Overview of the HLA competency directory*. Retrieved from: http://www.healthcareleadershipalliance.org/Overview%20of%20the%20HLA%20Competency%20Directory.pdf

Hess, C. A., Barss, C., & Stoller, J. K. (2014). Developing a leadership pipeline: the Cleveland Clinic experience. *Perspect Med Educ*. Retrieved from link.springer.com/article/10.1007/s40037-014-0135-y

Kouzes, J. M., & Posner, B. Z. (2012). *The leadership challenge workbook*. San Francisco: Jossey Bass.

Liang, Z., Howard, P. F., Koh, L. C., & Leggat, S. (2013). Competency requirements for middle and senior managers in community health services. *Australian Journal of Primary Health, 19*(3), 256–263. doi:10.1071/PY12041 PMID:23007275

Mandzuk, D., Hasinoff, S., & Seifert, K. (2003). Inside a student cohort: Teacher education from a social capital perspective. *Canadian Journal of Education, 28*(1&2), 168–184.

Noelke, N. (2009, March). Leverage the past to build the future: Executives at a Wisconsin healthcare network figured out how to fill its leadership pipeline. *HRMagazine*, 34–36.

Patel, N., Brennan, P. J., Metlay, J., Bellini, L., Shannon, R. P., & Myers, J. S. (2015). Building the pipeline: The creation of a residency training pathway for future physician leaders in health care quality. *Academic Medicine, 90*(2), 185–190. doi:10.1097/ACM.0000000000000546 PMID:25354070

Sarto, F., & Veronesi, G. (2016). Clinical leadership and hospital performance: Assessing the evidence base. *BMC Health Services Research, 16*(S2), 169. doi:10.118612913-016-1395-5 PMID:27230873

Shanafelt, T. D., Gorringe, G., Menaker, R., Storz, K. A., Reeves, D., Buskirk, S. J., ... Swensen, S. J. (2015). Impact of organizational leadership on physician burnout and satisfaction. *Mayo Clinic Proceedings, 90*(4), 432–440. doi:10.1016/j.mayocp.2015.01.012 PMID:25796117

Stoller, J. K. (2009). Developing physician-leaders: Need and rationale. *The Journal of Health Administration Education, 25*(4), 307–328. PMID:19655634

Stoller, J. K. (2013). Commentary: Recommendations and remaining questions for health care leadership training programs. *Academic Medicine, 88*(1), 12–15. doi:10.1097/ACM.0b013e318276bff1 PMID:23267224

Stoller, J. K. (2017). The clinician as leader: Why, how, and when. *American Thoracic Society, 14*(11), 1622–1626. doi:10.1513/AnnalsATS.201706-494PS PMID:28771027

Stoller, J. K., Berkowitz, E., & Bailin, P. B. (2007). Physician management and leadership education at the Cleveland Clinic Foundation: Programme impact and experience over 14 years. *The Journal of Medical Practice Management, 22*(4), 237–242. PMID:17425027

Strauss, S., Soobiah, C., & Levinson, W. (2013). The impact of leadership training programmes on physicians in academic medical centers: A systematic review. *Academic Medicine, 88*(5), 710–723. doi:10.1097/ACM.0b013e31828af493 PMID:23524921

Sunstein, C. R., & Hastie, R. (2015). *Wiser: Getting beyond groupthink to make groups smarter*. Boston, MA: Harvard Business Press.

Wenger, E. (1998). *Communities of practice: Learning, meaning, and identity*. Cambridge, UK: Cambridge University Press. doi:10.1017/CBO9780511803932

KEY TERMS AND DEFINITIONS

Clinical Collaboration: Interdisciplinary conversations create the necessary collaboration of care and individualization of care for each patient. The quality, reduction of patient harm, and improved team member success and engagement results.

Competency: Competencies are specific knowledge-based skills, abilities, or expertise in a subject area. When these skillsets are shared across a profession, they are said to have core competencies.

Dyad: A dyad model includes a physician leader as well as a manager that partner together to run the practice.

Intensivist Care Model: Physicians and providers that are trained in critical care medicine create a model of care for the ICU patient that recognizes early and important changes in the critically ill patients.

Leadership Development: Expansion of a person's capacity to be effective in leadership roles and processes is considered leadership development: those that facilitate setting direction, creating alignment, and maintaining commitment in groups of people who share common work.

APPENDIX: COMPETENCIES NEEDED TO LEAD IN HEALTHCARE

Table 3.

Competency	Demonstrable Skill
Emotional intelligence	Self-awareness & regulation of emotions, self-motivation, awareness of others' emotional states & proficiency in managing relationships
Professionalism	How we conduct ourselves as caregivers in our interactions with patients and society
Change management	Knowledge of change models, personal change readiness & avidity, timeliness of meeting deadlines
Communication	Teambuilding, active listening skills, negotiation, conflict resolution, giving feedback, awareness of Clinic resources, skills for interacting with the media
Commitment to lifelong learning	Openness to learning and trying new ideas and practices
Commitment to deliver observable results	Actively engaging in the planning, discussion and implementation phases of the project
Finance	Implementing a strategic plan, overall competence, reading a financial statement, developing a business plan, managing a budget, knowledge of reimbursement & insurance, creatively managing resources & people
Regulatory environment	Knowledge of resources for quality improvement, knowledge of organization's regulations as pertains to the individual's area
Marketing	Awareness of marketing resources, ability to develop a marketing plan
Recruiting & hiring	Awareness of resources for recruiting & hiring, sensitivity and attention to diversity & legal issues, identifying talent
Awareness of technology	Awareness of leaders & resources ('how things get done'), openness to learning new technologies & implementing new techniques in the workplace
Process assessment & management	Knowledge of resources for process improvement, knowledge of process improvement strategies
Philanthropy & development	Knowledge of resources for philanthropy & development, develop skills to solicit & cultivate potential donors
Medicolegal issues	Awareness of clinical legal issues, knowledge of strategies to avoid medical malpractice, skill to manage a malpractice claim
Managing physicians	Ability to recognize the physician in trouble, ability to manage the impaired physician & to motivate physicians
Clinic awareness	Knowledge of organizational leadership structures, knowledge of success metrics, informed about community service & volunteerism opportunities, knowledge of privileging issues & organization/system bylaws, personal collegiality

Adapted from Hess et al., (2014) with permission from Stoller (2009).

Compilation of References

12 Statistics on hospital profit and revenue in 2012. (2014, January 21). Retrieved from https://www.beckershospitalreview.com/finance/12-statistics-on-hospital-profit-and-revenue-in-2012.html

Accreditation Council for Graduate Medical Education (ACGME). (2001). *General competencies: ACGME outcome project*. Retrieved from http://www.acgme.org/What-We-Do/Accreditation/Common-Program-Requirements

Aki, S., & Mila, H. (2012). Building trust in high-performing teams. *Technology Innovation Management Review*, *38*, 38–41.

Alinier, G., Harwood, C., Harwood, P., Montague, S., Huish, E., Ruparelia, K., & Casey, B. (2009). Arts-based inquiry in nursing education. *Contemporary Nurse*, *32*(1-2), 69–82. doi:10.5172/conu.32.1-2.69 PMID:19697979

American Academy of Pediatrics. (2017). Retrieved from https://www.aap.org/en-us/about-the-aap/Committees-Councils-Sections/Neonatal-Perinatal-Medicine/TECAN/Pages/Leadership.aspx

American College of Healthcare Executives. (2015). *Healthcare executive competencies assessment tool.* Retrieved from https://www.ache.org/pdf/nonsecure/careers/competencies_booklet.pdf 201

American College of Surgeons. (2017). Retrieved from https://www.facs.org/education/division-of-education/courses/surgeons-as-leaders

American Hospital Association Division of Medical Affairs (AHA). (1992). *Medical Staff Report*. Chicago: The Association.

American Hospital Association. (2014). *Physician Leadership Education*. Chicago: Physician Leadership Forum.

Ancona, D., & Gregersen, H. (2018). *The power of leaders who focus on solving problems*. Retrieved from https://hbr.org/2018/04/the-power-of-leaders-who-focus-on-solving-problems

Arroliga, A. C., Huber, C., Myers, J. D., Dieckert, J. P., & Wesson, D. (2014). Leadership in health care for the 21st century: Challenges and opportunities. *The American Journal of Medicine*, *127*(3), 246–249. doi:10.1016/j.amjmed.2013.11.004 PMID:24280177

Artz, B., Goodall, A. H., & Oswald, A. J. (2016). Boss competence and worker well being. *Industrial & Labor Relations Review*.

Association of American Medical Colleges (AAMC). (2017). *Institutional GME leadership competencies*. GRA Core Competency Task Force of the Group on Resident Affairs (GRA). Retrieved from https://www.aamc.org/members/leadership/470170/gmeleadershipdevelopmentcertificateprogram.html

Bagaka's, J. G., Badillo, N., Bransteter, I., & Rispinto, S. (2015). Exploring student success in a doctoral program: The power of mentorship and research engagement. *International Journal of Doctoral Studies*, *10*, 323–342. doi:10.28945/2291

Barnett, B. G., Basom, M. R., Yerkes, D. M., & Norris, C. J. (2000). Cohorts in educational leadership programs: Benefits, difficulties, and the potential for developing school leaders. *Educational Administration Quarterly*, *36*(2), 255–282. doi:10.1177/0013161X00362005

Barnett, B. G., & Muse, I. D. (1993). Cohort groups in education: Promises and challenges. *Journal of School Leadership*, *3*, 400–415.

Bennett, C. (1975). Up the hierarchy. *Journal of Extension*, *13*(2). Retrieved from http://www.joe.org/joe/1975march/1975-2-a1.pdf

Bodenheimer, T., & Sinsky, C. (2014). From triple to quadruple aim: Care of the patient requires care of the provider. *Annals of Family Medicine*, *12*(6), 573–576. doi:10.1370/afm.1713 PMID:25384822

Britannica, T. E. (2017, November 15). *Hippocratic oath.* Retrieved from https://www.britannica.com/topic/Hippocratic-oath

Broom, K. D., Wood, S. J., & Sampson, C. J. (2013). Current trends in graduate-level healthcare management education: An examination of accreditation outcomes. *The Journal of Health Administration Education, 30*(3), 159–179.

Browne-Ferrigno, T., & Muth, R. (2003). Effects of cohorts on learners. *Journal of School Leadership, 13*, 621–643.

Buchholz, R., & Rosenthal, S. (2008). The unholy alliance of business and science. *Journal of Business Ethics, 78*(1-2), 199–206. doi:10.100710551-006-9329-5

Butcher, L. (2011). The rapid growth of MD/MBA programs: Are they worth it. *Physician Executive, 37*(1), 22–26. PMID:21302745

Carroll, L. (1865). *Alice's adventures in wonderland.* New York: MacMillan.

Chantler C. (1999). The role and education of doctors in the delivery of health care. *Lancet, 353*, 1178-81.

Chen, S. H. (2006). The merging of medicine and management--McGill University's MD-MBA degree. *McGill Journal of Medicine, 9*(1), 3–4. PMID:19529800

Choy, S., Edwards-Groves, C., & Grootenboer, P. (2017). Provoking a (re) newed frontier in theorising educational practice. In *Practice theory perspectives on pedagogy and education* (pp. 265–280). Singapore: Springer. doi:10.1007/978-981-10-3130-4_14

Clarke, A. E., & Friese, C. (2007). Situational analysis: Going beyond traditional grounded theory. Handbook of grounded theory, 694-743.

Clement, D. G., Hall, R. S., O'Connor, S. J., Qu, H., Stefl, M. E., & White, A. W. (2010). Competency development and validation: A collaborative approach among four graduate programs. *The Journal of Health Administration Education, 27*(3), 151–173.

Cochran, J., Kaplan, G. S., & Nesse, R. E. (2014). Physician leadership in changing times. *Health Care, 2*(1), 19–21. PMID:26250084

Cohen, K. R. (2008). *Best practices for developing effective and enduring board/CEO relationships*. American Hospital Association's Center for Healthcare Governance.

Collins, J. (2001). *Good to great*. New York, NY: HarperCollins Inc.

Collins, S. K., McKinnies, R., Lieneck, C., & Watts, S. (2016). A trend analysis of succession planning in health care as perceived by chief executive officers in US hospitals. *The Health Care Manager*, *35*(4), 333–339. doi:10.1097/HCM.0000000000000126 PMID:27669428

Conger, J. A., & Fulmer, R. M. (2003). Developing your leadership pipeline. *Harvard Business Review*, *81*(12), 76–84. PMID:14712546

Coroyannakis, C., Chandraharan, E., & Matiluko, A. (2013). Comparative analysis of the human 'WORM': Role of human factors on adverse incidents in two adjacent obstetric units in London. *British Journal of Obstetrics and Gynaecology*, *120*(1), 413.

Craft, M. (2005). Reflective writing and nursing education. *The Journal of Nursing Education*, *44*(2), 53–57. PMID:15719711

Cunningham, W. G., & Cordeiro, P. A. (2003). *Educational leadership: A problem-based approach*. Boston, MA: Pearson Education.

Darzi, A. (2007). *Healthcare for London: A framework for action*. London: NHS London.

Darzi, A. (2008). *High quality care for all: The NHS next stage review final report*. London: Department of Health.

Day, D. V., & Halpin, S. M. (2001). *Leadership development: A review of industry best practices. Review on corporate training*. Technical Report 1111. Retrieved from www.au.af.mil/au/awc/awcgate/army/tr1111.pdf

Diem, K. (1997). *Measuring impact of educational programs. Rutgers Cooperative Extension. Fact sheet #869*. New Brunswick, NJ: Rutgers University.

Doctors in Society. (2005). *Medical professionalism in a changing world*. London: Royal College of Physicians.

Drucker, P. (1985, May/June). Visions of empire: Some problems with the corporate model of hospitals. *Hospital Forum*, 50–52. Retrieved from www.healthfutures.net/text/w-visemp.doc PMID:10272322

Duke, L. M. (2015). *Penn Medicine: Lancaster General Health.* Progress Notes. Retrieved from http://www.lancastergeneralHealth.org/LG HEALTH/Healthcare-Professionals/Progress-Notes/Staff-Transitions/Meet-David-Polin,-MD-%E2%80%93-and-newly-minted-MBA.aspx

Duke, L. M. (2015). They're in business – 14 physicians earn MBAs. Retrieved from http://www.lancastergeneralhealth.org/LGH/Healthcare-Professionals/Progress-Notes/Staff-Transitions/They-re-in-business-14-physicians-earn-MBAs-Cap-an.aspx

Duke, M., Foley, R., Lauter, S., & Young, B. (2015). *Hospital Garrahan reflection paper*. Academic Press.

Dye, C. F. (2016, September/October). Selecting physician leaders. *Healthcare Executive*, 72–75. PMID:29693929

Employer health benefits survey - Summary of findings. (2018, February 21). Retrieved from https://www.kff.org/report-section/ehbs-2017-summary-of-findings/

Ethical Guidance Management for Doctors. (n.d.). Retrieved March 12, 2018, from http://www.gmcuk.org/guidance/ethical_guidance/management_for_doctors.asp

Evaluation Forum. (2000). *How to manage and analyze data for outcome-based evaluation*. Seattle, WA: Organizational Research Services Inc.

Faculty of Medical Leadership and Management. (2016). *Leadership and management standards for medical professionals* (2nd ed.). London: Faculty of Medical Leadership & Management.

Fibuch, E., & Van Way, C. W. III. (2012). Succession planning in health care organizations. *Physician Executive*, *38*(5), 44–54. PMID:23888663

Ford, J. D., & Ford, L. W. (2009). Resistance to change: A reexamination and extension. *Research in Organizational Change and Development*, *17*, 211–239. doi:10.1108/S0897-3016(2009)0000017008

Ford, J. D., & Ford, L. W. (2010). Stop blaming resistance to change and start using it. *Organizational Dynamics*, *39*(1), 24–36. doi:10.1016/j.orgdyn.2009.10.002

Foronda, C., Gattamorta, K., Snowden, K., & Bauman, E. B. (2014). Use of virtual clinical simulation to improve communication skills of baccalaureate nursing students: A pilot study. *Nurse Education Today*, *34*(6), e53–e57. doi:10.1016/j.nedt.2013.10.007 PMID:24231637

Fullan, M. (2001). *Leading in a culture of change*. San Francisco, CA: Jossey-Bass.

General Medical Council. (2012). *Leadership and management for all doctors*. London: GMC. Retrieved from: http:// www.gmc-uk.org/guidance

Goleman, D. (2009). *Emotional intelligence: Why it can matter more than IQ*. London: Bloomsbury.

Goodall, A. H. (2011). Physician-leaders and hospital performance: Is there an association? *Social Science & Medicine*, *73*(4), 535–539. doi:10.1016/j.socscimed.2011.06.025 PMID:21802184

Goodall, A. H. (2016). A theory of expert leadership (TEL) in psychiatry. *Australasian Psychiatry*, *24*(3), 231–234. doi:10.1177/1039856215609760 PMID:26460332

Goodall, A., & Stoller, J. K. (2017). The future of clinical leadership: Evidence for physician leadership and the educational pathway for new leaders. *BMJ Leader*, *1*(2), 8–11. doi:10.1136/leader-2017-000010

Goyal, R., Aung, K. K., Oh, B., Hwang, T. J., Besancon, E., & Jain, S. (2015). Survey of MD/MBA programs: Opportunities for physician management education. *Academic Medicine*, *90*(1), 121. doi:10.1097/ACM.0000000000000517 PMID:25229193

Greenleaf, R. K. (1977). *Servant leadership – A journey into the nature of legitimate power and greatness*. Paulist Press Mahwah.

Griffith, J. R. (1998). *Designing 21st century healthcare: Leadership in hospitals and healthcare systems*. Chicago, IL: Health Administration Press.

Gunderman, R., & Kanter, S. L. (2009). Perspective: Educating physicians to lead hospitals. *Academic Medicine*, *84*(10), 1348–1351. doi:10.1097/ACM.0b013e3181b6eb42 PMID:19881420

Gutteridge, D. (2015). Chronicle of a novice researcher: The Challenges and rewards. *International Journal of Training Research*, *13*(2), 159–170. doi:10.1080/14480220.2015.1077723

Ham, C., Clark, J., & Spurgeon, P. (2010). *Medical chief executives in the NHS: Facilitators and barriers to their career progress*. Coventry, UK: NHS Institute for Innovation & Improvement.

Hayes, C. (2014). *Professional practice for podiatric medicine*. M&K Publications.

Health Leadership Alliance. (2013). *Overview of the HLA competency directory*. Retrieved from: http://www.healthcareleadershipalliance.org/Overview%20of%20the%20HLA%20Competency%20Directory.pdf

Hess, C. A., Barss, C., & Stoller, J. K. (2014). Developing a leadership pipeline: the Cleveland Clinic experience. *Perspect Med Educ*. Retrieved from link.springer.com/article/10.1007/s40037-014-0135-y

Hess, C. (2013). Health care educators: New directions in leadership development. *The Journal of Leadership Studies*, *6*(4), 72–76. doi:10.1002/jls.21269

Hickman, S. E., Hammes, B. J., Torke, A. M., Sudore, R. L., & Sachs, G. A. (2017). The quality of physician orders for life-sustaining treatment decisions: A pilot study. *Journal of Palliative Medicine*, *20*(2), 155–162. doi:10.1089/jpm.2016.0059 PMID:27802064

Hilsenrath, P. E. (2012). Healthcare management education settings in the United States: History and perspective. *Journal of Management History*, *18*(4), 386–401. doi:10.1108/17511341211258738

Hinshaw, K. (2016a). Non-technical skills to improve obstetric practice. In S. Arulkumaren (Ed.), *Best practice in labour and delivery* (2nd ed.; pp. 389–390). Cambridge, UK: Cambridge University Press. doi:10.1017/9781316144961.035

Hinshaw, K. (2016b). Human factors in obstetrics and gynaecology. *Obstetrics, Gynaecology and Reproductive Medicine*, *26*(12), 368–370. doi:10.1016/j.ogrm.2016.09.002

Houghton, J. D., Neck, C. P., & Manz, C. C. (2002). Self-leadership and superleadership: The heart and art of creating shared leadership. In C. L. Pearce & J. A. Conger (Eds.), *Shared leadership: Reframing the hows and whys of leadership* (pp. 126–132). Thousand Oaks, CA: SAGE Publications.

Hughes, A. M., Gregory, M. E., Joseph, D. L., Sonesh, S. C., Marlow, S. L., Lacerenza, C. N., & Salas, E. (2016). Saving lives: A meta-analysis of team training in healthcare. *The Journal of Applied Psychology*, *101*(9), 1266–1304. doi:10.1037/apl0000120 PMID:27599089

Ibarra, H. (2016, April 18). *5 Misconceptions about networking*. Retrieved from https://hbr.org/2016/04/5-misconceptions-about-networking

Jarvenpaa, S., & Leidner, D. A. (1999). Communication and trust in global virtual teams. *Organization Science*, *10*(6), 791–815. doi:10.1287/orsc.10.6.791

Katzenbach, J. R., & Smith, D. K. (1993). *The wisdom of teams: Creating the high-performance organization*. Cambridge, MA: Harvard Business School Press.

Kirtman, L., & Fullan, M. (2016). *Leadership: Key competencies for whole-system change*. Bloomington, IN: Solution Tree Press.

Knight, M., Kenyon, S., Brocklehurst, P., Neilson, J., Shakespeare, J., & Kurinczuk, J. J. (Eds.). (2014). *Saving lives, improving mothers' care: Lessons learned to inform future maternity care from the UK and Ireland.* Confidential Enquiries into Maternal Deaths and Morbidity 2009-12. Oxford: National Perinatal Epidemiology Unit, University of Oxford. Retrieved from https://www.npeu.ox.ac.uk/mbrrace-uk/reports/confidential-enquiry-into-maternal-deaths

Kotter, J. P. (1990). *A force for change: How leadership differs from management*. New York: Free Press.

Kouzes, J. M., & Posner, B. Z. (2012). *The leadership challenge workbook*. San Francisco: Jossey Bass.

Krupat, E., Dienstag, J. L., Kester, W. C., & Finkelstein, S. N. (2017). Medical students who pursue a joint MD/MBA degree: Who are they and where are they heading? *Evaluation & the Health Professions*, *40*(2), 203–218. doi:10.1177/0163278715620831 PMID:26801747

Larson, D. B., Chandler, M., & Forman, H. P. (2003). MD/MBA programs in the United States: Evidence of a change in healthcare leadership. *Academic Medicine*, *78*(3), 335–341. doi:10.1097/00001888-200303000-00021 PMID:12634220

Lemon, J. D. (2018). The MD/MBA: An emerging dual degree in healthcare. *The Journal of Lancaster General Hospital*, *13*(2), 52–55.

Lencioni, P. (2012). *The advantage*. San Francisco, CA: Jossey-Bass.

Liang, Z., Howard, P. F., Koh, L. C., & Leggat, S. (2013). Competency requirements for middle and senior managers in community health services. *Australian Journal of Primary Health*, *19*(3), 256–263. doi:10.1071/PY12041 PMID:23007275

Ljuboja, D., Powers, B. W., Robbins, B., Huckman, R., Yeshwant, K., & Jain, S. H. (2016). When doctors go to business school: Career choices of physician-MBAs. *The American Journal of Managed Care*, *22*(6), 196–198. PMID:27355906

Mandzuk, D., Hasinoff, S., & Seifert, K. (2003). Inside a student cohort: Teacher education from a social capital perspective. *Canadian Journal of Education*, *28*(1&2), 168–184.

Marotti, A. (2016). Company support for MBAs fell off a cliff, so schools are getting creative. *Chicago Tribune*. Retrieved from http://www.chicagotribune.com/bluesky/originals/ct-mba-sponsorship-from-employers-bsi-20160811-story.html

Massachusetts Medical Society. (2017). *Leadership survey: Ability to lead does not come from a degree*. Waltham, MA: NEJM Catalyst Insight Council.

Merriman, C. D., Stayt, L. C., & Ricketts, B. (2014). Comparing the effectiveness of clinical simulation versus didactic methods to teach undergraduate adult nursing students to recognize and assess the deteriorating patient. *Clinical Simulation in Nursing*, *10*(3), e119–e127. doi:10.1016/j.ecns.2013.09.004

Mitchell, P. (2017). *Safer care – Human factors in healthcare training manual*. Retrieved from http://teamstepps.ahrq.gov/taq_index.htm

Morahan, P. S., Gleason, K. A., Richman, R. C., Dannels, S., & McDade, S. A. (2010). Advancing women faculty to senior leadership in U.S. academic health centers: Fifteen years of history in the making. *Journal About Women in Higher Education*, *3*(1), 137–161. doi:10.2202/1940-7890.1042

National Academies Press (NAP). (2012). *Improving the decision making abilities of small unit leaders*. Washington, DC: The National Academies Press.

National Health Accounts Historical. (2018). Retrieved from https://www.cms.gov/Research-Statistics-Data-and-Systems/Statistics-Trends-and-Reports/NationalHealthExpendData/NationalHealthAccountsHistorical.html

National Health Service (NHS) Institute for Innovation and Improvement & Academy of Medical Royal Colleges. (2010). *The medical leadership competency framework* (3rd ed.). The National Institute for Innovation and Improvement. Retrieved from http://www.institute.nhs.uk/assessment_tool/general/medical_leadership_competency_framework_-_homepage.html

National Health Service (NHS) Institute for Innovation and Improvement and Academy of Medical Royal Colleges. (2009). *The medical leadership competency framework* (2nd ed.). Coventry, UK: NHS Institute for Innovation & Improvement.

National Health Service (NHS) Leadership Academy. (2011). *Leadership framework: A summary*. Coventry, UK: NHS Institute for Innovation & Improvement.

National Institute for Health and Care Excellence. (2017). Intrapartum care: Care of healthy women and their babies during childbirth. *NICE Guidelines*, *133*(6), 614-21.

Nevin, C. R., Westfall, A. O., Rodriguez, J. M., Dempsey, D. M., Cherrington, A., Roy, B., & Willig, J. H. (2014). Gamification as a tool for enhancing graduate medical education. *Postgraduate Medical Journal*, *106*(4), 189–198. PMID:25352673

Noelke, N. (2009, March). Leverage the past to build the future: Executives at a Wisconsin healthcare network figured out how to fill its leadership pipeline. *HRMagazine*, 34–36.

Northouse, P. G. (2016). *Leadership: Theory and practice* (7th ed.). Thousand Oaks, CA: SAGE Publications.

Orr, S., & Shreeve, A. (2017). *Art and design pedagogy in higher education: Knowledge, values and ambiguity in the creative curriculum*. Abingdon, UK: Routledge. doi:10.4324/9781315415130

Patel, M. P., Arora, V., Patel, M. S., Kinney, J. M., Pauly, M. V., & Asch, D. A. (2014). The role of MD and MBA training in the professional development of a physician: A survey of 30 years of graduates from the Wharton Health Care Management program. *Academic Medicine*, *89*(9), 1282–1286. doi:10.1097/ACM.0000000000000366 PMID:24979286

Patel, N., Brennan, P. J., Metlay, J., Bellini, L., Shannon, R. P., & Myers, J. S. (2015). Building the pipeline: The creation of a residency training pathway for future physician leaders in health care quality. *Academic Medicine*, *90*(2), 185–190. doi:10.1097/ACM.0000000000000546 PMID:25354070

Pearce, C. L., & Conger, J. A. (2002). All those years ago: The historical underpinnings of shared leadership. In C. L. Pearce & J. A. Conger (Eds.), *Shared leadership: Reframing the hows and whys of leadership* (pp. 1–18). Thousand Oaks, CA: SAGE.

Pearl, R., & Fogle, A. L. (2016). New physicians will need business school skills. *New England Journal of Medicine Catalyst*. Retrieved from http://catalyst.nejm.org/new-physicians-need-business-school-skills/

Prouty Project L3 Invest in Your Best. (2017). Retrieved from http://www.proutyproject.com/l3---cohort-based-leadership-development

Richman, R. C., & Magrane, D. (2011). *The Executive Leadership in Academic Medicine (ELAM) program for women - Fourteen years of academic women leaders in medicine, dentistry, and public health*. Retrieved from https://www.aamc.org/members/gfa/faculty_vitae/148588/elam.html

Rider, E. A., & Keefer, C. H. (2006). Communication skills competencies: Definitions and a teaching toolbox. *Medical Education*, *40*(7), 624–629. doi:10.1111/j.1365-2929.2006.02500.x PMID:16836534

Robles, M. M. (2012). Executive perceptions of the top 10 soft skills needed in today's workplace. *Business Communication Quarterly*, *75*(4), 453–465. doi:10.1177/1080569912460400

Rosenthal, E. (2014, December 16). *The odd math of medical tests: One scan, two prices, both high*. Retrieved from https://www.nytimes.com/2014/12/16/health/the-odd-math-of-medical-tests-one-echocardiogram-two-prices-both-high.html

Royal College of Obstetricians and Gynaecologists. (2015). *Final report of the curriculum review group 2015*. RCOG. Retrieved from https://www.rcog.org.uk/globalassets/documents/careers-and-training/curriculum/curriculum2018/final-report-of-curriculum-review-working-group.pdf

Royal College of Obstetricians and Gynaecologists. (2018). *A new core curriculum for obstetrics & gynaecology – consultation document*. RCOG. Retrieved from https://www.rcog.org.uk/en/careers-training/specialty-training-curriculum/curriculum-2018/curriculum-2018-consultation.pdf

Saint Joseph's University's course catalog 2018. (n.d.). Retrieved from https://sites.sju.edu/catalog/

Sarto, F., & Veronesi, G. (2016). Clinical leadership and hospital performance: Assessing the evidence base. *BMC Health Services Research*, *16*(S2), 169. doi:10.118612913-016-1395-5 PMID:27230873

Savage, G. T., Duncan, W. J., Knowles, K. L., Nelson, K., Rogers, D. A., & Kennedy, K. N. (2014). Interprofessional academic health center leadership development: The case of the University of Alabama at Birmingham's Healthcare Leadership Academy. *Applied Nursing Research*, *27*(2), 104–108. doi:10.1016/j.apnr.2013.07.001 PMID:23993745

Serio, C. D., & Epperley, T. (2006). *Physician leadership: A new model for a new generation*. Retrieved from www.aafp.org/fpm

Shakeshaft, C., & Nowell, I. (1984). Research on theories, concepts, and models of organizational behavior: The influence of gender. *Issues in Education*, *2*(6), 186–200.

Shanafelt, T. D., Gorringe, G., Menaker, R., Storz, K. A., Reeves, D., Buskirk, S. J., ... Swensen, S. J. (2015). Impact of organizational leadership on physician burnout and satisfaction. *Mayo Clinic Proceedings*, *90*(4), 432–440. doi:10.1016/j.mayocp.2015.01.012 PMID:25796117

Siefert, K., & Mandzuk, D. (2006). Student cohorts in teacher education: Support groups or intellectual communities? *Teachers College Record, 108*(7), 1296–1320. doi:10.1111/j.1467-9620.2006.00694.x

Smith, P. (n.d.). *Shared leadership: New ways of leading*. Retrieved from http://www.opi-inc.com/shared_leadership.htm

Solomon, R. (2013). Skinship: An exchange of material understanding between plastic surgery and pattern cutting. *Collaboration through Craft*, 114.

Sonnino, R. E. (2013). Professional development and leadership training opportunities for healthcare professionals. *American Journal of Surgery, 206*(5), 727–731. doi:10.1016/j.amjsurg.2013.07.004 PMID:24011565

Sonnino, R. E. (2016). Health care leadership development and training: Progress and pitfalls. *Journal of Healthcare Leadership, 8*, 19–29. doi:10.2147/JHL.S68068 PMID:29355187

Squires, D., & Anderson, C. (2015, October 08). *U.S. health care from a global perspective*. Retrieved from http://www.commonwealthfund.org/publications/issue-briefs/2015/oct/us-health-care-from-a-global-perspective

Sternberg, S. (2017). Hospitals, doctors decry senate move toward Obamacare Repeal. *USA Today*. Retrieved from https://www.usnews.com/news/

Stoller, J. K. (2009). Developing physician-leaders: Need and rationale. *The Journal of Health Administration Education, 25*(4), 307–328. PMID:19655634

Stoller, J. K. (2013). Commentary: Recommendations and remaining questions for health care leadership training programs. *Academic Medicine, 88*(1), 12–15. doi:10.1097/ACM.0b013e318276bff1 PMID:23267224

Stoller, J. K. (2014). Help wanted: Developing clinician leaders. *Perspectives on Medical Education, 3*(3), 233–237. doi:10.100740037-014-0119-y PMID:24865886

Stoller, J. K. (2017). The clinician as leader: Why, how, and when. *American Thoracic Society, 14*(11), 1622–1626. doi:10.1513/AnnalsATS.201706-494PS PMID:28771027

Stoller, J. K., Berkowitz, E., & Bailin, P. B. (2007). Physician management and leadership education at the Cleveland Clinic Foundation: Programme impact and experience over 14 years. *The Journal of Medical Practice Management*, *22*(4), 237–242. PMID:17425027

Storey, V. A., & Asadoorian, M. O. III. (2014, March 24). The political sense of urgency for educational leadership preparation programs to show impact data: The case of Florida. *The International Journal of Educational Leadership Preparation*, *1*(9). Retrieved from files.eric.ed.gov/fulltext/EJ1024106.pdf

Strauss, S., Soobiah, C., & Levinson, W. (2013). The impact of leadership training programmes on physicians in academic medical centers: A systematic review. *Academic Medicine*, *88*(5), 710–723. doi:10.1097/ACM.0b013e31828af493 PMID:23524921

Sunstein, C. R., & Hastie, R. (2015). *Wiser: Getting beyond groupthink to make groups smarter*. Boston, MA: Harvard Business Press.

Synergy. (n.d.). Retrieved from: www.synergyorg.com

Taleb, N. (2010). *The black swan: The impact of the highly improbable*. New York: Random House.

The Physicians Foundation. (n.d.). Retrieved from http://www.physiciansfundation.org/healthcare-grants/portfolio/physician-leadership-grants

Tuckman, B. W. (1965). Developmental sequence in small groups. *Psychological Bulletin*, *63*(6), 384–399. doi:10.1037/h0022100 PMID:14314073

U.S. News and World Report. (2013). Retrieved from http://health.usnews.com/health-news/best-hospitals/articies/2013/07/16/besthospitals-

Viswanathan, V. (2014). *The rise of the MD/MBA degree*. Retrieved from https://www.theatlantic.com/education/archive/2014/09/the-rise-of-the-mdmba-degree/380683/

Warren, O. J., & Carnall, R. (2017). Medical leadership: Why it's important, what is required, and how we develop it. *Postgraduate Medical Journal*, *87*(1023), 27–32. doi:10.1136/pgmj.2009.093807 PMID:20935344

Wenger, E. (1998). *Communities of practice: Learning, meaning, and identity*. Cambridge, UK: Cambridge University Press. doi:10.1017/CBO9780511803932

Wingfield, N., Thomas, K., & Abelson, R. (2018, January 30). *Amazon, Berkshire Hathaway and JPMorgan team up to try to disrupt health care*. Retrieved from https://www.nytimes.com/2018/01/30/technology/amazon-berkshire-hathaway-jpmorgan-health-care.html

Related References

To continue our tradition of advancing information science and technology research, we have compiled a list of recommended IGI Global readings. These references will provide additional information and guidance to further enrich your knowledge and assist you with your own research and future publications.

Abu Seman, S. A., & Ramayah, T. (2017). Are We Ready to App?: A Study on mHealth Apps, Its Future, and Trends in Malaysia Context. In J. Pelet (Ed.), *Mobile Platforms, Design, and Apps for Social Commerce* (pp. 69–83). Hershey, PA: IGI Global. doi:10.4018/978-1-5225-2469-4.ch005

Aggarwal, S., & Azad, V. (2017). A Hybrid System Based on FMM and MLP to Diagnose Heart Disease. In S. Bhattacharyya, S. De, I. Pan, & P. Dutta (Eds.), *Intelligent Multidimensional Data Clustering and Analysis* (pp. 293–325). Hershey, PA: IGI Global. doi:10.4018/978-1-5225-1776-4.ch011

Akaichi, J., & Mhadhbi, L. (2016). A Clinical Decision Support System: Ontology-Driven Approach for Effective Emergency Management. In J. Moon & M. Galea (Eds.), *Improving Health Management through Clinical Decision Support Systems* (pp. 270–294). Hershey, PA: IGI Global. doi:10.4018/978-1-4666-9432-3.ch013

Akerkar, R. (2016). Towards an Intelligent Integrated Approach for Clinical Decision Support. In A. Aggarwal (Ed.), *Managing Big Data Integration in the Public Sector* (pp. 187–205). Hershey, PA: IGI Global. doi:10.4018/978-1-4666-9649-5.ch011

Al-Busaidi, S. S. (2018). Interdisciplinary Relationships Between Medicine and Social Sciences. In M. Al-Suqri, A. Al-Kindi, S. AlKindi, & N. Saleem (Eds.), *Promoting Interdisciplinarity in Knowledge Generation and Problem Solving* (pp. 124–137). Hershey, PA: IGI Global. doi:10.4018/978-1-5225-3878-3.ch009

Al Kareh, T., & Thoumy, M. (2018). The Impact of Health Information Digitization on the Physiotherapist-Patient Relationship: A Pilot Study of the Lebanese Community. *International Journal of Healthcare Information Systems and Informatics, 13*(2), 29–53. doi:10.4018/IJHISI.2018040103

Alenzuela, R. (2017). Research, Leadership, and Resource-Sharing Initiatives: The Role of Local Library Consortia in Access to Medical Information. In S. Ram (Ed.), *Library and Information Services for Bioinformatics Education and Research* (pp. 199–211). Hershey, PA: IGI Global. doi:10.4018/978-1-5225-1871-6.ch012

Ameri, H., Alizadeh, S., & Noughabi, E. A. (2017). Application of Data Mining Techniques in Clinical Decision Making: A Literature Review and Classification. In E. Noughabi, B. Raahemi, A. Albadvi, & B. Far (Eds.), *Handbook of Research on Data Science for Effective Healthcare Practice and Administration* (pp. 257–295). Hershey, PA: IGI Global. doi:10.4018/978-1-5225-2515-8.ch012

Anand, S. (2017). Medical Image Enhancement Using Edge Information-Based Methods. In B. Singh (Ed.), *Computational Tools and Techniques for Biomedical Signal Processing* (pp. 123–148). Hershey, PA: IGI Global. doi:10.4018/978-1-5225-0660-7.ch006

Angjellari-Dajci, F., Sapienza, C., Lawless, W. F., & Kavanagh, K. (2016). Human Capital Accumulation in Medical Simulated Learning Environments: A Framework for Economic Evaluation. In M. Russ (Ed.), *Quantitative Multidisciplinary Approaches in Human Capital and Asset Management* (pp. 65–88). Hershey, PA: IGI Global. doi:10.4018/978-1-4666-9652-5.ch004

Anil, M., Ayyildiz-Tamis, D., Tasdemir, S., Sendemir-Urkmez, A., & Gulce-Iz, S. (2016). Bioinspired Materials and Biocompatibility. In M. Bououdina (Ed.), *Emerging Research on Bioinspired Materials Engineering* (pp. 294–322). Hershey, PA: IGI Global. doi:10.4018/978-1-4666-9811-6.ch011

Anton, J. L., Soriano, J. V., Martinez, M. I., & Garcia, F. B. (2018). Comprehensive E-Learning Appraisal System. In M. Khosrow-Pour, D.B.A. (Ed.), Encyclopedia of Information Science and Technology, Fourth Edition (pp. 5787-5799). Hershey, PA: IGI Global. doi:10.4018/978-1-5225-2255-3.ch503

Arabi, M. (2016). Redesigning the Organizational Structure to Reach Efficiency: The Case of Ministry of Health and Medical Education of Iran. In R. Gholipour & K. Rouzbehani (Eds.), *Social, Economic, and Political Perspectives on Public Health Policy-Making* (pp. 257–294). Hershey, PA: IGI Global. doi:10.4018/978-1-4666-9944-1.ch012

Assis-Hassid, S., Heart, T., Reychav, I., & Pliskin, J. S. (2016). Modelling Factors Affecting Patient-Doctor-Computer Communication in Primary Care. *International Journal of Reliable and Quality E-Healthcare*, *5*(1), 1–17. doi:10.4018/IJRQEH.2016010101

Atzori, B., Hoffman, H. G., Vagnoli, L., Messeri, A., & Grotto, R. L. (2018). Virtual Reality as Distraction Technique for Pain Management in Children and Adolescents. In M. Khosrow-Pour, D.B.A. (Ed.), Encyclopedia of Information Science and Technology, Fourth Edition (pp. 5955-5965). Hershey, PA: IGI Global. doi:10.4018/978-1-5225-2255-3.ch518

Audibert, M., Mathonnat, J., Pélissier, A., & Huang, X. X. (2018). The Impact of the New Rural Cooperative Medical Scheme on Township Hospitals' Utilization and Income Structure in Weifang Prefecture, China. In I. Management Association (Ed.), Health Economics and Healthcare Reform: Breakthroughs in Research and Practice (pp. 109-121). Hershey, PA: IGI Global. doi:10.4018/978-1-5225-3168-5.ch007

Ayyachamy, S. (2016). Analysis and Comparison of Developed 2D Medical Image Database Design using Registration Scheme, Retrieval Scheme, and Bag-of-Visual-Words. In N. Dey & A. Ashour (Eds.), *Classification and Clustering in Biomedical Signal Processing* (pp. 149–168). Hershey, PA: IGI Global. doi:10.4018/978-1-5225-0140-4.ch007

Babalola, A. C. (2016). Literacy and Decision Making on Health Issues among Married Women in Southwest Nigeria. In V. Wang (Ed.), *Handbook of Research on Advancing Health Education through Technology* (pp. 191–212). Hershey, PA: IGI Global. doi:10.4018/978-1-4666-9494-1.ch009

Babu, A., & Ayyappan, S. (2017). A Methodological Evaluation of Crypto-Watermarking System for Medical Images. In C. Bhatt & S. Peddoju (Eds.), *Cloud Computing Systems and Applications in Healthcare* (pp. 189–217). Hershey, PA: IGI Global. doi:10.4018/978-1-5225-1002-4.ch010

Bakke, A. (2017). Ethos in E-Health: From Informational to Interactive Websites. In M. Folk & S. Apostel (Eds.), *Establishing and Evaluating Digital Ethos and Online Credibility* (pp. 85–103). Hershey, PA: IGI Global. doi:10.4018/978-1-5225-1072-7.ch005

Bali, S. (2018). Enhancing the Reach of Health Care Through Telemedicine: Status and New Possibilities in Developing Countries. In U. Pandey & V. Indrakanti (Eds.), *Open and Distance Learning Initiatives for Sustainable Development* (pp. 339–354). Hershey, PA: IGI Global. doi:10.4018/978-1-5225-2621-6.ch019

Barrett, T. E. (2018). Essentials for Education and Training for Tomorrow's Physicians. In C. Smith (Ed.), *Exploring the Pressures of Medical Education From a Mental Health and Wellness Perspective* (pp. 230–252). Hershey, PA: IGI Global. doi:10.4018/978-1-5225-2811-1.ch010

Barrett, T. J. (2016). Knowledge in Action: Fostering Health Education through Technology. In V. Wang (Ed.), *Handbook of Research on Advancing Health Education through Technology* (pp. 39–62). Hershey, PA: IGI Global. doi:10.4018/978-1-4666-9494-1.ch003

Berrahal, S., & Boudriga, N. (2017). The Risks of Wearable Technologies to Individuals and Organizations. In A. Marrington, D. Kerr, & J. Gammack (Eds.), *Managing Security Issues and the Hidden Dangers of Wearable Technologies* (pp. 18–46). Hershey, PA: IGI Global. doi:10.4018/978-1-5225-1016-1.ch002

Bhagat, A. P., & Atique, M. (2016). Medical Image Mining Using Fuzzy Connectedness Image Segmentation: Efficient Retrieval of Patients' Stored Images. In W. Karâa & N. Dey (Eds.), *Biomedical Image Analysis and Mining Techniques for Improved Health Outcomes* (pp. 184–209). Hershey, PA: IGI Global. doi:10.4018/978-1-4666-8811-7.ch009

Bhargava, P. (2018). Blended Learning: An Effective Application to Clinical Teaching. In S. Tang & C. Lim (Eds.), *Preparing the Next Generation of Teachers for 21st Century Education* (pp. 302–320). Hershey, PA: IGI Global. doi:10.4018/978-1-5225-4080-9.ch018

Binh, N. T., & Tuyet, V. T. (2016). The Combination of Adaptive Filters to Improve the Quality of Medical Images in New Wavelet Domain. In N. Dey & A. Ashour (Eds.), *Classification and Clustering in Biomedical Signal Processing* (pp. 46–76). Hershey, PA: IGI Global. doi:10.4018/978-1-5225-0140-4.ch003

Bird, J. L. (2017). Writing Healing Narratives. In V. Bryan & J. Bird (Eds.), *Healthcare Community Synergism between Patients, Practitioners, and Researchers* (pp. 1–28). Hershey, PA: IGI Global. doi:10.4018/978-1-5225-0640-9.ch001

Bottrighi, A., Leonardi, G., Piovesan, L., & Terenziani, P. (2016). Knowledge-Based Support to the Treatment of Exceptions in Computer Interpretable Clinical Guidelines. *International Journal of Knowledge-Based Organizations, 6*(3), 1–27. doi:10.4018/IJKBO.2016070101

Bougoulias, K., Kouris, I., Prasinos, M., Giokas, K., & Koutsouris, D. (2017). Ob/Gyn EMR Software: A Solution for Obstetricians and Gynecologists. In A. Moumtzoglou (Ed.), *Design, Development, and Integration of Reliable Electronic Healthcare Platforms* (pp. 101–111). Hershey, PA: IGI Global. doi:10.4018/978-1-5225-1724-5.ch006

Bouslimi, R., Ayadi, M. G., & Akaichi, J. (2018). Medical Image Retrieval in Healthcare Social Networks. *International Journal of Healthcare Information Systems and Informatics, 13*(2), 13–28. doi:10.4018/IJHISI.2018040102

Bouzaabia, O., Bouzaabia, R., & Mejri, K. (2017). Role of Internet in the Development of Medical Tourism Service in Tunisia. In A. Capatina & E. Rancati (Eds.), *Key Challenges and Opportunities in Web Entrepreneurship* (pp. 211–241). Hershey, PA: IGI Global. doi:10.4018/978-1-5225-2466-3.ch009

Briz-Ponce, L., Juanes-Méndez, J. A., & García-Peñalvo, F. J. (2016). The Role of Gender in Technology Acceptance for Medical Education. In M. Cruz-Cunha, I. Miranda, R. Martinho, & R. Rijo (Eds.), *Encyclopedia of E-Health and Telemedicine* (pp. 1013–1027). Hershey, PA: IGI Global. doi:10.4018/978-1-4666-9978-6.ch079

Briz-Ponce, L., Juanes-Méndez, J. A., & García-Peñalvo, F. J. (2016). A Research Contribution to the Analysis of Mobile Devices in Higher Education from Medical Students' Point of View. In L. Briz-Ponce, J. Juanes-Méndez, & F. García-Peñalvo (Eds.), *Handbook of Research on Mobile Devices and Applications in Higher Education Settings* (pp. 196–221). Hershey, PA: IGI Global. doi:10.4018/978-1-5225-0256-2.ch009

Brown-Jackson, K. L. (2018). Telemedicine and Telehealth: Academics Engaging the Community in a Call to Action. In S. Burton (Ed.), *Engaged Scholarship and Civic Responsibility in Higher Education* (pp. 166–193). Hershey, PA: IGI Global. doi:10.4018/978-1-5225-3649-9.ch008

Bwalya, K. J. (2017). Next Wave of Tele-Medicine: Virtual Presence of Medical Personnel. In K. Moahi, K. Bwalya, & P. Sebina (Eds.), *Health Information Systems and the Advancement of Medical Practice in Developing Countries* (pp. 168–180). Hershey, PA: IGI Global. doi:10.4018/978-1-5225-2262-1.ch010

Carlton, E. L., Holsinger, J. W. Jr, & Anunobi, N. (2016). Physician Engagement with Health Information Technology: Implications for Practice and Professionalism. *International Journal of Computers in Clinical Practice, 1*(2), 51–73. doi:10.4018/IJCCP.2016070103

Castillo-Page, L., Eliason, J., Conrad, S. S., & Nivet, M. A. (2016). Diversity in Undergraduate Medical Education: An Examination of Organizational Culture and Climate in Medical Schools. In C. Scott & J. Sims (Eds.), *Developing Workforce Diversity Programs, Curriculum, and Degrees in Higher Education* (pp. 304–326). Hershey, PA: IGI Global. doi:10.4018/978-1-5225-0209-8.ch016

Cebeci, H. I., & Hiziroglu, A. (2016). Review of Business Intelligence and Intelligent Systems in Healthcare Domain. In N. Celebi (Ed.), *Intelligent Techniques for Data Analysis in Diverse Settings* (pp. 192–206). Hershey, PA: IGI Global. doi:10.4018/978-1-5225-0075-9.ch009

Celik, G. (2018). Determining Headache Diseases With Genetic Algorithm. In U. Kose, G. Guraksin, & O. Deperlioglu (Eds.), *Nature-Inspired Intelligent Techniques for Solving Biomedical Engineering Problems* (pp. 249–262). Hershey, PA: IGI Global. doi:10.4018/978-1-5225-4769-3.ch012

Chakraborty, C., Gupta, B., & Ghosh, S. K. (2016). Mobile Telemedicine Systems for Remote Patient's Chronic Wound Monitoring. In A. Moumtzoglou (Ed.), *M-Health Innovations for Patient-Centered Care* (pp. 213–239). Hershey, PA: IGI Global. doi:10.4018/978-1-4666-9861-1.ch011

Chakraborty, S., Chatterjee, S., Ashour, A. S., Mali, K., & Dey, N. (2018). Intelligent Computing in Medical Imaging: A Study. In N. Dey (Ed.), *Advancements in Applied Metaheuristic Computing* (pp. 143–163). Hershey, PA: IGI Global. doi:10.4018/978-1-5225-4151-6.ch006

Chavez, A., & Kovarik, C. (2017). Open Source Technology for Medical Practice in Developing Countries. In K. Moahi, K. Bwalya, & P. Sebina (Eds.), *Health Information Systems and the Advancement of Medical Practice in Developing Countries* (pp. 33–59). Hershey, PA: IGI Global. doi:10.4018/978-1-5225-2262-1.ch003

Chen, E. T. (2016). Examining the Influence of Information Technology on Modern Health Care. In P. Manolitzas, E. Grigoroudis, N. Matsatsinis, & D. Yannacopoulos (Eds.), *Effective Methods for Modern Healthcare Service Quality and Evaluation* (pp. 110–136). Hershey, PA: IGI Global. doi:10.4018/978-1-4666-9961-8.ch006

Chin, S. (2016). Surviving Sandy: Recovering Collections after a Natural Disaster. In E. Decker & J. Townes (Eds.), *Handbook of Research on Disaster Management and Contingency Planning in Modern Libraries* (pp. 366–388). Hershey, PA: IGI Global. doi:10.4018/978-1-4666-8624-3.ch016

Chojnacki, M., & Wójcik, A. (2016). Security and the Role of New Technologies and Innovation in Medical Ethics. In A. Rosiek & K. Leksowski (Eds.), *Organizational Culture and Ethics in Modern Medicine* (pp. 52–77). Hershey, PA: IGI Global. doi:10.4018/978-1-4666-9658-7.ch003

Cılız, N., Yıldırım, H., & Temizel, Ş. (2016). Structure Development for Effective Medical Waste and Hazardous Waste Management System. In U. Akkucuk (Ed.), *Handbook of Research on Waste Management Techniques for Sustainability* (pp. 303–327). Hershey, PA: IGI Global. doi:10.4018/978-1-4666-9723-2.ch016

Ciufudean, C. (2018). Innovative Formalism for Biological Data Analysis. In M. Khosrow-Pour, D.B.A. (Ed.), Encyclopedia of Information Science and Technology, Fourth Edition (pp. 1814-1824). Hershey, PA: IGI Global. doi:10.4018/978-1-5225-2255-3.ch158

Ciufudean, C., & Ciufudean, O. (2016). Tele-Monitoring for Medical Diagnosis Availability. In M. Cruz-Cunha, I. Miranda, R. Martinho, & R. Rijo (Eds.), *Encyclopedia of E-Health and Telemedicine* (pp. 401–411). Hershey, PA: IGI Global. doi:10.4018/978-1-4666-9978-6.ch032

Colaguori, R., & Danesi, M. (2017). Medical Semiotics: A Revisitation and an Exhortation. *International Journal of Semiotics and Visual Rhetoric, 1*(1), 11–18. doi:10.4018/IJSVR.2017010102

Cole, A. W., & Salek, T. A. (2017). Adopting a Parasocial Connection to Overcome Professional Kakoethos in Online Health Information. In M. Folk & S. Apostel (Eds.), *Establishing and Evaluating Digital Ethos and Online Credibility* (pp. 104–120). Hershey, PA: IGI Global. doi:10.4018/978-1-5225-1072-7.ch006

Contreras, E. C., & Puente, G. J. (2016). How to Identify Rheumatic Diseases by General Physicians. In T. Gasmelseid (Ed.), *Advancing Pharmaceutical Processes and Tools for Improved Health Outcomes* (pp. 136–166). Hershey, PA: IGI Global. doi:10.4018/978-1-5225-0248-7.ch006

D'Andrea, A., Ferri, F., & Grifoni, P. (2016). RFID Technologies in Healthcare Setting: Applications and Future Perspectives. *International Journal of Computers in Clinical Practice, 1*(1), 15–27. doi:10.4018/IJCCP.2016010102

Damianakis, A., Kallonis, P., Loudos, G., Tsatsos, D., & Tsoukalis, A. (2016). Exploiting 3D Medical Equipment Simulations to Support Biomedical Engineering Academic Courses: Design Methodology and Implementation in a Small Scale National Project. In B. Khan (Ed.), *Revolutionizing Modern Education through Meaningful E-Learning Implementation* (pp. 277–295). Hershey, PA: IGI Global. doi:10.4018/978-1-5225-0466-5.ch015

Demiroz, E. (2016). Principles of Instructional Design for E-Learning and Online Learning Practices: Implications for Medical Education. In V. Wang (Ed.), *Handbook of Research on Advancing Health Education through Technology* (pp. 419–451). Hershey, PA: IGI Global. doi:10.4018/978-1-4666-9494-1.ch018

Deperlioglu, O. (2018). Intelligent Techniques Inspired by Nature and Used in Biomedical Engineering. In U. Kose, G. Guraksin, & O. Deperlioglu (Eds.), *Nature-Inspired Intelligent Techniques for Solving Biomedical Engineering Problems* (pp. 51–77). Hershey, PA: IGI Global. doi:10.4018/978-1-5225-4769-3.ch003

Dey, N., & Ashour, A. S. (2018). Meta-Heuristic Algorithms in Medical Image Segmentation: A Review. In N. Dey (Ed.), *Advancements in Applied Metaheuristic Computing* (pp. 185–203). Hershey, PA: IGI Global. doi:10.4018/978-1-5225-4151-6.ch008

Dey, N., Ashour, A. S., & Althoupety, A. S. (2017). Thermal Imaging in Medical Science. In V. Santhi (Ed.), *Recent Advances in Applied Thermal Imaging for Industrial Applications* (pp. 87–117). Hershey, PA: IGI Global. doi:10.4018/978-1-5225-2423-6.ch004

Di Virgilio, F., Camillo, A. A., & Camillo, I. C. (2017). The Impact of Social Network on Italian Users' Behavioural Intention for the Choice of a Medical Tourist Destination. *International Journal of Tourism and Hospitality Management in the Digital Age, 1*(1), 36–49. doi:10.4018/IJTHMDA.2017010103

Dias, C. M., Ribeiro, A. G., & Furtado, S. F. (2016). An Overview about the Use of Healthcare Applications on Mobile Devices. In M. Cruz-Cunha, I. Miranda, R. Martinho, & R. Rijo (Eds.), *Encyclopedia of E-Health and Telemedicine* (pp. 285–298). Hershey, PA: IGI Global. doi:10.4018/978-1-4666-9978-6.ch024

Dogra, A. K., & Dogra, P. (2017). The Medical Tourism Industry in the BRIC Nations: An Indian Analysis. In M. Dhiman (Ed.), *Opportunities and Challenges for Tourism and Hospitality in the BRIC Nations* (pp. 320–336). Hershey, PA: IGI Global. doi:10.4018/978-1-5225-0708-6.ch020

Drowos, J. L., & Wood, S. K. (2017). Preparing Future Physicians to Adapt to the Changing Health Care System: Promoting Humanism through Curricular Design. In V. Bryan & J. Bird (Eds.), *Healthcare Community Synergism between Patients, Practitioners, and Researchers* (pp. 106–125). Hershey, PA: IGI Global. doi:10.4018/978-1-5225-0640-9.ch006

Dulam, K. (2017). Medical Patents and Impact on Availability and Affordability of Essential Medicines in India. In R. Aggarwal & R. Kaur (Eds.), *Patent Law and Intellectual Property in the Medical Field* (pp. 41–57). Hershey, PA: IGI Global. doi:10.4018/978-1-5225-2414-4.ch003

Dutta, P. (2017). Decision Making in Medical Diagnosis via Distance Measures on Interval Valued Fuzzy Sets. *International Journal of System Dynamics Applications*, *6*(4), 63–83. doi:10.4018/IJSDA.2017100104

Edoh, T. O., Pawar, P. A., Brügge, B., & Teege, G. (2016). A Multidisciplinary Remote Healthcare Delivery System to Increase Health Care Access, Pathology Screening, and Treatment in Developing Countries: The Case of Benin. *International Journal of Healthcare Information Systems and Informatics*, *11*(4), 1–31. doi:10.4018/IJHISI.2016100101

El Guemhioui, K., & Demurjian, S. A. (2017). Semantic Reconciliation of Electronic Health Records Using Semantic Web Technologies. *International Journal of Information Technology and Web Engineering*, *12*(2), 26–48. doi:10.4018/IJITWE.2017040102

Ellouze, N., Rekhis, S., & Boudriga, N. (2016). Forensic Investigation of Digital Crimes in Healthcare Applications. In O. Isafiade & A. Bagula (Eds.), *Data Mining Trends and Applications in Criminal Science and Investigations* (pp. 169–210). Hershey, PA: IGI Global. doi:10.4018/978-1-5225-0463-4.ch007

Eneanya, A. N. (2016). Health Policy Implementation and Its Barriers: The Case Study of US Health System. In R. Gholipour & K. Rouzbehani (Eds.), *Social, Economic, and Political Perspectives on Public Health Policy-Making* (pp. 42–63). Hershey, PA: IGI Global. doi:10.4018/978-1-4666-9944-1.ch003

Entico, G. J. (2016). Knowledge Management and the Medical Health Librarians: A Perception Study. In J. Yap, M. Perez, M. Ayson, & G. Entico (Eds.), *Special Library Administration, Standardization and Technological Integration* (pp. 52–77). Hershey, PA: IGI Global. doi:10.4018/978-1-4666-9542-9.ch003

Ferradji, M. A., & Zidani, A. (2016). Collaborative Environment for Remote Clinical Reasoning Learning. *International Journal of E-Health and Medical Communications*, *7*(4), 62–81. doi:10.4018/IJEHMC.2016100104

Fisher, J. (2018). Sociological Perspectives on Improving Medical Diagnosis Emphasizing CAD. In M. Khosrow-Pour, D.B.A. (Ed.), Encyclopedia of Information Science and Technology, Fourth Edition (pp. 1017-1024). Hershey, PA: IGI Global. doi:10.4018/978-1-5225-2255-3.ch088

Flores, C. D., Respício, A., Coelho, H., Bez, M. R., & Fonseca, J. M. (2016). Simulation for Medical Training. In M. Cruz-Cunha, I. Miranda, R. Martinho, & R. Rijo (Eds.), *Encyclopedia of E-Health and Telemedicine* (pp. 827–842). Hershey, PA: IGI Global. doi:10.4018/978-1-4666-9978-6.ch064

Frank, E. M. (2018). Healthcare Education: Integrating Simulation Technologies. In V. Bryan, A. Musgrove, & J. Powers (Eds.), *Handbook of Research on Human Development in the Digital Age* (pp. 163–182). Hershey, PA: IGI Global. doi:10.4018/978-1-5225-2838-8.ch008

Garner, G. (2018). Foundations for Yoga Practice in Rehabilitation. In S. Telles & N. Singh (Eds.), *Research-Based Perspectives on the Psychophysiology of Yoga* (pp. 263–307). Hershey, PA: IGI Global. doi:10.4018/978-1-5225-2788-6.ch015

Gasmelseid, T. M. (2016). Improving Pharmaceutical Care through the Use of Intelligent Pharmacoinformatics. In T. Gasmelseid (Ed.), *Advancing Pharmaceutical Processes and Tools for Improved Health Outcomes* (pp. 167–188). Hershey, PA: IGI Global. doi:10.4018/978-1-5225-0248-7.ch007

Gavurová, B., Kováč, V., & Šoltés, M. (2018). Medical Equipment and Economic Determinants of Its Structure and Regulation in the Slovak Republic. In M. Khosrow-Pour, D.B.A. (Ed.), Encyclopedia of Information Science and Technology, Fourth Edition (pp. 5841-5852). Hershey, PA: IGI Global. doi:10.4018/978-1-5225-2255-3.ch508

Ge, X., Wang, Q., Huang, K., Law, V., & Thomas, D. C. (2017). Designing Simulated Learning Environments and Facilitating Authentic Learning Experiences in Medical Education. In J. Stefaniak (Ed.), *Advancing Medical Education Through Strategic Instructional Design* (pp. 77–100). Hershey, PA: IGI Global. doi:10.4018/978-1-5225-2098-6.ch004

Gewald, H., & Gewald, C. (2018). Inhibitors of Physicians' Use of Mandatory Hospital Information Systems (HIS). *International Journal of Healthcare Information Systems and Informatics*, *13*(1), 29–44. doi:10.4018/IJHISI.2018010103

Ghosh, D., & Dinda, S. (2017). Health Infrastructure and Economic Development in India. In R. Das (Ed.), *Social, Health, and Environmental Infrastructures for Economic Growth* (pp. 99–119). Hershey, PA: IGI Global. doi:10.4018/978-1-5225-2364-2.ch006

Ghosh, K., & Sen, K. C. (2017). The Potential of Crowdsourcing in the Health Care Industry. In N. Wickramasinghe (Ed.), *Handbook of Research on Healthcare Administration and Management* (pp. 418–427). Hershey, PA: IGI Global. doi:10.4018/978-1-5225-0920-2.ch024

Ghrab, S., & Saad, I. (2016). Identifying Crucial Know-How and Knowing-That for Medical Decision Support. *International Journal of Decision Support System Technology*, *8*(4), 14–33. doi:10.4018/IJDSST.2016100102

Giokas, K., Tsirmpas, C., Anastasiou, A., Iliopoulou, D., Costarides, V., & Koutsouris, D. (2016). Contemporary Heart Failure Treatment Based on Improved Knowledge and Personalized Care of Comorbidities. In D. Fotiadis (Ed.), *Handbook of Research on Trends in the Diagnosis and Treatment of Chronic Conditions* (pp. 301–314). Hershey, PA: IGI Global. doi:10.4018/978-1-4666-8828-5.ch014

Gopalan, V., Chan, E., & Ho, D. T. (2018). Deliberate Self-Harm and Suicide Ideology in Medical Students. In C. Smith (Ed.), *Exploring the Pressures of Medical Education From a Mental Health and Wellness Perspective* (pp. 122–143). Hershey, PA: IGI Global. doi:10.4018/978-1-5225-2811-1.ch005

Goswami, S., Dey, U., Roy, P., Ashour, A., & Dey, N. (2017). Medical Video Processing: Concept and Applications. In N. Dey, A. Ashour, & P. Patra (Eds.), *Feature Detectors and Motion Detection in Video Processing* (pp. 1–17). Hershey, PA: IGI Global. doi:10.4018/978-1-5225-1025-3.ch001

Goswami, S., Mahanta, K., Goswami, S., Jigdung, T., & Devi, T. P. (2018). Ageing and Cancer: The Epigenetic Basis, Alternative Treatment, and Care. In B. Prasad & S. Akbar (Eds.), *Handbook of Research on Geriatric Health, Treatment, and Care* (pp. 206–235). Hershey, PA: IGI Global. doi:10.4018/978-1-5225-3480-8.ch012

Gouva, M. I. (2017). The Psychological Impact of Medical Error on Patients, Family Members, and Health Professionals. In M. Riga (Ed.), *Impact of Medical Errors and Malpractice on Health Economics, Quality, and Patient Safety* (pp. 171–196). Hershey, PA: IGI Global. doi:10.4018/978-1-5225-2337-6.ch007

Gürcü, M., & Tengilimoğlu, D. (2017). Health Tourism-Based Destination Marketing. In A. Bayraktar & C. Uslay (Eds.), *Strategic Place Branding Methodologies and Theory for Tourist Attraction* (pp. 308–331). Hershey, PA: IGI Global. doi:10.4018/978-1-5225-0579-2.ch015

Gürsel, G. (2016). Mobility in Healthcare: M-Health. In A. Panagopoulos (Ed.), *Handbook of Research on Next Generation Mobile Communication Systems* (pp. 485–511). Hershey, PA: IGI Global. doi:10.4018/978-1-4666-8732-5.ch019

Gürsel, G. (2017). For Better Healthcare Mining Health Data. In S. Bhattacharyya, S. De, I. Pan, & P. Dutta (Eds.), *Intelligent Multidimensional Data Clustering and Analysis* (pp. 135–158). Hershey, PA: IGI Global. doi:10.4018/978-1-5225-1776-4.ch006

Guzman-Lugo, G., Lopez-Martinez, M., Lopez-Ramirez, B., & Avila-Vazquez, D. (2016). City-Driven Approach to Determine Health Services Based on Current User Location and Collaborative Information. *International Journal of Knowledge Society Research*, *7*(1), 53–62. doi:10.4018/IJKSR.2016010104

Gyaase, P. O., Darko-Lartey, R., William, H., & Borkloe, F. (2017). Towards an Integrated Electronic Medical Records System for Quality Healthcare in Ghana: An Exploratory Factor Analysis. *International Journal of Computers in Clinical Practice*, *2*(2), 38–55. doi:10.4018/IJCCP.2017070103

Handayani, P. W., Sandhyaduhita, P. I., Hidayanto, A. N., Pinem, A. A., Fajrina, H. R., Junus, K. M., ... Ayuningtyas, D. (2016). Integrated Hospital Information System Architecture Design in Indonesia. In T. Iyamu & A. Tatnall (Eds.), *Maximizing Healthcare Delivery and Management through Technology Integration* (pp. 207–236). Hershey, PA: IGI Global. doi:10.4018/978-1-4666-9446-0.ch013

Hanel, P. (2017). Is China Catching Up?: Health-Related Applications of Biotechnology. In T. Bas & J. Zhao (Eds.), *Comparative Approaches to Biotechnology Development and Use in Developed and Emerging Nations* (pp. 465–520). Hershey, PA: IGI Global. doi:10.4018/978-1-5225-1040-6.ch016

Harmsen, C. A., & Royle, R. N. (2016). St. Stephen's Hospital Hervey Bay: Study of Developing a Digital Hospital. In J. Moon & M. Galea (Eds.), *Improving Health Management through Clinical Decision Support Systems* (pp. 127–153). Hershey, PA: IGI Global. doi:10.4018/978-1-4666-9432-3.ch006

Harp, D., Shim, R. S., Johnson, J., Harp, J. A., Wilcox, W. C., & Wilcox, J. K. (2016). Race and Gender Inequalities in Medicine and Biomedical Research. In U. Thomas & J. Drake (Eds.), *Critical Research on Sexism and Racism in STEM Fields* (pp. 115–134). Hershey, PA: IGI Global. doi:10.4018/978-1-5225-0174-9.ch006

Hartman, A., & Brown, S. (2017). Synergism through Therapeutic Visual Arts. In V. Bryan & J. Bird (Eds.), *Healthcare Community Synergism between Patients, Practitioners, and Researchers* (pp. 29–48). Hershey, PA: IGI Global. doi:10.4018/978-1-5225-0640-9.ch002

Hazra, J., Chowdhury, A. R., & Dutta, P. (2016). Cluster Based Medical Image Registration Using Optimized Neural Network. In S. Bhattacharyya, P. Banerjee, D. Majumdar, & P. Dutta (Eds.), *Handbook of Research on Advanced Hybrid Intelligent Techniques and Applications* (pp. 551–581). Hershey, PA: IGI Global. doi:10.4018/978-1-4666-9474-3.ch018

Hung, S., Huang, W., Yen, D. C., Chang, S., & Lu, C. (2016). Effect of Information Service Competence and Contextual Factors on the Effectiveness of Strategic Information Systems Planning in Hospitals. *Journal of Global Information Management, 24*(1), 14–36. doi:10.4018/JGIM.2016010102

Iltchev, P., Śliwczyński, A., Szynkiewicz, P., & Marczak, M. (2016). Mobile Health Applications Assisting Patients with Chronic Diseases: Examples from Asthma Care. In A. Moumtzoglou (Ed.), *M-Health Innovations for Patient-Centered Care* (pp. 170–196). Hershey, PA: IGI Global. doi:10.4018/978-1-4666-9861-1.ch009

Iqbal, S., Ahmad, S., & Willis, I. (2017). Influencing Factors for Adopting Technology Enhanced Learning in the Medical Schools of Punjab, Pakistan. *International Journal of Information and Communication Technology Education, 13*(3), 27–39. doi:10.4018/IJICTE.2017070103

Jagan, J., Dalkiliç, Y., & Samui, P. (2016). Utilization of SVM, LSSVM and GP for Predicting the Medical Waste Generation. In G. Hua (Ed.), *Smart Cities as a Solution for Reducing Urban Waste and Pollution* (pp. 224–251). Hershey, PA: IGI Global. doi:10.4018/978-1-5225-0302-6.ch008

Jagiello, K., Sosnowska, A., Mikolajczyk, A., & Puzyn, T. (2017). Nanomaterials in Medical Devices: Regulations' Review and Future Perspectives. *Journal of Nanotoxicology and Nanomedicine, 2*(2), 1–11. doi:10.4018/JNN.2017070101

Jena, T. K. (2018). Skill Training Process in Medicine Through Distance Mode. In U. Pandey & V. Indrakanti (Eds.), *Optimizing Open and Distance Learning in Higher Education Institutions* (pp. 228–243). Hershey, PA: IGI Global. doi:10.4018/978-1-5225-2624-7.ch010

Jesus, Â., & Gomes, M. J. (2016). Web 2.0 Tools in Biomedical and Pharmaceutical Education: Updated Review and Commentary. In T. Gasmelseid (Ed.), *Advancing Pharmaceutical Processes and Tools for Improved Health Outcomes* (pp. 52–78). Hershey, PA: IGI Global. doi:10.4018/978-1-5225-0248-7.ch003

Joseph, V., & Miller, J. M. (2018). Medical Students' Perceived Stigma in Seeking Care: A Cultural Perspective. In C. Smith (Ed.), *Exploring the Pressures of Medical Education From a Mental Health and Wellness Perspective* (pp. 44–67). Hershey, PA: IGI Global. doi:10.4018/978-1-5225-2811-1.ch002

Joyce, B. L., & Swanberg, S. M. (2017). Using Backward Design for Competency-Based Undergraduate Medical Education. In J. Stefaniak (Ed.), *Advancing Medical Education Through Strategic Instructional Design* (pp. 53–76). Hershey, PA: IGI Global. doi:10.4018/978-1-5225-2098-6.ch003

Kaljo, K., & Jacques, L. (2018). Flipping the Medical School Classroom. In M. Khosrow-Pour, D.B.A. (Ed.), Encyclopedia of Information Science and Technology, Fourth Edition (pp. 5800-5809). Hershey, PA: IGI Global. doi:10.4018/978-1-5225-2255-3.ch504

Karon, R. (2016). Utilisation of Health Information Systems for Service Delivery in the Namibian Environment. In T. Iyamu & A. Tatnall (Eds.), *Maximizing Healthcare Delivery and Management through Technology Integration* (pp. 169–183). Hershey, PA: IGI Global. doi:10.4018/978-1-4666-9446-0.ch011

Kasina, H., Bahubalendruni, M. V., & Botcha, R. (2017). Robots in Medicine: Past, Present and Future. *International Journal of Manufacturing, Materials, and Mechanical Engineering*, *7*(4), 44–64. doi:10.4018/IJMMME.2017100104

Katehakis, D. G. (2018). Electronic Medical Record Implementation Challenges for the National Health System in Greece. *International Journal of Reliable and Quality E-Healthcare*, *7*(1), 16–30. doi:10.4018/IJRQEH.2018010102

Katz, A., & Shtub, A. (2016). Design and Build a Wizard of Oz (WOZ) Telemedicine Simulator Platform. In M. Cruz-Cunha, I. Miranda, R. Martinho, & R. Rijo (Eds.), *Encyclopedia of E-Health and Telemedicine* (pp. 128–141). Hershey, PA: IGI Global. doi:10.4018/978-1-4666-9978-6.ch011

Kaur, P. D., & Sharma, P. (2017). Success Dimensions of ICTs in Healthcare. In B. Singh (Ed.), *Computational Tools and Techniques for Biomedical Signal Processing* (pp. 149–173). Hershey, PA: IGI Global. doi:10.4018/978-1-5225-0660-7.ch007

Kaushik, P. (2018). Comorbidity of Medical and Psychiatric Disorders in Geriatric Population: Treatment and Care. In B. Prasad & S. Akbar (Eds.), *Handbook of Research on Geriatric Health, Treatment, and Care* (pp. 448–474). Hershey, PA: IGI Global. doi:10.4018/978-1-5225-3480-8.ch025

Khachane, M. Y. (2017). Organ-Based Medical Image Classification Using Support Vector Machine. *International Journal of Synthetic Emotions*, *8*(1), 18–30. doi:10.4018/IJSE.2017010102

Kirci, P. (2018). Intelligent Techniques for Analysis of Big Data About Healthcare and Medical Records. In N. Shah & M. Mittal (Eds.), *Handbook of Research on Promoting Business Process Improvement Through Inventory Control Techniques* (pp. 559–582). Hershey, PA: IGI Global. doi:10.4018/978-1-5225-3232-3.ch029

Kldiashvili, E. (2016). Cloud Computing as the Useful Resource for Application of the Medical Information System for Quality Assurance Purposes. *International Journal of Computers in Clinical Practice*, *1*(2), 1–23. doi:10.4018/IJCCP.2016070101

Kldiashvili, E. (2018). Cloud Approach for the Medical Information System: MIS on Cloud. In M. Khosrow-Pour (Ed.), *Incorporating Nature-Inspired Paradigms in Computational Applications* (pp. 238–261). Hershey, PA: IGI Global. doi:10.4018/978-1-5225-5020-4.ch008

Kldiashvili, E., Burduli, A., Ghortlishvili, G., & Sheklashvili, I. (2016). Georgian Experience in Telecytology. In M. Cruz-Cunha, I. Miranda, R. Martinho, & R. Rijo (Eds.), *Encyclopedia of E-Health and Telemedicine* (pp. 62–71). Hershey, PA: IGI Global. doi:10.4018/978-1-4666-9978-6.ch006

Ko, H., Mesicek, L., Choi, J., Choi, J., & Hwang, S. (2018). A Study on Secure Contents Strategies for Applications With DRM on Cloud Computing. *International Journal of Cloud Applications and Computing*, *8*(1), 143–153. doi:10.4018/IJCAC.2018010107

Komendziński, T., Dreszer-Drogorób, J., Mikołajewska, E., Mikołajewski, D., & Bałaj, B. (2016). Interdisciplinary Education for Research and Everyday Clinical Practice: Lessons Learned from InteRDoCTor Project. In A. Rosiek & K. Leksowski (Eds.), *Organizational Culture and Ethics in Modern Medicine* (pp. 78–110). Hershey, PA: IGI Global. doi:10.4018/978-1-4666-9658-7.ch004

Komendziński, T., Mikołajewska, E., & Mikołajewski, D. (2018). Cross-Cultural Decision-Making in Healthcare: Theory and Practical Application in Real Clinical Conditions. In A. Rosiek-Kryszewska & K. Leksowski (Eds.), *Healthcare Administration for Patient Safety and Engagement* (pp. 276–298). Hershey, PA: IGI Global. doi:10.4018/978-1-5225-3946-9.ch015

Konecny, L. T. (2018). Medical School Wellness Initiatives. In C. Smith (Ed.), *Exploring the Pressures of Medical Education From a Mental Health and Wellness Perspective* (pp. 209–228). Hershey, PA: IGI Global. doi:10.4018/978-1-5225-2811-1.ch009

Konieczna, A., & Słomkowski, P. (2016). Confrontation of Human Rights in Daily Clinical Situations. In A. Rosiek & K. Leksowski (Eds.), *Organizational Culture and Ethics in Modern Medicine* (pp. 255–281). Hershey, PA: IGI Global. doi:10.4018/978-1-4666-9658-7.ch011

Kromrei, H., Solomonson, W. L., & Juzych, M. S. (2017). Teaching Residents How to Teach. In J. Stefaniak (Ed.), *Advancing Medical Education Through Strategic Instructional Design* (pp. 164–185). Hershey, PA: IGI Global. doi:10.4018/978-1-5225-2098-6.ch008

Kulkarni, S., Savyanavar, A., Kulkarni, P., Stranieri, A., & Ghorpade, V. (2018). Framework for Integration of Medical Image and Text-Based Report Retrieval to Support Radiological Diagnosis. In M. Kolekar & V. Kumar (Eds.), *Biomedical Signal and Image Processing in Patient Care* (pp. 86–122). Hershey, PA: IGI Global. doi:10.4018/978-1-5225-2829-6.ch006

Kumar, A., & Sarkar, B. K. (2018). Performance Analysis of Nature-Inspired Algorithms-Based Bayesian Prediction Models for Medical Data Sets. In U. Singh, A. Tiwari, & R. Singh (Eds.), *Soft-Computing-Based Nonlinear Control Systems Design* (pp. 134–155). Hershey, PA: IGI Global. doi:10.4018/978-1-5225-3531-7.ch007

Kurtz, R. S. (2016). Fortitude: A Study of African Americans in Surgery in New York City. In U. Thomas & J. Drake (Eds.), *Critical Research on Sexism and Racism in STEM Fields* (pp. 153–169). Hershey, PA: IGI Global. doi:10.4018/978-1-5225-0174-9.ch009

Labbadi, W., & Akaichi, J. (2017). Efficient Algorithm for Answering Fuzzy Medical Requests in Pervasive Healthcare Information Systems. *International Journal of Healthcare Information Systems and Informatics, 12*(2), 46–64. doi:10.4018/IJHISI.2017040103

Lagumdzija, A., & Swing, V. K. (2017). Health, Digitalization, and Individual Empowerment. In F. Topor (Ed.), *Handbook of Research on Individualism and Identity in the Globalized Digital Age* (pp. 380–402). Hershey, PA: IGI Global. doi:10.4018/978-1-5225-0522-8.ch017

Lamey, T. W., & Davidson-Shivers, G. V. (2017). Instructional Strategies and Sequencing. In J. Stefaniak (Ed.), *Advancing Medical Education Through Strategic Instructional Design* (pp. 30–52). Hershey, PA: IGI Global. doi:10.4018/978-1-5225-2098-6.ch002

Leon, G. (2017). The Role of Forensic Medicine in Medical Errors. In M. Riga (Ed.), *Impact of Medical Errors and Malpractice on Health Economics, Quality, and Patient Safety* (pp. 144–170). Hershey, PA: IGI Global. doi:10.4018/978-1-5225-2337-6.ch006

Lidia, B., Federica, G., & Maria, V. E. (2016). The Patient-Centered Medicine as the Theoretical Framework for Patient Engagement. In G. Graffigna (Ed.), *Promoting Patient Engagement and Participation for Effective Healthcare Reform* (pp. 25–39). Hershey, PA: IGI Global. doi:10.4018/978-1-4666-9992-2.ch002

Love, L., & McDowelle, D. (2018). Developing a Comprehensive Wellness Program for Medical Students. In C. Smith (Ed.), *Exploring the Pressures of Medical Education From a Mental Health and Wellness Perspective* (pp. 190–208). Hershey, PA: IGI Global. doi:10.4018/978-1-5225-2811-1.ch008

Lovell, K. L. (2017). Development and Evaluation of Neuroscience Computer-Based Modules for Medical Students: Instructional Design Principles and Effectiveness. In J. Stefaniak (Ed.), *Advancing Medical Education Through Strategic Instructional Design* (pp. 262–276). Hershey, PA: IGI Global. doi:10.4018/978-1-5225-2098-6.ch013

Lubin, R., & Hamlin, M. D. (2018). Medical Student Burnout: A Social Cognitive Learning Perspective on Medical Student Mental Health and Wellness. In C. Smith (Ed.), *Exploring the Pressures of Medical Education From a Mental Health and Wellness Perspective* (pp. 92–121). Hershey, PA: IGI Global. doi:10.4018/978-1-5225-2811-1.ch004

Luk, C. Y. (2018). Moving Towards Universal Health Coverage: Challenges for the Present and Future in China. In B. Fong, A. Ng, & P. Yuen (Eds.), *Sustainable Health and Long-Term Care Solutions for an Aging Population* (pp. 19–45). Hershey, PA: IGI Global. doi:10.4018/978-1-5225-2633-9.ch002

Mahat, M., & Pettigrew, A. (2017). The Regulatory Environment of Non-Profit Higher Education and Research Institutions and Its Implications for Managerial Strategy: The Case of Medical Education and Research. In L. West & A. Worthington (Eds.), *Handbook of Research on Emerging Business Models and Managerial Strategies in the Nonprofit Sector* (pp. 336–351). Hershey, PA: IGI Global. doi:10.4018/978-1-5225-2537-0.ch017

Maitra, I. K., & Bandhyopadhyaay, S. K. (2017). Adaptive Edge Detection Method towards Features Extraction from Diverse Medical Imaging Technologies. In S. Bhattacharyya, S. De, I. Pan, & P. Dutta (Eds.), *Intelligent Multidimensional Data Clustering and Analysis* (pp. 159–192). Hershey, PA: IGI Global. doi:10.4018/978-1-5225-1776-4.ch007

Mangu, V. P. (2017). Mobile Health Care: A Technology View. In C. Bhatt & S. Peddoju (Eds.), *Cloud Computing Systems and Applications in Healthcare* (pp. 1–18). Hershey, PA: IGI Global. doi:10.4018/978-1-5225-1002-4.ch001

Manirabona, A., Fourati, L. C., & Boudjit, S. (2017). Investigation on Healthcare Monitoring Systems: Innovative Services and Applications. *International Journal of E-Health and Medical Communications*, *8*(1), 1–18. doi:10.4018/IJEHMC.2017010101

Mannai, M. M., & Karâa, W. B. (2016). Biomedical Image Processing Overview. In W. Karâa & N. Dey (Eds.), *Biomedical Image Analysis and Mining Techniques for Improved Health Outcomes* (pp. 1–12). Hershey, PA: IGI Global. doi:10.4018/978-1-4666-8811-7.ch001

Manzoor, A. (2016). RFID in Health Care-Building Smart Hospitals for Quality Healthcare. *International Journal of User-Driven Healthcare*, *6*(2), 21–45. doi:10.4018/IJUDH.2016070102

Marwan, M., Kartit, A., & Ouahmane, H. (2018). A Framework to Secure Medical Image Storage in Cloud Computing Environment. *Journal of Electronic Commerce in Organizations, 16*(1), 1–16. doi:10.4018/JECO.2018010101

Masoud, M. P., Nejad, M. K., Darebaghi, H., Chavoshi, M., & Farahani, M. (2018). The Decision Support System and Conventional Method of Telephone Triage by Nurses in Emergency Medical Services: A Comparative Investigation. *International Journal of E-Business Research, 14*(1), 77–88. doi:10.4018/IJEBR.2018010105

McDonald, W. G., Martin, M., & Salzberg, L. D. (2018). From Medical Student to Medical Resident: Graduate Medical Education and Mental Health in the United States. In C. Smith (Ed.), *Exploring the Pressures of Medical Education From a Mental Health and Wellness Perspective* (pp. 145–169). Hershey, PA: IGI Global. doi:10.4018/978-1-5225-2811-1.ch006

Medhekar, A. (2017). The Role of Social Media for Knowledge Dissemination in Medical Tourism: A Case of India. In R. Chugh (Ed.), *Harnessing Social Media as a Knowledge Management Tool* (pp. 25–54). Hershey, PA: IGI Global. doi:10.4018/978-1-5225-0495-5.ch002

Medhekar, A., & Haq, F. (2018). Urbanization and New Jobs Creation in Healthcare Services in India: Challenges and Opportunities. In U. Benna & I. Benna (Eds.), *Urbanization and Its Impact on Socio-Economic Growth in Developing Regions* (pp. 198–218). Hershey, PA: IGI Global. doi:10.4018/978-1-5225-2659-9.ch010

Mehta, G., Dutta, M. K., & Kim, P. S. (2016). An Efficient and Lossless Cryptosystem for Security in Tele-Ophthalmology Applications Using Chaotic Theory. *International Journal of E-Health and Medical Communications, 7*(4), 28–47. doi:10.4018/IJEHMC.2016100102

Mehta, P. (2017). Framework of Indian Healthcare System and its Challenges: An Insight. In V. Bryan & J. Bird (Eds.), *Healthcare Community Synergism between Patients, Practitioners, and Researchers* (pp. 247–271). Hershey, PA: IGI Global. doi:10.4018/978-1-5225-0640-9.ch011

Metelmann, B., & Metelmann, C. (2016). M-Health in Prehospital Emergency Medicine: Experiences from the EU funded Project LiveCity. In A. Moumtzoglou (Ed.), *M-Health Innovations for Patient-Centered Care* (pp. 197–212). Hershey, PA: IGI Global. doi:10.4018/978-1-4666-9861-1.ch010

Mi, M. (2017). Informal Learning in Medical Education. In J. Stefaniak (Ed.), *Advancing Medical Education Through Strategic Instructional Design* (pp. 225–244). Hershey, PA: IGI Global. doi:10.4018/978-1-5225-2098-6.ch011

Miglioretti, M., Mariani, F., & Vecchio, L. (2016). Could Patient Engagement Promote a Health System Free From Malpractice Litigation Risk? In G. Graffigna (Ed.), *Promoting Patient Engagement and Participation for Effective Healthcare Reform* (pp. 240–264). Hershey, PA: IGI Global. doi:10.4018/978-1-4666-9992-2.ch012

Misra, S. C., & Bisui, S. (2016). Feasibility of Large Scale Implementation of Personalized Medicine in the Current Scenario. *International Journal of E-Health and Medical Communications*, *7*(2), 30–49. doi:10.4018/IJEHMC.2016040103

Misra, S. C., Bisui, S., & Fantazy, K. (2016). Identifying Critical Changes in Adoption of Personalized Medicine (PM) in Healthcare Management. *International Journal of E-Health and Medical Communications*, *7*(3), 1–15. doi:10.4018/IJEHMC.2016070101

Mohammadian, M., Hatzinakos, D., Spachos, P., & Jentzsh, R. (2016). An Intelligent and Secure Framework for Wireless Information Technology in Healthcare for User and Data Classification in Hospitals. In V. Wang (Ed.), *Handbook of Research on Advancing Health Education through Technology* (pp. 452–479). Hershey, PA: IGI Global. doi:10.4018/978-1-4666-9494-1.ch019

Mokeddem, S., & Atmani, B. (2016). Assessment of Clinical Decision Support Systems for Predicting Coronary Heart Disease. *International Journal of Operations Research and Information Systems*, *7*(3), 57–73. doi:10.4018/IJORIS.2016070104

Mokrzycka, A., & Kowalska-Bobko, I. (2016). Public Health Legislation and Patient's Rights: Health2020 Strategy, European Perspective. In A. Rosiek & K. Leksowski (Eds.), *Organizational Culture and Ethics in Modern Medicine* (pp. 298–322). Hershey, PA: IGI Global. doi:10.4018/978-1-4666-9658-7.ch013

Moon, J. D., & Galea, M. P. (2016). Overview of Clinical Decision Support Systems in Healthcare. In J. Moon & M. Galea (Eds.), *Improving Health Management through Clinical Decision Support Systems* (pp. 1–27). Hershey, PA: IGI Global. doi:10.4018/978-1-4666-9432-3.ch001

Mosadeghrad, A. M., & Woldemichael, A. (2017). Application of Quality Management in Promoting Patient Safety and Preventing Medical Errors. In M. Riga (Ed.), *Impact of Medical Errors and Malpractice on Health Economics, Quality, and Patient Safety* (pp. 91–112). Hershey, PA: IGI Global. doi:10.4018/978-1-5225-2337-6.ch004

Moumtzoglou, A. (2017). Digital Medicine: The Quality Standpoint. In A. Moumtzoglou (Ed.), *Design, Development, and Integration of Reliable Electronic Healthcare Platforms* (pp. 179–195). Hershey, PA: IGI Global. doi:10.4018/978-1-5225-1724-5.ch011

Moumtzoglou, A., & Pouliakis, A. (2018). Population Health Management and the Science of Individuality. *International Journal of Reliable and Quality E-Healthcare*, *7*(2), 1–26. doi:10.4018/IJRQEH.2018040101

Mpofu, C. (2016). International Medical Experiences Outbound New Zealand: An Economic and Medical Workforce Strategy. In D. Velliaris & D. Coleman-George (Eds.), *Handbook of Research on Study Abroad Programs and Outbound Mobility* (pp. 446–469). Hershey, PA: IGI Global. doi:10.4018/978-1-5225-0169-5.ch018

Mukhtar, W. F., & Abuelyaman, E. S. (2017). Opportunities and Challenges of Big Data in Healthcare. In N. Wickramasinghe (Ed.), *Handbook of Research on Healthcare Administration and Management* (pp. 47–58). Hershey, PA: IGI Global. doi:10.4018/978-1-5225-0920-2.ch004

Munugala, S., Brar, G. K., Syed, A., Mohammad, A., & Halgamuge, M. N. (2018). The Much Needed Security and Data Reforms of Cloud Computing in Medical Data Storage. In M. Lytras & P. Papadopoulou (Eds.), *Applying Big Data Analytics in Bioinformatics and Medicine* (pp. 99–113). Hershey, PA: IGI Global. doi:10.4018/978-1-5225-2607-0.ch005

Narasimhamurthy, A. (2016). An Overview of Machine Learning in Medical Image Analysis: Trends in Health Informatics. In N. Dey & A. Ashour (Eds.), *Classification and Clustering in Biomedical Signal Processing* (pp. 23–45). Hershey, PA: IGI Global. doi:10.4018/978-1-5225-0140-4.ch002

Ngara, R. (2017). Multiple Voices, Multiple Paths: Towards Dialogue between Western and Indigenous Medical Knowledge Systems. In P. Ngulube (Ed.), *Handbook of Research on Theoretical Perspectives on Indigenous Knowledge Systems in Developing Countries* (pp. 332–358). Hershey, PA: IGI Global. doi:10.4018/978-1-5225-0833-5.ch015

O'Connor, Y., & Heavin, C. (2018). Defining and Characterising the Landscape of eHealth. In M. Khosrow-Pour, D.B.A. (Ed.), Encyclopedia of Information Science and Technology, Fourth Edition (pp. 5864-5875). Hershey, PA: IGI Global. doi:10.4018/978-1-5225-2255-3.ch510

Ochonogor, W. C., & Okite-Amughoro, F. A. (2018). Building an Effective Digital Library in a University Teaching Hospital (UTH) in Nigeria. In A. Tella & T. Kwanya (Eds.), *Handbook of Research on Managing Intellectual Property in Digital Libraries* (pp. 184–204). Hershey, PA: IGI Global. doi:10.4018/978-1-5225-3093-0.ch010

Olaniran, B. A. (2016). ICTs, E-health, and Multidisciplinary Healthcare Teams: Promises and Challenges. *International Journal of Privacy and Health Information Management*, *4*(2), 62–75. doi:10.4018/IJPHIM.2016070105

Olaniran, B. A. (2016). ICT Use and Multidisciplinary Healthcare Teams in the Age of e-Health. *International Journal of Reliable and Quality E-Healthcare*, *5*(1), 18–31. doi:10.4018/IJRQEH.2016010102

Olivares, S. L., Cruz, A. G., Cabrera, M. V., Regalado, A. I., & García, J. E. (2017). An Assessment Study of Quality Model for Medical Schools in Mexico. In S. Mukerji & P. Tripathi (Eds.), *Handbook of Research on Administration, Policy, and Leadership in Higher Education* (pp. 404–439). Hershey, PA: IGI Global. doi:10.4018/978-1-5225-0672-0.ch016

Omidoyin, E. O., Opeke, R. O., & Osagbemi, G. K. (2016). Utilization Pattern and Privacy Issues in the use of Health Records for Research Practice by Doctors: Selected Nigerian Teaching Hospitals as Case Study. *International Journal of Privacy and Health Information Management*, *4*(1), 1–11. doi:10.4018/IJPHIM.2016010101

Omoruyi, E. A., & Omidele, F. (2018). Resident Physician and Medical Academic Faculty Burnout: A Review of Current Literature. In C. Smith (Ed.), *Exploring the Pressures of Medical Education From a Mental Health and Wellness Perspective* (pp. 171–189). Hershey, PA: IGI Global. doi:10.4018/978-1-5225-2811-1.ch007

Osop, H., & Sahama, T. (2016). Data-Driven and Practice-Based Evidence: Design and Development of Efficient and Effective Clinical Decision Support System. In J. Moon & M. Galea (Eds.), *Improving Health Management through Clinical Decision Support Systems* (pp. 295–328). Hershey, PA: IGI Global. doi:10.4018/978-1-4666-9432-3.ch014

Ossowski, R., & Izdebski, P. (2016). Ethical Aspects of Talking to a Patient. In A. Rosiek & K. Leksowski (Eds.), *Organizational Culture and Ethics in Modern Medicine* (pp. 203–235). Hershey, PA: IGI Global. doi:10.4018/978-1-4666-9658-7.ch009

Pandian, P. S. (2016). An Overview of Telemedicine Technologies for Healthcare Applications. *International Journal of Biomedical and Clinical Engineering*, *5*(2), 29–52. doi:10.4018/IJBCE.2016070103

Papadopoulou, P., Lytras, M., & Marouli, C. (2018). Bioinformatics as Applied to Medicine: Challenges Faced Moving from Big Data to Smart Data to Wise Data. In M. Lytras & P. Papadopoulou (Eds.), *Applying Big Data Analytics in Bioinformatics and Medicine* (pp. 1–25). Hershey, PA: IGI Global. doi:10.4018/978-1-5225-2607-0.ch001

Paraskou, A., & George, B. P. (2018). An Overview of Reproductive Tourism. In *Legal and Economic Considerations Surrounding Reproductive Tourism: Emerging Research and Opportunities* (pp. 1–17). Hershey, PA: IGI Global. doi:10.4018/978-1-5225-2694-0.ch001

Park, S., & Moon, J. (2016). Strategic Approach towards Clinical Information Security. In J. Moon & M. Galea (Eds.), *Improving Health Management through Clinical Decision Support Systems* (pp. 329–359). Hershey, PA: IGI Global. doi:10.4018/978-1-4666-9432-3.ch015

Pereira, D., Castro, A., Gomes, P., Areias, J. C., Reis, Z. S., Coimbra, M. T., & Cruz-Correia, R. (2016). Digital Auscultation: Challenges and Perspectives. In M. Cruz-Cunha, I. Miranda, R. Martinho, & R. Rijo (Eds.), *Encyclopedia of E-Health and Telemedicine* (pp. 910–927). Hershey, PA: IGI Global. doi:10.4018/978-1-4666-9978-6.ch070

Peters, R. A., & Cruz, M. (2016). The States as Generators of Incremental Change in American Health Care Policy: 1935 to 1965. In R. Gholipour & K. Rouzbehani (Eds.), *Social, Economic, and Political Perspectives on Public Health Policy-Making* (pp. 86–114). Hershey, PA: IGI Global. doi:10.4018/978-1-4666-9944-1.ch005

Phuritsabam, B., & Devi, A. B. (2017). Information Seeking Behavior of Medical Scientists at Jawaharlal Nehru Institute of Medical Science: A Study. In S. Ram (Ed.), *Library and Information Services for Bioinformatics Education and Research* (pp. 177–187). Hershey, PA: IGI Global. doi:10.4018/978-1-5225-1871-6.ch010

Pieczka, B. (2018). Management of Risk and Adverse Events in Medical Entities. In A. Rosiek-Kryszewska & K. Leksowski (Eds.), *Healthcare Administration for Patient Safety and Engagement* (pp. 31–46). Hershey, PA: IGI Global. doi:10.4018/978-1-5225-3946-9.ch003

Poduval, J. (2016). Curriculum Development. In *Optimizing Medicine Residency Training Programs* (pp. 45–102). Hershey, PA: IGI Global. doi:10.4018/978-1-4666-9527-6.ch003

Poduval, J. (2016). Ethics and Professionalism. In *Optimizing Medicine Residency Training Programs* (pp. 103–133). Hershey, PA: IGI Global. doi:10.4018/978-1-4666-9527-6.ch004

Poduval, J. (2016). Management Skills and Leadership. In *Optimizing Medicine Residency Training Programs* (pp. 182–205). Hershey, PA: IGI Global. doi:10.4018/978-1-4666-9527-6.ch008

Poduval, J. (2016). Medicine Residency Training. In *Optimizing Medicine Residency Training Programs* (pp. 1–27). Hershey, PA: IGI Global. doi:10.4018/978-1-4666-9527-6.ch001

Poduval, J. (2016). Personal Issues. In *Optimizing Medicine Residency Training Programs* (pp. 206–221). Hershey, PA: IGI Global. doi:10.4018/978-1-4666-9527-6.ch009

Poduval, J. (2017). Medical Errors: Impact on Health Care Quality. In M. Riga (Ed.), *Impact of Medical Errors and Malpractice on Health Economics, Quality, and Patient Safety* (pp. 33–60). Hershey, PA: IGI Global. doi:10.4018/978-1-5225-2337-6.ch002

Politis, D., Stagiopoulos, P., Aidona, S., Kyriafinis, G., & Constantinidis, I. (2018). Autonomous Learning and Skill Accreditation: A Paradigm for Medical Studies. In A. Kumar (Ed.), *Optimizing Student Engagement in Online Learning Environments* (pp. 266–296). Hershey, PA: IGI Global. doi:10.4018/978-1-5225-3634-5.ch012

Pomares-Quimbaya, A., Gonzalez, R. A., Quintero, S., Muñoz, O. M., Bohórquez, W. R., García, O. M., & Londoño, D. (2016). A Review of Existing Applications and Techniques for Narrative Text Analysis in Electronic Medical Records. In M. Cruz-Cunha, I. Miranda, R. Martinho, & R. Rijo (Eds.), *Encyclopedia of E-Health and Telemedicine* (pp. 796–811). Hershey, PA: IGI Global. doi:10.4018/978-1-4666-9978-6.ch062

Pomares-Quimbaya, A., González, R. A., Sierra, A., Daza, J. C., Muñoz, O., García, A., ... Bohórquez, W. R. (2017). ICT for Enabling the Quality Evaluation of Health Care Services: A Case Study in a General Hospital. In A. Moumtzoglou (Ed.), *Design, Development, and Integration of Reliable Electronic Healthcare Platforms* (pp. 196–210). Hershey, PA: IGI Global. doi:10.4018/978-1-5225-1724-5.ch012

Pouliakis, A., Margari, N., Karakitsou, E., Archondakis, S., & Karakitsos, P. (2018). Emerging Technologies Serving Cytopathology: Big Data, the Cloud, and Mobile Computing. In I. El Naqa (Ed.), *Emerging Developments and Practices in Oncology* (pp. 114–152). Hershey, PA: IGI Global. doi:10.4018/978-1-5225-3085-5.ch005

Queirós, A., Silva, A. G., Ferreira, A., Caravau, H., Cerqueira, M., & Rocha, N. P. (2016). Assessing Mobile Applications Considered Medical Devices. In M. Cruz-Cunha, I. Miranda, R. Martinho, & R. Rijo (Eds.), *Encyclopedia of E-Health and Telemedicine* (pp. 111–127). Hershey, PA: IGI Global. doi:10.4018/978-1-4666-9978-6.ch010

Raffaeli, L., Spinsante, S., & Gambi, E. (2016). Integrated Smart TV-Based Personal e-Health System. *International Journal of E-Health and Medical Communications*, *7*(1), 48–64. doi:10.4018/IJEHMC.2016010103

Rai, A., Kothari, R., & Singh, D. P. (2017). Assessment of Available Technologies for Hospital Waste Management: A Need for Society. In R. Singh, A. Singh, & V. Srivastava (Eds.), *Environmental Issues Surrounding Human Overpopulation* (pp. 172–188). Hershey, PA: IGI Global. doi:10.4018/978-1-5225-1683-5.ch010

Ramamoorthy, S., & Sivasubramaniam, R. (2018). Image Processing Including Medical Liver Imaging: Medical Image Processing from Big Data Perspective, Ultrasound Liver Images, Challenges. In M. Lytras & P. Papadopoulou (Eds.), *Applying Big Data Analytics in Bioinformatics and Medicine* (pp. 380–392). Hershey, PA: IGI Global. doi:10.4018/978-1-5225-2607-0.ch016

Rathor, G. P., & Gupta, S. K. (2017). Improving Multimodality Image Fusion through Integrate AFL and Wavelet Transform. In V. Tiwari, B. Tiwari, R. Thakur, & S. Gupta (Eds.), *Pattern and Data Analysis in Healthcare Settings* (pp. 143–157). Hershey, PA: IGI Global. doi:10.4018/978-1-5225-0536-5.ch008

Rawat, D. B., & Bhattacharya, S. (2016). Wireless Body Area Network for Healthcare Applications. In N. Meghanathan (Ed.), *Advanced Methods for Complex Network Analysis* (pp. 343–358). Hershey, PA: IGI Global. doi:10.4018/978-1-4666-9964-9.ch014

Rea, P. M. (2016). Advances in Anatomical and Medical Visualisation. In M. Pinheiro & D. Simões (Eds.), *Handbook of Research on Engaging Digital Natives in Higher Education Settings* (pp. 244–264). Hershey, PA: IGI Global. doi:10.4018/978-1-5225-0039-1.ch011

Rexhepi, H., & Persson, A. (2017). Challenges to Implementing IT Support for Evidence Based Practice Among Nurses and Assistant Nurses: A Qualitative Study. *Journal of Electronic Commerce in Organizations*, *15*(2), 61–76. doi:10.4018/JECO.2017040105

Reychav, I., & Azuri, J. (2016). Including Elderly Patients in Decision Making via Electronic Health Literacy. In M. Cruz-Cunha, I. Miranda, R. Martinho, & R. Rijo (Eds.), *Encyclopedia of E-Health and Telemedicine* (pp. 241–249). Hershey, PA: IGI Global. doi:10.4018/978-1-4666-9978-6.ch020

Richards, D., & Caldwell, P. H. (2016). Gamification to Improve Adherence to Clinical Treatment Advice: Improving Adherence to Clinical Treatment. In D. Novák, B. Tulu, & H. Brendryen (Eds.), *Handbook of Research on Holistic Perspectives in Gamification for Clinical Practice* (pp. 47–77). Hershey, PA: IGI Global. doi:10.4018/978-1-4666-9522-1.ch004

Rissman, B. (2016). Medical Conditions Associated with NLD. In B. Rissman (Ed.), *Medical and Educational Perspectives on Nonverbal Learning Disability in Children and Young Adults* (pp. 27–66). Hershey, PA: IGI Global. doi:10.4018/978-1-4666-9539-9.ch002

Rosiek, A. (2018). The Assessment of Actions of the Environment and the Impact of Preventive Medicine for Public Health in Poland. In A. Rosiek-Kryszewska & K. Leksowski (Eds.), *Healthcare Administration for Patient Safety and Engagement* (pp. 106–119). Hershey, PA: IGI Global. doi:10.4018/978-1-5225-3946-9.ch006

Rosiek, A., Leksowski, K., Goch, A., Rosiek-Kryszewska, A., & Leksowski, Ł. (2016). Medical Treatment and Difficult Ethical Decisions in Interdisciplinary Hospital Teams. In A. Rosiek & K. Leksowski (Eds.), *Organizational Culture and Ethics in Modern Medicine* (pp. 121–153). Hershey, PA: IGI Global. doi:10.4018/978-1-4666-9658-7.ch006

Rosiek, A., & Rosiek-Kryszewska, A. (2018). Managed Healthcare: Doctor Life Satisfaction and Its Impact on the Process of Communicating With the Patient. In A. Rosiek-Kryszewska & K. Leksowski (Eds.), *Healthcare Administration for Patient Safety and Engagement* (pp. 244–261). Hershey, PA: IGI Global. doi:10.4018/978-1-5225-3946-9.ch013

Rosiek-Kryszewska, A., Leksowski, Ł., Rosiek, A., Leksowski, K., & Goch, A. (2016). Clinical Communication in the Aspect of Development of New Technologies and E-Health in the Doctor-Patient Relationship. In A. Rosiek & K. Leksowski (Eds.), *Organizational Culture and Ethics in Modern Medicine* (pp. 18–51). Hershey, PA: IGI Global. doi:10.4018/978-1-4666-9658-7.ch002

Rosiek-Kryszewska, A., & Rosiek, A. (2018). The Involvement of the Patient and his Perspective Evaluation of the Quality of Healthcare. In A. Rosiek-Kryszewska & K. Leksowski (Eds.), *Healthcare Administration for Patient Safety and Engagement* (pp. 121–144). Hershey, PA: IGI Global. doi:10.4018/978-1-5225-3946-9.ch007

Rosiek-Kryszewska, A., & Rosiek, A. (2018). The Impact of Management and Leadership Roles in Building Competitive Healthcare Units. In A. Rosiek-Kryszewska & K. Leksowski (Eds.), *Healthcare Administration for Patient Safety and Engagement* (pp. 13–30). Hershey, PA: IGI Global. doi:10.4018/978-1-5225-3946-9.ch002

Roşu, S. M., Păvăloiu, I. B., Dragoi, G., Apostol, C. G., & Munteanu, D. (2016). Telemedicine Based on LMDS in the Urban/Metropolitan Area: A Romanian Case Study. In M. Cruz-Cunha, I. Miranda, R. Martinho, & R. Rijo (Eds.), *Encyclopedia of E-Health and Telemedicine* (pp. 96–109). Hershey, PA: IGI Global. doi:10.4018/978-1-4666-9978-6.ch009

Rouzbehani, K. (2017). Health Policy Implementation: Moving Beyond Its Barriers in United States. In N. Wickramasinghe (Ed.), *Handbook of Research on Healthcare Administration and Management* (pp. 541–552). Hershey, PA: IGI Global. doi:10.4018/978-1-5225-0920-2.ch032

Ruiz, I. M., Cohen, D. S., & Marco, Á. M. (2016). ISO/IEEE11073 Family of Standards: Trends and Applications on E-Health Monitoring. In M. Cruz-Cunha, I. Miranda, R. Martinho, & R. Rijo (Eds.), *Encyclopedia of E-Health and Telemedicine* (pp. 646–660). Hershey, PA: IGI Global. doi:10.4018/978-1-4666-9978-6.ch050

Sam, S. (2017). Mobile Phones and Expanding Human Capabilities in Plural Health Systems. In K. Moahi, K. Bwalya, & P. Sebina (Eds.), *Health Information Systems and the Advancement of Medical Practice in Developing Countries* (pp. 93–114). Hershey, PA: IGI Global. doi:10.4018/978-1-5225-2262-1.ch006

Sankaranarayanan, S., & Ganesan, S. (2016). Applications of Intelligent Agents in Health Sector-A Review. *International Journal of E-Health and Medical Communications*, *7*(1), 1–30. doi:10.4018/IJEHMC.2016010101

Santos-Trigo, M., Suaste, E., & Figuerola, P. (2018). Technology Design and Routes for Tool Appropriation in Medical Practices. In M. Khosrow-Pour, D.B.A. (Ed.), Encyclopedia of Information Science and Technology, Fourth Edition (pp. 3794-3804). Hershey, PA: IGI Global. doi:10.4018/978-1-5225-2255-3.ch329

Sarivougioukas, J., Vagelatos, A., Parsopoulos, K. E., & Lagaris, I. E. (2018). Home UbiHealth. In M. Khosrow-Pour, D.B.A. (Ed.), Encyclopedia of Information Science and Technology, Fourth Edition (pp. 7765-7774). Hershey, PA: IGI Global. doi:10.4018/978-1-5225-2255-3.ch675

Sarkar, B. K. (2017). Big Data and Healthcare Data: A Survey. *International Journal of Knowledge-Based Organizations*, *7*(4), 50–77. doi:10.4018/IJKBO.2017100104

Saxena, K., & Banodha, U. (2017). An Essence of the SOA on Healthcare. In R. Bhadoria, N. Chaudhari, G. Tomar, & S. Singh (Eds.), *Exploring Enterprise Service Bus in the Service-Oriented Architecture Paradigm* (pp. 283–304). Hershey, PA: IGI Global. doi:10.4018/978-1-5225-2157-0.ch018

Schmeida, M., & McNeal, R. (2016). Consulting Online Healthcare Information: E-Caregivers as Knowledgeable Decision Makers. *International Journal of Computers in Clinical Practice*, *1*(1), 42–52. doi:10.4018/IJCCP.2016010104

Sen, K., & Ghosh, K. (2018). Incorporating Global Medical Knowledge to Solve Healthcare Problems: A Framework for a Crowdsourcing System. *International Journal of Healthcare Information Systems and Informatics*, *13*(1), 1–14. doi:10.4018/IJHISI.2018010101

Shakdher, A., & Pandey, K. (2017). REDAlert+: Medical/Fire Emergency and Warning System using Android Devices. *International Journal of E-Health and Medical Communications*, *8*(1), 37–51. doi:10.4018/IJEHMC.2017010103

Shekarian, E., Abdul-Rashid, S. H., & Olugu, E. U. (2017). An Integrated Fuzzy VIKOR Method for Performance Management in Healthcare. In M. Tavana, K. Szabat, & K. Puranam (Eds.), *Organizational Productivity and Performance Measurements Using Predictive Modeling and Analytics* (pp. 40–61). Hershey, PA: IGI Global. doi:10.4018/978-1-5225-0654-6.ch003

Shi, J., Erdem, E., & Liu, H. (2016). Expanding Role of Telephone Systems in Healthcare: Developments and Opportunities. In A. Dwivedi (Ed.), *Reshaping Medical Practice and Care with Health Information Systems* (pp. 87–131). Hershey, PA: IGI Global. doi:10.4018/978-1-4666-9870-3.ch004

Shijina, V., & John, S. J. (2017). Multiple Relations and its Application in Medical Diagnosis. *International Journal of Fuzzy System Applications*, *6*(4), 47–62. doi:10.4018/IJFSA.2017100104

Shipley, N., & Chakraborty, J. (2018). Big Data and mHealth: Increasing the Usability of Healthcare Through the Customization of Pinterest – Literary Perspective. In J. Machado, A. Abelha, M. Santos, & F. Portela (Eds.), *Next-Generation Mobile and Pervasive Healthcare Solutions* (pp. 46–66). Hershey, PA: IGI Global. doi:10.4018/978-1-5225-2851-7.ch004

Singh, A., & Dutta, M. K. (2017). A Reversible Data Hiding Scheme for Efficient Management of Tele-Ophthalmological Data. *International Journal of E-Health and Medical Communications*, *8*(3), 38–54. doi:10.4018/IJEHMC.2017070103

Sivaji, A., Radjo, H. K., Amin, M., & Abu Hashim, M. A. (2016). Design of a Hospital Interactive Wayfinding System: Designing for Malaysian Users. In N. Mohamed, T. Mantoro, M. Ayu, & M. Mahmud (Eds.), *Critical Socio-Technical Issues Surrounding Mobile Computing* (pp. 88–123). Hershey, PA: IGI Global. doi:10.4018/978-1-4666-9438-5.ch005

Skourti, P. K., & Pavlakis, A. (2017). The Second Victim Phenomenon: The Way Out. In M. Riga (Ed.), *Impact of Medical Errors and Malpractice on Health Economics, Quality, and Patient Safety* (pp. 197–222). Hershey, PA: IGI Global. doi:10.4018/978-1-5225-2337-6.ch008

Smith, C. R. (2018). Medical Students' Quest Towards the Long White Coat: Impact on Mental Health and Well-Being. In C. Smith (Ed.), *Exploring the Pressures of Medical Education From a Mental Health and Wellness Perspective* (pp. 1–42). Hershey, PA: IGI Global. doi:10.4018/978-1-5225-2811-1.ch001

Smith, S. I., & Dandignac, M. (2018). Perfectionism: Addressing Lofty Expectations in Medical School. In C. Smith (Ed.), *Exploring the Pressures of Medical Education From a Mental Health and Wellness Perspective* (pp. 68–91). Hershey, PA: IGI Global. doi:10.4018/978-1-5225-2811-1.ch003

Sobrinho, Á. A., Dias da Silva, L., Perkusich, A., Cunha, P., Pinheiro, M. E., & Melo de Medeiros, L. (2016). Towards Medical Systems to Aid the Detection and Treatment of Chronic Diseases. In D. Fotiadis (Ed.), *Handbook of Research on Trends in the Diagnosis and Treatment of Chronic Conditions* (pp. 50–69). Hershey, PA: IGI Global. doi:10.4018/978-1-4666-8828-5.ch003

Soczywko, J., & Rutkowska, D. (2018). The Patient/Provider Relationship in Emergency Medicine: Organization, Communication, and Understanding. In A. Rosiek-Kryszewska & K. Leksowski (Eds.), *Healthcare Administration for Patient Safety and Engagement* (pp. 74–105). Hershey, PA: IGI Global. doi:10.4018/978-1-5225-3946-9.ch005

Sołtysik-Piorunkiewicz, A., Furmankiewicz, M., & Ziuziański, P. (2016). Web Healthcare Applications in Poland: Trends, Standards, Barriers and Possibilities of Implementation and Usage of E-Health Systems. In I. Deliyannis, P. Kostagiolas, & C. Banou (Eds.), *Experimental Multimedia Systems for Interactivity and Strategic Innovation* (pp. 258–283). Hershey, PA: IGI Global. doi:10.4018/978-1-4666-8659-5.ch013

Soni, P. (2018). Implications of HIPAA and Subsequent Regulations on Information Technology. In M. Gupta, R. Sharman, J. Walp, & P. Mulgund (Eds.), *Information Technology Risk Management and Compliance in Modern Organizations* (pp. 71–98). Hershey, PA: IGI Global. doi:10.4018/978-1-5225-2604-9.ch004

Spinelli, R., & Benevolo, C. (2016). From Healthcare Services to E-Health Applications: A Delivery System-Based Taxonomy. In A. Dwivedi (Ed.), *Reshaping Medical Practice and Care with Health Information Systems* (pp. 205–245). Hershey, PA: IGI Global. doi:10.4018/978-1-4666-9870-3.ch007

Srivastava, A., & Aggarwal, A. K. (2018). Medical Image Fusion in Spatial and Transform Domain: A Comparative Analysis. In M. Anwar, A. Khosla, & R. Kapoor (Eds.), *Handbook of Research on Advanced Concepts in Real-Time Image and Video Processing* (pp. 281–300). Hershey, PA: IGI Global. doi:10.4018/978-1-5225-2848-7.ch011

Srivastava, S. K., & Roy, S. N. (2018). Recommendation System: A Potential Tool for Achieving Pervasive Health Care. In J. Machado, A. Abelha, M. Santos, & F. Portela (Eds.), *Next-Generation Mobile and Pervasive Healthcare Solutions* (pp. 111–127). Hershey, PA: IGI Global. doi:10.4018/978-1-5225-2851-7.ch008

Stancu, A. (2016). Correlations and Patterns of Food and Health Consumer Expenditure. In A. Jean-Vasile (Ed.), *Food Science, Production, and Engineering in Contemporary Economies* (pp. 44–101). Hershey, PA: IGI Global. doi:10.4018/978-1-5225-0341-5.ch003

Stanimirovic, D. (2017). Digitalization of Death Certification Model: Transformation Issues and Implementation Concerns. In S. Saeed, Y. Bamarouf, T. Ramayah, & S. Iqbal (Eds.), *Design Solutions for User-Centric Information Systems* (pp. 22–43). Hershey, PA: IGI Global. doi:10.4018/978-1-5225-1944-7.ch002

Stavros, A., Vavoulidis, E., & Nasioutziki, M. (2016). The Use of Mobile Health Applications for Quality Control and Accreditational Purposes in a Cytopathology Laboratory. In A. Moumtzoglou (Ed.), *M-Health Innovations for Patient-Centered Care* (pp. 262–283). Hershey, PA: IGI Global. doi:10.4018/978-1-4666-9861-1.ch013

Sukkird, V., & Shirahada, K. (2018). E-Health Service Model for Asian Developing Countries: A Case of Emergency Medical Service for Elderly People in Thailand. In M. Khosrow-Pour (Ed.), *Optimizing Current Practices in E-Services and Mobile Applications* (pp. 214–232). Hershey, PA: IGI Global. doi:10.4018/978-1-5225-5026-6.ch011

Sygit, B., & Wąsik, D. (2016). Patients' Rights and Medical Personnel Duties in the Field of Hospital Care. In A. Rosiek & K. Leksowski (Eds.), *Organizational Culture and Ethics in Modern Medicine* (pp. 282–297). Hershey, PA: IGI Global. doi:10.4018/978-1-4666-9658-7.ch012

Sygit, B., & Wąsik, D. (2016). The Idea of Human Rights in Conditions of Hospital Treatment. In A. Rosiek & K. Leksowski (Eds.), *Organizational Culture and Ethics in Modern Medicine* (pp. 236–254). Hershey, PA: IGI Global. doi:10.4018/978-1-4666-9658-7.ch010

Talbot, T. B. (2017). Making Lifelike Medical Games in the Age of Virtual Reality: An Update on "Playing Games with Biology" from 2013. In B. Dubbels (Ed.), *Transforming Gaming and Computer Simulation Technologies across Industries* (pp. 103–119). Hershey, PA: IGI Global. doi:10.4018/978-1-5225-1817-4.ch006

Tamposis, I., Pouliakis, A., Fezoulidis, I., & Karakitsos, P. (2016). Mobile Platforms Supporting Health Professionals: Need, Technical Requirements, and Applications. In A. Moumtzoglou (Ed.), *M-Health Innovations for Patient-Centered Care* (pp. 91–114). Hershey, PA: IGI Global. doi:10.4018/978-1-4666-9861-1.ch005

Tiago, M. T., Tiago, F., Amaral, F. E., & Silva, S. (2016). Healthy 3.0: Healthcare Digital Dimensions. In A. Dwivedi (Ed.), *Reshaping Medical Practice and Care with Health Information Systems* (pp. 287–322). Hershey, PA: IGI Global. doi:10.4018/978-1-4666-9870-3.ch010

Tripathy, B. (2016). Application of Rough Set Based Models in Medical Diagnosis. In S. Dash & B. Subudhi (Eds.), *Handbook of Research on Computational Intelligence Applications in Bioinformatics* (pp. 144–168). Hershey, PA: IGI Global. doi:10.4018/978-1-5225-0427-6.ch008

Turcu, C. E., & Turcu, C. O. (2017). Social Internet of Things in Healthcare: From Things to Social Things in Internet of Things. In C. Reis & M. Maximiano (Eds.), *Internet of Things and Advanced Application in Healthcare* (pp. 266–295). Hershey, PA: IGI Global. doi:10.4018/978-1-5225-1820-4.ch010

Unwin, D. W., Sanzogni, L., & Sandhu, K. (2017). Developing and Measuring the Business Case for Health Information Technology. In K. Moahi, K. Bwalya, & P. Sebina (Eds.), *Health Information Systems and the Advancement of Medical Practice in Developing Countries* (pp. 262–290). Hershey, PA: IGI Global. doi:10.4018/978-1-5225-2262-1.ch015

Urooj, S., & Singh, S. P. (2016). Wavelet Transform-Based Soft Computational Techniques and Applications in Medical Imaging. In P. Saxena, D. Singh, & M. Pant (Eds.), *Problem Solving and Uncertainty Modeling through Optimization and Soft Computing Applications* (pp. 339–363). Hershey, PA: IGI Global. doi:10.4018/978-1-4666-9885-7.ch016

Vasant, P. (2018). A General Medical Diagnosis System Formed by Artificial Neural Networks and Swarm Intelligence Techniques. In U. Kose, G. Guraksin, & O. Deperlioglu (Eds.), *Nature-Inspired Intelligent Techniques for Solving Biomedical Engineering Problems* (pp. 130–145). Hershey, PA: IGI Global. doi:10.4018/978-1-5225-4769-3.ch006

Waegemann, C. P. (2016). mHealth: History, Analysis, and Implementation. In A. Moumtzoglou (Ed.), M-Health Innovations for Patient-Centered Care (pp. 1-19). Hershey, PA: IGI Global. doi:10.4018/978-1-4666-9861-1.ch001

Watfa, M. K., Majeed, H., & Salahuddin, T. (2016). Computer Based E-Healthcare Clinical Systems: A Comprehensive Survey. *International Journal of Privacy and Health Information Management*, *4*(1), 50–69. doi:10.4018/IJPHIM.2016010104

Wietholter, J. P., Coetzee, R., Nardella, B., Kincaid, S. E., & Slain, D. (2016). International Healthcare Experiences: Caring While Learning and Learning While Caring. In D. Velliaris & D. Coleman-George (Eds.), *Handbook of Research on Study Abroad Programs and Outbound Mobility* (pp. 470–496). Hershey, PA: IGI Global. doi:10.4018/978-1-5225-0169-5.ch019

Witzke, K., & Specht, O. (2017). M-Health Telemedicine and Telepresence in Oral and Maxillofacial Surgery: An Innovative Prehospital Healthcare Concept in Structurally Weak Areas. *International Journal of Reliable and Quality E-Healthcare*, *6*(4), 37–48. doi:10.4018/IJRQEH.2017100105

Wójcik, A., & Chojnacki, M. (2016). Behavior and Ethical Problems in the Functioning of the Operating Theater (Case Study). In A. Rosiek & K. Leksowski (Eds.), *Organizational Culture and Ethics in Modern Medicine* (pp. 154–179). Hershey, PA: IGI Global. doi:10.4018/978-1-4666-9658-7.ch007

Wolk, K., & Marasek, K. P. (2016). Translation of Medical Texts using Neural Networks. *International Journal of Reliable and Quality E-Healthcare*, *5*(4), 51–66. doi:10.4018/IJRQEH.2016100104

Wong, A. K., & Lo, M. F. (2018). Using Pervasive Computing for Sustainable Healthcare in an Aging Population. In B. Fong, A. Ng, & P. Yuen (Eds.), *Sustainable Health and Long-Term Care Solutions for an Aging Population* (pp. 187–202). Hershey, PA: IGI Global. doi:10.4018/978-1-5225-2633-9.ch010

Wu, W., Martin, B. C., & Ni, C. (2017). A Systematic Review of Competency-Based Education Effort in the Health Professions: Seeking Order Out of Chaos. In K. Rasmussen, P. Northrup, & R. Colson (Eds.), *Handbook of Research on Competency-Based Education in University Settings* (pp. 352–378). Hershey, PA: IGI Global. doi:10.4018/978-1-5225-0932-5.ch018

Yadav, N., Aliasgari, M., & Poellabauer, C. (2016). Mobile Healthcare in an Increasingly Connected Developing World. *International Journal of Privacy and Health Information Management*, *4*(2), 76–97. doi:10.4018/IJPHIM.2016070106

Yadav, S., Ekbal, A., Saha, S., Pathak, P. S., & Bhattacharyya, P. (2017). Patient Data De-Identification: A Conditional Random-Field-Based Supervised Approach. In S. Saha, A. Mandal, A. Narasimhamurthy, S. V, & S. Sangam (Eds.), Handbook of Research on Applied Cybernetics and Systems Science (pp. 234-253). Hershey, PA: IGI Global. doi:10.4018/978-1-5225-2498-4.ch011

Yu, B., Wijesekera, D., & Costa, P. C. (2017). Informed Consent in Healthcare: A Study Case of Genetic Services. In A. Moumtzoglou (Ed.), *Design, Development, and Integration of Reliable Electronic Healthcare Platforms* (pp. 211–242). Hershey, PA: IGI Global. doi:10.4018/978-1-5225-1724-5.ch013

Yu, B., Wijesekera, D., & Costa, P. C. (2017). Informed Consent in Electronic Medical Record Systems. In I. Management Association (Ed.), Healthcare Ethics and Training: Concepts, Methodologies, Tools, and Applications (pp. 1029-1049). Hershey, PA: IGI Global. doi:10.4018/978-1-5225-2237-9.ch049

Yu, M., Li, J., & Wang, W. (2017). Creative Life Experience among Students in Medical Education. In C. Zhou (Ed.), *Handbook of Research on Creative Problem-Solving Skill Development in Higher Education* (pp. 158–184). Hershey, PA: IGI Global. doi:10.4018/978-1-5225-0643-0.ch008

Zarour, K. (2017). Towards a Telehomecare in Algeria: Case of Diabetes Measurement and Remote Monitoring. *International Journal of E-Health and Medical Communications*, *8*(4), 61–80. doi:10.4018/IJEHMC.2017100104

Zavyalova, Y. V., Korzun, D. G., Meigal, A. Y., & Borodin, A. V. (2017). Towards the Development of Smart Spaces-Based Socio-Cyber-Medicine Systems. *International Journal of Embedded and Real-Time Communication Systems*, *8*(1), 45–63. doi:10.4018/IJERTCS.2017010104

Zeinali, A. A. (2018). Word Formation Study in Developing Naming Guidelines in the Translation of English Medical Terms Into Persian. In M. Khosrow-Pour, D.B.A. (Ed.), Encyclopedia of Information Science and Technology, Fourth Edition (pp. 5136-5147). Hershey, PA: IGI Global. doi:10.4018/978-1-5225-2255-3.ch446

Ziminski, T. B., Demurjian, S. A., Sanzi, E., & Agresta, T. (2016). Toward Integrating Healthcare Data and Systems: A Study of Architectural Alternatives. In T. Iyamu & A. Tatnall (Eds.), *Maximizing Healthcare Delivery and Management through Technology Integration* (pp. 270–304). Hershey, PA: IGI Global. doi:10.4018/978-1-4666-9446-0.ch016

Ziminski, T. B., Demurjian, S. A., Sanzi, E., Baihan, M., & Agresta, T. (2016). An Architectural Solution for Health Information Exchange. *International Journal of User-Driven Healthcare*, *6*(1), 65–103. doi:10.4018/IJUDH.2016010104

Zineldin, M., & Vasicheva, V. (2018). Reducing Medical Errors and Increasing Patient Safety: TRM and 5 Q's Approaches for Better Quality of Life. In *Technological Tools for Value-Based Sustainable Relationships in Health: Emerging Research and Opportunities* (pp. 87–115). Hershey, PA: IGI Global. doi:10.4018/978-1-5225-4091-5.ch005

About the Contributors

Valerie A. Storey is an Associate Professor in the School of Teaching, Learning and Leadership at the University of Central Florida. She is the author of more that 40 publications in the areas of organizational leadership, professional doctoral program design, Dissertation in Practice design, and community-based learning. Recent works include the edited book *International Perspectives on Designing Professional Practice Doctorates,* in which scholars from Australia, Canada, Ireland, Israel, New Zealand, and the United Kingdom develop collective knowledge of professional practice doctoral programs through ongoing critical friends' discourse, offering insights on current important global issues in professional practice doctoral programs. Current leadership roles in professional organizations include serving as President of Florida Association of Professors of Educational Leadership (FAPEL), Chair of the American Educational Research Association, Division A, Educational Leadership Dissertation Award Committee, and Chair of the Faculty Council in the College of Education and Human Performance, UCF. Dr. Storey received her undergraduate degree from Leeds University (UK), her master's from Manchester University (UK) and her PhD. in Educational Leadership, Policy and Organizations from Peabody College, Vanderbilt University (USA).

Thomas E. Beeman has been a healthcare executive for over 44 years both in the civilian and military sector. Beeman most recently was the COO of Regional Operations at Penn Medicine and prior to that had 27 years of experience as a CEO of several large Health Systems. He served 33 years in the US Navy attaining the rank of Rear Admiral (U). His last duty station was the Bureau of Medicine and Surgery as the Assistant Deputy Surgeon General of the Navy. Beeman was the CEO at Lancaster General Health a large complex healthcare system in Pennsylvania and also the CEO of Saint Thomas Health a multi-hospital system in Nashville, Tennessee. He was appointed by the President to sit on the COVER Commission, which is looking at ways to enhance mental healthcare for veterans. Beeman holds numerous military awards including the Legion of Merit (3 awards). He serves on various University Boards and in his new role of Executive in Residence for Penn Medicine enjoys teaching, mentoring and writing. He is the co-author of two books and a myriad of academic articles. Beeman holds a PhD. from Vanderbilt University, an MBA from Widener University, and MA and BS from Saint Joseph University.

* * *

Kenneth R. Cohen, the Founder/Chief Executive Officer of The Synergy Organization, Inc., established an evidence-Based Healthcare Executive Search, Executive Assessments and Consulting firm in 1989. An Organizational Psychologist and Leadership Consultant, Dr. Cohen has dedicated his career to helping progressive health systems and hospitals to recruit, select, develop and retain their leaders most effectively and cost-efficiently while simultaneously enabling healthcare leaders to love what they do. This is accomplished through the application of Evidence-Based industry Best Practices, proven science, the proprietary Synergy Screening System®, his own specialized expertise and 35+ years of experience, findings from the firm's multiple innovative national leadership research studies, and Baldrige Performance Excellence Program standards across all of Synergy's business practices. He has conducted hundreds of projects including Evidence-Based Selection and Developmental Assessments, Executive Coaching, and Evidence-Based Succession Planning; presented numerous seminars on effective leadership, recruitment, selection, executive development, and retention strategies for respected healthcare organizations; and has served as a Recommended Speaker for the American Hospital Association's Center for Healthcare Governance. He has taught at both the graduate and undergraduate level. In addition, Dr. Cohen has written, been published in or interviewed by numerous professional journals and publications. Dr. Cohen earned both his Master's and PhD as a Psychologist with Distinction Honors at Temple University. He graduated from Dickinson College with a Bachelor's Degree in Psychology.

Genevieve (Genny) Mak Dean serves as the Director for Regional Planning, Penn Medicine Medical Group at Penn Medicine. Genny's experience in strategic planning, systems integration, process development and project management have been applied in academic, community and military health settings. Genny received her undergraduate degree in process management and consulting from the College of William and Mary and her Executive MBA from St. Joseph's University's Haub School of Business. Prior to her role at Penn Medicine, Genny served as the Chief of Staff to the CEO at Lancaster General Health.

Anthony DelConte is an Assistant Professor of Pharmaceutical and Healthcare Marketing at Saint Joseph's University Erivan K. Haub School of Business. Dr. DelConte also serves as the Chief Medical Director for Lipocine, a specialty pharmaceutical company. Previously Dr. DelConte was Chief Medical Officer at Auxilium Pharmaceuticals and also served on the faculty at Jefferson Medical College. Dr. DelConte holds a Bachelor of Science in Biology from Saint Joseph's University and earned his Medical Degree from the University of Pittsburgh. His research interests include access to healthcare, service learning, and professional interactions with pharmaceutical and biotech companies.

Joseph A. DiAngelo, Ed.D., has served as a business school dean for two Philadelphia-area universities -- Widener University (1988 to 2000) and Saint Joseph's University (from 2000 to present) which represents a 30+ year career in business school leadership. Highly respected by business school deans and academic leaders from across the country and the globe, DiAngelo is considered a foremost authority on higher education issues and topics, and has served in leadership roles for the premier global business school accrediting organization – AACSB, where he led the organization as chairman and now as an ex officio supporter to the board and its members. At Saint Joseph's University, Joe's leadership has allowed the Haub School of Business to grow by 100 percent in nearly two decades with the introduction and expansion of a graduate school that fosters the growth of more than 1,150 students annually.

Karen Flaherty-Oxler, MSN, RN, is a seasoned healthcare and Nursing Executive who has dedicated her career to inspiring others as a servant leader to care for and improve the health of those we are honored to serve. Rear Admiral Flaherty retired from the United States Navy on January 1, 2012 after thirty-eight years of dedicated service, culminating in her role as the Deputy Surgeon General of Navy Medicine at the Bureau of Medicine and Surgery which she assumed August 6, 2010. Prior to these duties Flaherty served as the 22nd director of the Nurse Corps as well as the deputy chief, Wounded, Ill, and Injured at the Bureau of Medicine and Surgery. Flaherty received her Master's of Science from the University of Pennsylvania and has held senior executive leadership positions at Thomas Jefferson University Hospital in Philadelphia, Pennsylvania, St. Francis Hospital in Wilmington, Delaware, and the Philadelphia Veterans Affairs Medical Center in Philadelphia, Pennsylvania. She served as the Senior Vice President of Hospital Operations/ Chief Nursing Executive, President of Lancaster General Hospital and the Chief Nursing Officer of Lancaster General Health in Lancaster, Pennsylvania. Most recently she served as the Senior Vice President Chief Nurse and Patient Experience Executive, Atlantic Health System in Morristown, NJ.

Michael J. Gast received his MD from The Ohio State University College of Medicine in 1973. He completed his residency in Obstetrics and Gynecology at Barnes Hospital, Washington University School of Medicine in 1976. Following residency, Dr. Gast completed a PhD in Molecular Biology at Washington University and two fellowships (in Maternal/Fetal Medicine and Reproductive Endocrinology and Infertility). He has participated on numerous Boards and in key executive positions in the field of Women's and Children's Health and has an extensive history of legislative and regulatory activity at local, state and national levels in the areas of maternal/child and reproductive health. Dr. Gast currently holds an adjunct faculty position in the Haub School of Business at Saint Joseph's University. He served on the Board of Supervisors of Thornbury Township, Chester County from 2007-13, serving as Chairman in 2010-11. Prior to that time, Dr. Gast worked as an executive in the biopharmaceutical industry, leading management and research teams in various areas including women's health.

Kenneth Hanover brings over forty years of executive level experience in health system and hospital management and in the medical device industry to his current position as President, Healthcare Solutions with The Synergy Organization. Previously, he served as the Chief Executive Officer of Prezio Health, a private equity owned, surgical and endoscopic management, maintenance, and repair company serving over 1000 hospitals and other health care institutions across the United States. Prior to joining Prezio in September 2013, Mr. Hanover spent his career managing a diverse array of hospital and health care delivery systems. He has served as the President and Chief Executive Officer of major health care delivery systems in Pennsylvania, Ohio, and Massachusetts and has a successful track-record of strategically repositioning the product portfolio, service mix and market distribution of these organizations to build market share, enhance clinical quality and drive financial performance. His organizational efforts to lower operating costs, improve productivity, and increase revenue have improved management performance and strengthened community trust and confidence.

Catherine Hayes is a Reader in Health Professions Pedagogic Practice, Faculty of Health Sciences and Wellbeing at the University of Sunderland. Qualified in podiatric medicine, Catherine is a Founding Fellow of the Faculty of Podiatric Medicine (Royal College of Physicians and Surgeons, Glasgow) and a Fellow of the College of Podiatry and General Practice (London). She leads and undertakes pedagogical research at the University of Sunderland alongside the supervision of doctoral candidates. She is national Convenor of the RAISE Network's Postgraduate and Professional Practice Special Interest Group (SIG) and holds Visiting Professorships at the Universities of Cumbria and Liverpool Hope in the UK. She also holds a National Teaching Fellowship and is a Principal Fellow of the Higher Education Academy. In addition to her Readership role, Catherine has published widely on qualitative research methodologies and the development of professional practice in health. She has an active interest in transcending disciplinarity between science and arts as signature pedagogies and is currently working on a monograph titled 'Beyond Disciplinarity in Social Science', with Routledge. She has been a UK Advisor in Podiatric Medicine for the Royal College of Physicians and Surgeons and was awarded Honorary Membership by Distinction of the Faculty of Public Health in 2015 and elected to the Royal Society of Arts in 2016. Catherine was formally elected to the role of Secretary of the Faculty of Podiatric Medicine at the Royal College of Physicians and Surgeons (Glasgow) in 2018.

Kim Hinshaw has been a National Health Service consultant in Obstetrics and Gynecology at City Hospitals Sunderland NHS Trust 1994, prior to which he was a Lecturer in Obstetrics and Gynecology at the University of Aberdeen. He has clinical sessions in both Obstetrics and Gynecology and has active research interests in the contexts of labour management and miscarriage. He is Director of Research for the Trust and Visiting Professor in the Faculty of Health Science, University of Sunderland, where he regularly leads interdisciplinary clinical simulation events. These focus specifically on emergency care in Obstetrics and the development of specific skill sets to provide optimal care for women and their children. Kim also works in Private Practice and has published widely in his field of practice.

Kevin Petrie, as of Head of the School of Art and Design, National Glass Centre, University of Sunderland, provides academic leadership with a key purpose of engendering an exciting, dynamic and relevant scholarly environment that encourages curiosity and creativity amongst staff and students. Kevin is also Professor of Glass and Ceramics and world renowned for his creative practice in 'blending' printmaking and glass/ceramics for creative use. His most recent creative practice focuses on drawing, painting and glass inspired by movement though landscape. Kevin's artwork focuses on drawing and painting as well as glass and ceramics. His research has previously focused on methods of printmaking for glass and ceramics. He has published two books on this subject 'Glass and Print' and 'Ceramic Transfer Printing'. Other publications include a chapter on the prints of Erwin Eisch (a seminal figure in the studio glass movement) and other chapters for books in relation to learning and teaching. More recently, he has focused on bringing together critical writing on glass and ceramics and he has co-edited 'The Ceramics Reader' published by Bloomsbury. He is currently working on 'The Glass Reader'. Kevin was awarded a National Teaching Fellowship for his contribution to Higher Education.

Stephen J. Porth is Professor of Management at the Haub School of Business, Saint Joseph's University (SJU), Philadelphia, PA, USA. He also serves as the Senior Editor of the *Journal of Jesuit Business Education*. Steve has chaired three academic departments at SJU and served for 17 years as Associate Dean of the business school and Executive Director of Graduate Business Programs. He is the chair of the Atlantic 10 Conference Council of Faculty Athletic Representatives (FARs). Steve's research and teaching interests are in the areas of strategic management, leadership and ethics. He provides consulting services specializing in leadership development and strategic management programs. He has written two books, one of which is now in its sixth edition and is translated into Chinese, and he has published extensively in management journals. Steve serves on the Executive Committee of the Board of *Colleagues in Jesuit Business Education* and on the Governance Board of *IgnitEd*, the platform to support Jesuit higher education.

George P. Sillup is an Associate Professor in the Pharmaceutical & Healthcare Marketing Department and Fellow in the Pedro Arrupe Center for Business Ethics and the Institute of Catholic Bioethics at Saint Joseph's University. Prior to transitioning to academia in 2004, he worked in the diagnostic, pharmaceutical and medical device industries where he held positions from salesman to COO. He guided numerous product launches that included attaining reimbursement coverage and coding to support products in the U.S. and global markets. As a professor, Dr. Sillup emphasizes teaching at the undergraduate and graduate levels and utilizes his industry experience to generate publications about different facets of healthcare delivery. His most recent forthcoming publication with colleagues is about a non-pharmacologic treatment alternative, TimeSlips™, for dementia patients in nursing homes. Dr. Sillup is currently on sabbatical to assess care in nursing homes as well as to implement alternative learning programs. A collegiate athlete, Dr. Sillup earned his undergraduate degree from the U.S. Military Academy and Wilkes University and his graduate degrees from Drexel University and the Fielding Institute.

Terese W. Waldron, MS, has worked at Saint Joseph's University for nearly 18 years. Shifting from the private sector to academia, Waldron brought with her a unique business development capacity and skill set from her career in Marketing and Advertising. While at Saint Joseph's University, she has directed a portfolio of Executive MBA and Pharmaceutical and Healthcare Marketing MBA and Food Marketing MBA/MS programs, as well as customized certificate programs, customized degree programs, and more to students, to clients, and to the industry.

Index

R

S

T

www.ingramcontent.com/pod-product-compliance
Lightning Source LLC
LaVergne TN
LVHW081326300926
849161LV00008B/1886
* 9 7 8 1 5 2 2 5 7 5 7 6 4 *